The Complete Idiot's Reference Card

Five Ways to Analyze an Advertisement

1. **Who is the target audience?** Women, men, young people, baby boomers, the elderly, a specific class or "type?"

2. **What is the ad selling?** First, what is the actual product? Second, what are the adjunct elements that the ad is trying to sell? What is the emotional appeal—fear, mystery, confidence, sex appeal, freedom, safety, acceptance, sense of self-worth? Is the ad negative or positive?

3. **How does the ad get the message across?** Notice things like sound effects, music, camera angles and movement, setting, black and white or color, highlighted color within black and white, special effects, graphics, repetition, celebrities, and celebrity voice-overs.

4. **What facts are being used in the ads?** Who's providing the facts and where did they get them? If there's a demonstration, how might that demonstration be "rigged?" If there's a testimonial, who's giving the testimonial and why should you believe him or her?

5. **Be aware of advertising that's subtle, maybe even hardly noticeable.** How many visible labels or logos can you spot? Play this game with your kids while you're waiting for something. Play "spot the ad" in TV shows and movies and talk about how placement in that particular program or movie affects one's perception of that product.

Ten Principles of Simple Living

1. Consume less.
2. Love people, use things. Put people before things.
3. Live lightly on the land and close to the earth.
4. Choose locally whenever possible.
5. Less is usually more.
6. Insist on quality.
7. Live from your vision.
8. Check in with yourself regularly.
9. Simple solutions are usually better than complicated ones.
10. Everything and everyone is connected.

alpha
books

Six Simple Living Lessons from Thoreau

1. We tend to interpret the phrase "freedom from want" as having everything we want. To Thoreau, real freedom meant wanting little: "A man is rich in proportion to the number of things which he can afford to let alone."

2. Solitude is an important part of everyday life. According to Thoreau, "The man who goes alone can start today; but he who travels with another must wait till that other is ready."

3. Simple living is not an end in itself but a means to knowing oneself and living a happy life through the pursuit of deeper and more spiritual things. People can live simply and be base and spiritless as well. It's the vision and purpose behind our living choices that count most.

4. Technology, though exciting, distracts us from the important questions in life, and it isn't worth the price if it destroys nature. Thoreau argued, "Our inventions are wont to be pretty toys, which distract our attention from serious things. They are but improved means to an unimproved end, an end which it was already but too easy to arrive at."

5. Nature is one of our most important teachers. We need to learn about it—the names of the plants, the constellations, the habits of animals—if we are to understand the universe, both without and within.

6. If we reduce our wants to our true needs, we'll be able to work less and spend more time doing the things we enjoy most and find the most fulfilling.

Six Simple Living Lessons from Helen and Scott Nearing

1. Know what you believe and set up your living plan according to those beliefs. Write them down. Refer to them daily. Revise as the need arises.

2. Have a clear plan every day as to what you want to accomplish. Spend time each morning mapping out the day and adjust for circumstances.

3. Prepare yourself for each major project or change. Do your homework, decide on a method, take your time, and evaluate as you go along.

4. Decide what your essentials are and get rid of the rest. Simplify the basic areas of existence: food, clothing, and shelter. Do you really need to cook every meal? How would a partially raw diet affect the time it takes to prepare meals?

5. Choose work that is a pleasure. Downsize so you can support your lifestyle with work you enjoy.

6. Wherever possible, work cooperatively with neighbors and friends. Trade, share, borrow, and lend. Learn from each other.

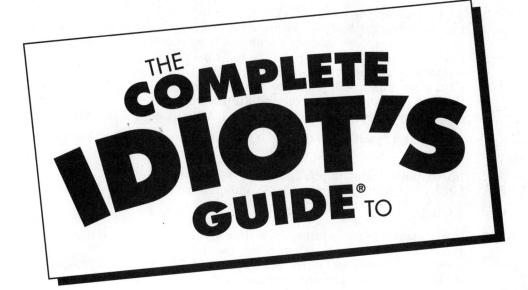

THE COMPLETE IDIOT'S GUIDE® TO

Simple Living

by Georgene Lockwood

alpha
books

A Pearson Education Company

Publisher
Marie Butler-Knight

Product Manager
Phil Kitchel

Managing Editor
Cari Luna

Acquisitions Editor
Randy Ladenheim-Gil

Development Editor
Jennifer Moore

Production Editor
Billy Fields

Copy Editor
Amy Lepore

Illustrator
Jody P. Shaeffer

Cover Designers
Mike Freeland
Kevin Spear

Book Designers
Scott Cook and Amy Adams of DesignLab

Indexer
Amy Lawrence

Layout/Proofreading
Ayanna Lacey
Mary Hunt
Heather Hiatt Miller
Stacey Richwine-DeRome
Michael J. Poor

Contents at a Glance

Contents

Foreword

For whatever reason, you have picked up this book and started to read. I don't know what brought you to this page—an advertisement, advice from a friend, serendipity on the internet, or the elegance of the words "simple living." Perhaps you have found that living at the edge of the twenty-first century is anything but simple and you are looking for some answers. You are ready to make some adjustments.

To benefit from the wealth of knowledge and vast array of resources offered in this book, the only thing required of you is the recognition that there are some things—large or small—you would like to change in your personal life, community, company, country, or planet.

In my work and travels I have discovered that for many people there is a vague sense that the "American Dream" has become something of a nightmare—one that threatens to completely consume the earth. There is a growing understanding that the more, more, more, bigger, bigger, better mentality just isn't sustainable. We are in debt up to our eyeballs. We feel trapped in nine-to-five-until-we-die jobs that are sucking away our life energy and killing the natural world in the process. Too many of us are isolated, even though we live in big cities surrounded by hundreds of thousands of people. We have too little time for family and friends. At the end of the day when we finally get a chance to prop up our feet and zone out in front of the tube, we are left with an overwhelming feeling that there is nothing we can do about the whole situation.

Fortunately, *there are* things you can do. There are a growing number of people from all walks of life, educational levels, income brackets, ethnic and religious backgrounds, and political persuasions that have discovered the alternatives. What they have discovered is something called: simple living (a.k.a. voluntary simplicity).

So, what is simple living?

As far as I know, there is not a standard definition. When put together, these two words mean different things to different people. The reasons people choose simplicity as a lifestyle are as many as there are ... well ... people. Perhaps it is easier to begin by explaining what simple living is not.

Simple living is not about depravation. Simple living is not about living in poverty or going without the things you need to feel comfortable. Simple living is not something you can buy (as Madison Avenue would have you believe). Simple living is not a get-rich-quick scheme. And, perhaps the most important thing to understand is that "simple," when chosen as a way of living, does not necessarily equate with "easy."

Simple living *is* about carefully evaluating every aspect of your life, learning what is important to you, taking positive steps to discard the fluff and junk, and learning how to enjoy and celebrate what remains. Simple living is about having enough—no more, no less. Enough to eat and wear. Enough time and money. Enough peace of mind, joy and love. And, the exciting thing is that once you get a handle on what is enough for you, you may find that you have enough time and energy left over to do things you never dreamed were possible before—volunteer, teach, plant a garden, travel, sleep, write a novel, dream really big dreams ...

Simple living is about consciously changing your perspective and rearranging your priorities. And this book can show you how to do it.

I've spent the better part of the past 10 years learning everything I could about simple living. I've read volumes. I've met many of the key authors in the "movement." I've built an extensive Web site that provides tools for learning to simplify and live more lightly on the earth. And, I have to be honest; after 10 years of exposure to these ideas, I couldn't imagine that someone had come up with anything new to say about simple living. I was wrong.

This book is a gem. Georgene has created a resource that belongs on the bookshelf of anyone who wants to make positive changes in their life. It doesn't matter if you are just starting to simplify or you are a pro. The overviews, techniques and broad range of options presented herein have something to offer everyone. It is loaded front to back with personal insights and the wisdom of those who have traveled the path before us. It is also a gateway to further reading and research for anyone who wants to simplify just about any aspect of their life—from personal finances to raising children to relationships to food preparation to spirituality.

I know this may sound cliché, but this is a book that can change your life. Use it well.

For the earth,

Dave Wampler

Founder

The Simple Living Network

www.simpleliving.net

Introduction

Americans are enjoying record levels of prosperity. Even the poor in this country are more well off than the middle class of other nations. Increasingly, the measure of our prosperity seems to be our ability to consume in greater numbers the ever-increasing choices among goods and services created for our comfort, enjoyment, and amusement.

But does greater prosperity equal greater happiness? There's the nagging feeling among many of us that all these material possessions are not leading us to true happiness. Despite more and better "conveniences" available to us, we seem to have less time to do the things we most enjoy. Our relationships are stressed by high-pressure jobs, a lack of time, and social isolation as each of us pursues his or her own version of the American dream. There's an uneasiness that we may not be leaving a healthy world to our grandchildren and that, if the rest of the world were to attain the level of material wealth that we have achieved, Mother Earth would collapse and die under the strain.

No matter how successful we have become in our professional lives, we're ultimately dissatisfied with the meaning of such successes to our overall well-being. We're not sure what it is, but something seems amiss. In a search to gain control of our time and possessions, we try to streamline our lives and get more organized, both of which are steps in the right direction. But still we feel that the root of our dissatisfaction lies deeper below the surface.

This book is for people who want to figure out what that "something deeper" is and take steps toward simplifying their lives and living more lightly on the earth. It's for people who care about the land and the future of our planet, who want to conserve natural resources, and who want to add more meaning to everyday activities. It's for people who want to have more time for relationships and for doing things they truly enjoy. It's for those who are looking to go beyond simply organizing and decluttering their lives to making more fundamental changes leading to a lifestyle that's more sustainable for the future of this planet and our civilization.

I know all this might sound a bit heavy, but just like every other change we make in our lives, we begin by understanding our current situation and how we got here, we set reasonable goals, and then we take action, one step at a time.

The Complete Idiot's Guide to Simple Living is about starting where you are, thinking about your options, and then making choices that will lead to a more authentic, less complicated way of life. There will be loads of tips for getting started, resources for learning more, exercises to help you clarify your own goals and to decide what actions make the most sense for you, and thought-provoking messages from other writers, both those familiar to you and some who may not be.

How This Book Is Organized

To help you develop your own approach to simple living, this book is divided into five major sections:

Part 1, "What Is Simple Living?" gives you a concise overview of how our lives became so complicated to begin with; the spiritual aspects of simplifying; how to decide just what all this means for you, your family, and the future; and what history and other cultures can teach us about living simply.

Part 2, "Your Money IS Your Life!" examines how your relationship with money affects everything you do. It gives you a concrete plan to get out of debt, shows you how to create work that reflects your values, offers steps for becoming financially independent, and helps you decide whether staying in your present location or moving somewhere else is the best simple living move. You'll learn that simple living does not mean living in poverty, but at the same time, you learn how to live better on less money.

Part 3, "Simple Living Basics: Food, Clothing, and Shelter," gets down to the nitty-gritty, applying simple living principles to these three most basic areas of life. You'll have plenty of small day-to-day things to consider as well as ideas for broader changes you may wish to make.

Part 4, "Family, Friends, and Community," explores relationships and how they can be both enhanced and challenged by efforts to simplify your life. How do you raise kids who respect the earth and get their identity from values and ideals rather than material things? What role does your community play in your plan to uncomplicate your life? How will a simpler lifestyle affect your marriage, your friendships? You'll discover the answers to these questions and more including how to start a simplicity circle and benefit from the ideas and support of others.

Part 5, "What If Everybody Did It?" looks at the social, economic, and political impact of the simple living movement and poses some questions about how a large-scale change in our society toward voluntary simplicity would affect institutions like government agencies, the workplace, education, and the economy, to name a few. We'll also consider ways in which individuals can help with these transitions.

At the end of this book is a special appendix section that will help you take any of the subjects covered and find out lots of additional information. You'll find resources throughout the chapters as well, but this appendix gives you still more places to go if you want to know more. It also lists specific sources for more detailed instructions or companies where you can get the materials mentioned.

Extras

Throughout the book, you'll find boxes that will alert you to tips, resources, inspiring and helpful quotes, and things to avoid. These are indicated by their own special icons:

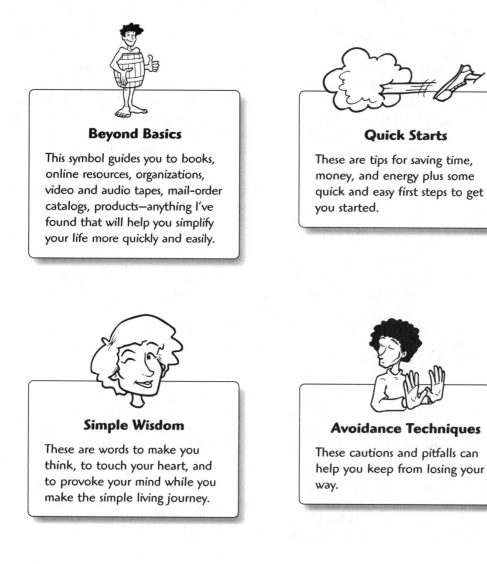

Beyond Basics

This symbol guides you to books, online resources, organizations, video and audio tapes, mail-order catalogs, products—anything I've found that will help you simplify your life more quickly and easily.

Quick Starts

These are tips for saving time, money, and energy plus some quick and easy first steps to get you started.

Simple Wisdom

These are words to make you think, to touch your heart, and to provoke your mind while you make the simple living journey.

Avoidance Techniques

These cautions and pitfalls can help you keep from losing your way.

Acknowledgments

I'd like to thank, as always, my dear husband, Jim, for his loving support during yet another intense research and writing project. My gratitude extends to all those who have shared their experiences with me as they strive to simplify and enrich their own lives. Thanks, too, to those who made the publication of this book possible. These include my agent, Carole Abel; Randy Ladenheim-Gil, Amy Lepore, Jennifer Moore, and the other editorial and production staff at Alpha Books; and Julie Woodman for her unfailingly sage advice and eagle eye for news. And deepest appreciation to my daughter, Rachel Griffiths, for her help on ecological and natural baby products and for sharing her simplicity circle experiences. What a great mom you're going to be!

Special Thanks to the Technical Reviewer

The Complete Idiot's Guide to Simple Living was reviewed by an expert who double-checked the accuracy of what you'll learn here to help us make sure this book gives you everything you need to know about simple living. Special thanks are extended Rita Cantu.

Trademarks

All terms mentioned in this book that are known to be or are suspected of being trademarks or service marks have been appropriately capitalized. Alpha Books and Pearson Education, Inc., cannot attest to the accuracy of this information. Use of a term in this book should not be regarded as affecting the validity of any trademark or service mark.

Part 1

What Is Simple Living?

You know your life is too complicated, but you're not sure how it got that way? And you certainly don't know how to fix it? The first step to understanding how you got here is realizing you're not alone. There's a reason so many of us feel like our lives are out of control and like we don't have time anymore for the things that really matter.

These first five chapters will give you the background you need so you can chart your own course to a simpler life, the life you design. You'll learn about people who extolled the pleasures of simple living in the past and about people who are choosing simple living right now. And you'll get to ask yourself some questions and consider some possible answers about the spiritual elements of the simple life.

Chapter 1

Consuming Passions: How the World Got Un-Simple

In This Chapter

➤ How consumerism works against our efforts to simplify

➤ Analyzing advertising to see how it persuades and moves you to action

➤ Developing a clearer definition of simple living

➤ Getting started on your own simple living program

If you're reading this book, you've already decided you'd like to simplify your life. But what made you determine this is necessary? How complicated is your life? What factors and feelings led you here? I'll hazard a guess:

➤ You're drowning in stuff you don't need or want, and you're not even sure how it got there.

➤ You have too little time, in spite of owning many modern "conveniences," to spend with the people you love doing what you enjoy most.

➤ You're on a "work and spend" merry-go-round, and you'd like to get off.

➤ You'd like to create a life that's more in line with your values, which may include consuming less and living more lightly on the earth.

So what's stopping you? It seems it should be simple to get simple, right? Not so fast! There are actually forces working against your efforts to simplify. You might recognize these:

Beyond Basics

The programs *Affluenza* and *Escape from Affluenza* may be available from your local library. If not, you can order them from a variety of sources including Bullfrog films at www.bullfrogfilms.com/catalog/affl.html. You might also enjoy taking a look at the PBS Affluenza site at www.pbs.org/kcts/affluenza/home.html.

➤ Consumerism, or "Affluenza" as a recent PBS documentary called it, a whole culture aimed at getting you to buy bigger and better things you don't need.

➤ The desire to belong and feel a part of your particular social group; not wanting to be different

➤ Coupling a sense of self-worth in our society with material success and conspicuous consumption

➤ Lack of information on how to simplify or where to begin

This chapter will take a brief look at how we all got here—surrounded by more and more stuff and enjoying it less—and how we can learn to recognize the forces in our lives that are undermining our efforts to attain a more simple life. It also discusses some easy first steps we can take to start us on the road to a less complex, more fulfilling existence.

In later chapters, you'll be able to examine specific areas of your life more closely, and I'll offer actions you can take from the immediate and easy to the more long-range and difficult. You'll hear from experts and people who've taken the simpler route themselves, providing thought-provoking ideas you can choose to use, leave for later, or skip altogether.

The Many Faces of Simple Living

First, let's take a look at some people in my own town who have chosen to downsize and simplify their lives. These stories will serve to illustrate how diverse the motivations for simple living are and how individual the solutions can be.

The Amateur Astronomer

Al and his wife Judy were living in a big midwestern city. On a trip west to check out a telescope he was interested in buying (he bought the telescope), Al stopped in northern Arizona on the advice of amateur astronomers he'd met who'd raved about its clear, dark skies and open spaces. He never left. Judy packed up their belongings, put their apartment up for sale, and came out to meet him. Al and Judy now live in a modest house close to town, walk or use their one well-used vehicle for transportation, and divide their time between a very manageable small publishing venture, lots of hiking, and reading. Al will tell you it was "all because of that telescope," but I suspect the move was really motivated by a strong desire to simplify their lives.

The Activist

Len worked in the upper levels of the aerospace industry but knew he wanted out. What he really wanted to do was live simply and work within the community to affect change in areas he truly cared about—like improving the environment and helping the local economy grow. He quit his job, drastically downsized his lifestyle, sold his car and bought a bicycle, and began working on small local projects that reflected his values. He has been carefully mapping area hiking trails, spearheading efforts to preserve them and create more, and is currently working on building a local bartering system. This is the life Len had envisioned.

Avoidance Techniques

Don't be afraid to be creative in the choices you make as you begin to live more simply. It's easy to judge yourself according to how other people live—especially if you admire them. Always remember that, even though the choices they made might be right for them, they're not necessarily right for you. You'll read about many different ways to achieve a simpler life in this book, and you'll probably read or hear about many more as you continue your research and start developing your own simple living plan. One of the most important things to remember is that the choices you make to live more simply must fit with your unique identity and goals—not the Jones'!

Leather and Lace

When I met my husband, I was writing for computer magazines and corporations as a freelancer. I was making a decent living but was not particularly enjoying the type of writing I was doing. I wanted to be more creative, and I had lots of subjects I wanted to research that I thought other people might enjoy reading about, too.

My husband owned a company, which he sold when the right offer came along, and we carefully invested the money so we could pursue the careers we'd always wanted without worrying about retirement benefits and health care. I wrote my first book shortly thereafter, on Victorian weddings, and Jim started a new business making reproduction leather goods from Hollywood westerns and history.

We then moved to northern Arizona, lowered our taxes and daily living expenses, and ultimately increased our living space so we could accommodate both our businesses and our living quarters in our home. We've worked to further lower our expenses, conserve natural resources, live closer to nature, and do more things for ourselves. We continue to move in this direction, and we couldn't be happier.

Quick Starts

Seek out people in your community who either have simplified their lives or are seeking to do so. We'll talk more in Chapter 19, "Circle of Community: You Can't Do It Alone," about how to locate or form a simplicity group, but for now, just start to collect information and notice what people are doing. By looking at what other people are doing, you can sort out what makes sense for you.

Quick Starts

Visit the dump! I know, sounds icky, but do it anyway. Pack the kids in the car and take a tour of your local landfill. What do you see that could be reused or recycled? What was once useful but is now outdated? What was a fad item that's no longer in vogue? What do you see that could have been repaired or restored?

These are just three real-life examples of simple living scenarios from real people in one community. There are thousands of others, and none is quite the same. The common threads are there, however. We all felt we needed to make a change to take more control of our lives. We all reduced our wants and needs to make the change possible. And we all are now living lives that are more in line with what we love and care about most. None of us would go back to our old ways of living.

A Simple Mathematics Lesson

While you're finding out more about real-life simplicity, let's take a look at the bigger picture as well. How did we get here and why are more people longing to make a change?

Since 1800, the world population has gone from staying level (for every person born, another person died) to an explosion of growth. As one population expert put it, "The balance between birth and death has been broken." The world's population just recently topped six billion, and every second five babies are born and two people die, a net gain of three people added to the world's population.

We are producing new goods and services every day and are using up the earth's resources at an alarming rate. In addition to new products, we are constantly upgrading existing ones, creating mounds of garbage and running out of places to put it.

If everyone in the world were to consume at the levels the wealthiest nations do, we would quickly run out of natural resources. Yet the experts agree that we cannot continue to ignore the impact of what we do on this planet's future, and these levels of growth and consumption are unsustainable. We must redefine progress and challenge ourselves to live sustainably.

Advertising and You

We often consume "stuff" because we are seduced by advertising—on billboards and television, in magazines and newspapers, in subways and airports … Advertising is ubiquitous in our society! On a fundamental level, advertising is a way of communicating our desire to sell so we can hopefully find someone who will buy what we're selling at the price we'd like to get.

But advertising today has become very sophisticated. Instead of selling a car, for example, an ad sells youth, sexiness, or intelligence. In spite of the rousing song, "serious freedom" isn't included in the sticker price. We're led to believe that, if we buy *this* car, we'll be happier, sexier, more alive, freer, safer. Now, we still may need a car to get to work or to see grandma on Sundays, but any reliable car that is comfortable for the family and relatively economical on gas would do the same thing. Advertising often taps into secondary needs and creates secondary motivations totally unrelated to the product itself. We invest inanimate objects with the power to invoke feelings and to give us something in our lives beyond their utilitarian value.

So how do you combat these multimillion dollar messages telling you continually to consume? One way is to turn them off—reduce the amount of television you watch, throw out that junk mail before opening it, avoid magazines that have more ads than editorial content. By limiting your exposure to these common advertising venues, you're lowering the number of messages you receive each day telling you to consume, and this can help you in your efforts to simplify your life.

Instead of letting television become a constant backdrop to your waking hours, try planning it into your schedule and switching it on only when you've decided there's something worthwhile to spend your time watching. Or tape programs you want to see and watch them when it's convenient for you, fast-forwarding through the ads. Notice how often you switch on the TV for company or let your kids watch it to keep them busy. If you

Beyond Basics

Wondering how you score in your efforts to live more environmentally friendly? Test yourself with *How Earth-Friendly Are You? A Lifestyle Self-Assessment Questionnaire*, created by the New Road Map Foundation and *EarthScore: Your Personal Environment Audit and Guide*, by Donald W. Lotter. For information on how to obtain these self-tests, see the Appendix, "Resource Guide."

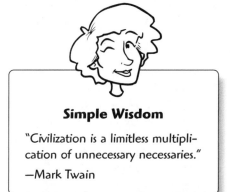

Simple Wisdom

"Civilization is a limitless multiplication of unnecessary necessaries."
—Mark Twain

were selective, how many television shows would you actually watch each week? Which ones would they be? If you missed them, what would be the result? Do you watch certain shows so you can discuss them with your friends?

Quick Starts

In one hour of network television viewing, count the number of ads you see. Don't forget to include products shown or mentioned within shows. Notice things like logos and labels. Write down the name of the product and any secondary motivations being portrayed such as status, acceptance, self-worth, or freedom, to name a few. Make this a game with your kids.

Beyond Basics

Although it's out of print, if you can find a copy of Jerry Mander's book *Four Arguments for the Elimination of Television* in the library or a used book store, I highly recommend it. You may not get rid of the set, but you'll become a lot more critical of what you see.

Become an Analyst

Another way to combat the consumer culture is to become a critic. Analyze the ads you see. Take them apart. What a great skill to teach your kids! Here are a few questions to ask:

➤ **Who is the target audience?** Women, men, young people, baby boomers, elderly, a specific class or "type?"

➤ **What is the ad selling?** First, what is the actual product, then what are the adjunct elements the ad is trying to sell? What is the emotional appeal—fear, mystery, confidence, sex appeal, freedom, safety, acceptance, sense of self-worth? Is the ad negative or positive?

➤ **How does the ad get across the message?** Notice things like sound effects, music, camera angles and movement, setting, black and white or color, highlighted color within black and white, special effects, graphics, repetition, celebrities and celebrity voice-overs.

➤ **What facts are being used in the ads?** Who's providing the facts and where did they get them? If there's a demonstration, how might that demonstration be "rigged"? If there's a testimonial, who's giving the testimonial and why should you believe him?

Be aware of advertising that's subtle and maybe even hardly noticeable. How many visible labels or logos can you spot? Play "spot the ad" in TV shows and movies with your kids and talk about how placement in that particular program or movie affects the perception of that product. We have to teach ourselves and our kids to be critical since we often don't learn these skills in school or at least haven't learned to apply them to how we consume.

Toward a Definition of Simple Living

Still not sure what simple living is? As I said before, it's not that simple. Well, once you decide what it is for you, then it gets simple, but there's some brainwork and emotional stuff you have to do first before you arrive at the definition that makes sense for you.

Is simple living the same as poverty? Poverty means not having enough to take care of yourself. The poor are malnourished, don't have health care, and have inadequate shelter. True poverty impoverishes the spirit as well as the body. World poverty also means a negative impact on the environment as people try to raise themselves out of substandard living by ravaging rain forests, poaching near-extinct animals, and raising crops like cocaine that ruin the land and lead to a variety of social ills. No, simple living isn't poverty; it's voluntarily living with less. It could be described as having enough, with "enough" being contained within the Golden Rule of sustainability that "each generation should meet its needs without jeopardizing the prospects for future generations to meet their own needs."

Don't let the fear of poverty prevent you from living a more simple life. Just because you want to live more simply doesn't mean you will have to be worried about where your next meal is coming from or how you'll pay to heat your house next winter. Simple living is about making choices that put you in the position of being more in control of how you choose to spend your money, not shunning money altogether. While you may choose to make "poverty wages"—and this is by no means necessary—as established by the federal government, you'll be living within your means and according to your goals.

Simple Wisdom

"When twenty-somethings can't afford much more than a utilitarian studio but think they should have a New York apartment to match the ones they see on *Friends,* they are setting unattainable consumption goals for themselves, with dissatisfaction as a predictable result."

—Juliet B. Schor, *The Overspent American*

Quick Starts

Another way to interrupt the "see, buy" process is to delay it. Write down what you think you need in a wish list and give it time. Then decide if it fits into your real values, the goals you've set for yourself, the bigger picture of who you are and who you want to be. The longer you wait, the less likely you are to "need" or "want" it.

Simple Wisdom

The Golden Rule of sustainability is that "each generation should meet its needs without jeopardizing the prospects for future generations to meet their own needs."

—Duane Elgin

If it doesn't mean poverty, then it certainly means frugality, right? Well, yes and no. The frugal living movement and the voluntary simplicity movement are close cousins. However, some frugal living folks aren't really into simple living. To live simply means to save money only if it also means simplifying your life. In some cases, a simple living choice might actually be more expensive, at least initially.

Does simple living mean a rural lifestyle? Again, the answer is "not necessarily." Although moving to a rural area may be the direction some of us want to take, there are many people living the simple life in the hearts of cities. We'll discuss location in more detail in Chapter 8, "Location, Location! The Truth About Where You Live," but for now, you can begin right where you are!

Does simple living mean living without technology? I don't think so, but it may if that's the direction you want to go. You may choose instead to resist all the hype about having the most up-to-date technology or the latest electronic gadget and buy only what you can truly use. For some of us, technology is what allows us to simplify our lives by starting our own business in a remote location or telecommuting.

Does simple living mean less work? Not necessarily. Some things take more time, some things less. What simple living points to is the inherent value in the tasks we do. I, for one, would rather take more time making foods from scratch than clipping coupons or searching for prepackaged bargains. I'd rather take the extra time to make handmade gifts than go shopping. We generally get better quality if we do or make things ourselves. You must decide which things are worth it to do the longer way or the harder way and which things you'd rather purchase.

If it's something you don't want to do yourself, perhaps you can find someone who does and trade something you *do* want to do. An entire simple living community can develop once you start on this path. I didn't want to keep chickens but wanted fresh eggs. Someone else in my community does keep chickens. I trade the herbs I enjoy growing for the extra eggs her chickens produce.

The 10 Simple Living Principles

We'll spend a lot more time discussing the philosophical and spiritual underpinnings of the simple living movement, but I wanted to start you off with some clear principles that might get you thinking in the right direction. Here's what I've come up with. Feel free to add to my list!

1. Consume less.
2. Love people; use things. Put people before things.
3. Live lightly on the land and close to the earth.
4. Choose locally whenever possible.
5. Less is usually more.
6. Insist on quality.
7. Live from your vision.
8. Check in with yourself regularly.
9. Simple solutions are usually better than complicated ones.
10. Everything and everyone is connected.

You'll have a chance in Chapter 5, "Finding Your Own Simple Living Way," to further refine your simple living definition and to decide, after learning a bit about simple living in the past and in other cultures, what simple living might mean for you. But these principles should help get you started.

First Steps

I've given you some exercises to help you think more critically, but you may ask, what can I do right now to get the ball rolling?

Start by Stopping

One of the best ways to begin is to try an experiment. Stop consuming for a week. Just seven days. If you can make it last longer, by all means do so. Before you begin, buy only the basic foods you need for the week and fill up the gas tank. When you shop for food, try to stick to things like eggs, bread, and milk and use up what you already have in the refrigerator and pantry. If there's nothing there (what would you ever do if there's a blizzard?), you'll have to do some additional food shopping, but as much as possible live off what you already have.

Again, that's *no shopping!* And that includes online or by phone. During the time you've designated, make a list of what you really need (or think you do) but don't buy it. At the end of your shopless stint, see if you really do need the items you listed. Notice which are genuine consumables, like food and paper goods, and which are not. In what different forms can you get it (fresh, canned, frozen, and so on) and which form has the least impact on the environment? Which is cheapest? Later we'll be looking at specific areas like food, clothing, and shelter, but for now, just notice these things in a broader context.

Quick Starts

Use the library! Don't buy that book you'll only read once and then put on a shelf to gather dust—borrow it! Libraries are incredible resources—not just for books but for CDs, videos, computer programs, patterns, and a whole lot more. Kids love the library, too, and most libraries have fun educational programs for children that keep them busy and are free.

Now, what have you learned? How did you feel? Did you feel a sense of resourcefulness? Frustration? Independence? Rebellion? Did you feel stifled or freer? How long did you make this period last? Did watching television make it more difficult or easier? How about looking at catalogs and junk mail? Reading magazines or newspapers? Surfing the Web? Being with friends?

Notice where the strongest tugs came from and when. What things were you most tempted by? When you look at your wish list, are there any things you could create or grow or borrow or produce yourself instead of buying them?

Unstuff Yourself!

Now that you've had a chance to experience "consumer withdrawal," the next thing to experiment with is "unstuffing." This is also known as decluttering or paring down. If you need help, pick up a copy of my book *The Complete Idiot's Guide to Organizing Your Life* and pick a project or life area you'd most like to tackle. We'll be going into this in more detail later, but for now, get your mind set on these two ideas—stop buying and pare down what you already own. When you think about acquiring new things, make them tools and skills rather than just more stuff. Think in terms of seeds and materials for growing and making. And when looking at what you have, think about how you can reuse it, share it, or pass it on.

Now you've had a chance to explore the simple living mindset. Throughout this book, we'll refine this together in a way that makes sense to you. What I'm doing with my life in semirural northern Arizona may be different from what you may decide to do in downtown Chicago, suburban Florida, or rural New England. I'm doing this in stages; others I know have jumped in with both feet. See what feels right to you and set your own game plan and schedule when you're ready. As you go through this book, you'll get to decide whether this is even a direction you want to go in and what areas seem the most crucial to you. The main point of this book is to get you thinking in a new way—to get you thinking! The rest is up to you.

The Least You Need to Know

➤ In order to have a high quality of life for everyone, we need to learn how to lower consumption and conserve natural resources.

➤ Advertising helps create our consumerist culture, along with peer pressure and unfulfilled emotional needs.

➤ We can begin to simplify our lives by becoming more critical of "buy" messages, experimenting with lowering our consumption, and paring down what we already have.

➤ Simple living doesn't mean poverty and doesn't necessarily mean relocating or living without technology.

Chapter 2

Simplicity and the Spirit

In This Chapter

➤ Understanding the spiritual side of simple living and how it will make your journey easier

➤ How the concepts of choice, stillness, gratitude, and creativity contribute to living more simply

➤ How to deepen your relationship with nature and find greater contentment

---

Although the choice to begin simplifying our lives may at first seem like a strictly practical decision—we want to get out of debt, save money, have more time to spend doing the things we enjoy, and get organized—if we scratch the surface, there are probably some more profound reasons why we've decided to make the change. It can even be a sick or troubled spirit that drives us to consider simplicity as a way of life.

In this chapter, we'll examine some of the possible spiritual reasons you may have for making things simpler so you'll be clearer as you develop your own personalized plan and will be more likely to experience lasting results. You'll find ways of exploring your spirituality that can be tailored to whatever religious, philosophical, or spiritual beliefs you may already have.

The Importance of Choice

At the core of the simple living movement is a desire to have more choices about the things that matter. We long for this increased self-determination while in the midst of more choices than we can cope with about the things that don't matter. There may be 10 different kinds of mushrooms to choose from at the local gourmet food market, but we may feel trapped in our present job or feel we "have" to do far too many things we don't feel good about or really want to do. Which kind of freedom of choice is more meaningful? Choices about where and how we live, what kind of work we do, how we spend our time, and who we spend it with are, in the long run, the kinds of choices that really count.

The desire to live more simply is often fueled by a need to gain more control over our lives, to have more valid and significant choices. We're tired of being passive consumers of life. We want to take charge and create different choices than those offered to us. We want to have more of a say.

Simple living at its core is about making conscious daily choices. The very process involves bringing creativity into these choices and engaging the imagination as well searching out our true meaning and purpose in the scheme of things.

In a simpler life, the choices are increasingly ours. Ultimately, we decide how and when to work, what environment we want to surround ourselves with, what clothes we wear, what food we eat, and with whom we associate.

Beyond Basics

If you'd like to read more about the process of making choices, try Lewis B. Smedes' *Choices: Making Right Decisions in a Complex World.* Smedes' perspective is a Christian one, but this book contains valid information for people of all faiths and spiritual perspectives.

Now you may not be able to rethink all these choices right now, but you can start right where you are within your own existing framework. How many of the things you think you have to do, do you really *have* to do? Where could you make different choices based more on what you care about or believe in? How much does "fitting in" matter to you when faced with these broader possibilities? What risks are you willing to take if it means having more freedom and living more in harmony with your values?

One new choice I've made, for example, is to stop using plastic bags from stores. I mean, *stop*, completely. I'm not there yet. Sometimes I forget to bring a canvas bag. It's so easy to just walk without thinking into a store, make my purchase and take the plastic bag from the clerk. But I'm really working on it. All it really takes is keeping the canvas bags in the car and returning them each time I bring them into the house to empty.

Notice all the choices you have every day: what products to use in your daily personal-care routine, what fabrics and clothing you wear, what you eat for breakfast, what mode of transportation you choose, how you decide to behave at work, how you spend your lunch hour, how you use your speech, who you associate with, what you do with your evenings and weekends, where your money goes, and so on. Examine whether you exist mostly in limitations ("I can't do that. People will think I'm odd." or "It takes too much effort.") or are open to the possibilities and the power of your freedom of choice.

We think of ourselves as a free society with more choices than anywhere else in the world. But we have to exercise our freedom to keep it. The choices are there, but we are responsible for making them in the widest realm of possibilities. So how free are you, really?

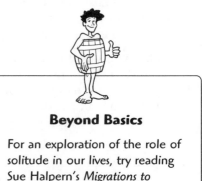

Beyond Basics

For an exploration of the role of solitude in our lives, try reading Sue Halpern's *Migrations to Solitude: The Quest for Privacy in a Crowded World*.

Simplicity Lives in Silence

Another spiritual key to simplifying your life is seeking and finding quiet. In silence, we get to listen to our inner voice. We discover our purpose when we take time away from the "noise." New ideas are born when we listen to ourselves closely. How much time do you allow in your life for silence? Is there always a radio playing or a television droning on in the background? Are you always making "small talk"? Is it hard for you to hold your tongue? How often are you just "still"?

It's amazing how immediately life gets simpler when we just "turn it off." Have you ever had the electricity go out and notice how different the silence is? We hardly notice the hum of the refrigerator day and night, but when it's no longer there, we notice.

Consciously try to incorporate quiet time into your daily routine. Many spiritual disciplines advise setting aside time to be still at the beginning and end of each day. Try it. Regardless of your religious beliefs, I think you'll find it brings you closer to both

Quick Starts

Try going through a whole day without anything in the background. Try not speaking unless spoken to. Keep to yourself and close the door. Do you find you're uncomfortable with silence? Don't be alarmed. You're having a natural reaction to a significant change in your environment. If you practice being quiet more often, it will bother you less. You may even look forward to it!

yourself and your idea of the divine, whatever that may be. If you know how to meditate and want to do that, fine. If you're inclined to pray, then do so but silently. If you can take some of this quiet time outside in the fresh air, all the better! Be conscious of your senses. Let your mind wander and then bring it back. Breathe more slowly and deeply. Notice your breathing and your body.

Give yourself at least one hour a day to be silent. You'll very likely find you crave more. Try half an hour in the morning and half an hour at night. Morning contemplation sets you up for a more productive *and* more relaxed day. In the evening, it helps you put the day to rest and helps you sleep better. Remind yourself of all you have. Give yourself this gift and defend it every day.

If you can't get the quiet you need where you are, take a long walk alone. Listen to your thoughts as you walk. Don't stop to chat with a neighbor, keep walking. Breathe deeply and walk some more.

Beyond Basics

To learn more about deep breathing, its benefits, and other deep-breathing techniques, check out *Breathe Deep, Laugh Loudly: The Joy of Transformational Breathing*, by Judy I. Kravitz. Now breathe!

Simple Wisdom

"Find and honor your own pace."
—Sarah Ban Breathnach

Breathing Lessons

If you're having trouble getting quiet, just try concentrating on *breathing*. Practice slowing down through breathing by simply taking in a breath through your nose, counting slowly to four, filling your lungs, ribs, and chest cavity. Be sure to push out your abdomen as you breathe in as well. Hold the breath for four seconds and then exhale completely. Repeat.

Try this exercise for five minutes before you begin your quiet time or any time you need to slow down during the day. If you become lightheaded at any time, you can alternate regular breaths with deep breaths.

Another time to be quiet is when you're trying to sleep. Sounds obvious, right? Yet many of us attempt to sleep under all kinds of adverse conditions. Guard your sleep. Create an environment conducive to real rest and add rituals in addition to some quiet time before retiring that will help you prepare for sleep. Pay attention to your sleeping space and create the optimum conditions for deep, restful sleep.

When you're struggling with something, take it to silence. Ask questions and wait for the answers. You'll be surprised at the results you get if you truly quiet yourself and learn to listen.

Meditate Your Way to Simplicity

For many people, meditation is how they spend their quiet time. The practice of meditation can be used to relax, to improve breathing, to increase creativity, to heal, and some believe to discover and maintain a deeper relationship with the divine. One of the most poetic phrases I've seen to describe this phenomenon is "the thunder of silence." It can be a very powerful experience. Regardless of your religious tradition or beliefs, meditation can open doors to your inner self and can help you on your path to simplicity. Give it a try.

Beyond Basics

There are lots of good books on meditation, some from a Christian perspective, some from an Eastern one, and you can certainly choose one that's more specific to your beliefs. However, here are three excellent beginner's guides that are more general in nature:

The Best Guide to Meditation, by Victor N. Davich is a nice overview of the different traditions and very helpful for beginners.

Journey to the Center: A Meditation Workbook, by Matthew Flickstein has an Eastern point of view.

The Complete Idiot's Guide to Meditation, by Joan Budilovsky and Eve Adamson is a good beginner's guide to several different approaches to meditation.

In addition to these quiet periods during which you commune with yourself, try setting aside some time for spiritual study as part of your simple living path. In the morning, read a passage from a book that speaks to you spiritually, then close your eyes and give yourself time to think on it. You might make it the focus of your meditation, your prayer, or your daily walk.

The practice of silence forces you to slow down, and slowing down is the beginning of simplifying your life. Slowing down allows you to distinguish between needs and wants. It allows you to break the frantic pace, to figure out what really satisfies you, to appreciate what you already have, and to experience true satisfaction. Slowing down lets you try things on for size mentally, develop your imagination, and nurture yourself.

You Are What You Speak

In seeking more quiet in your life, try speaking less. When you do speak, make a concentrated effort to communicate more honestly. Make greater eye contact. Really look at someone when you speak to him or her and allow silent spaces. Truly listen. Start eliminating garbage from your communication. By garbage, I mean all the meaningless chatter we use to fill the spaces between others and ourselves instead of allowing for intimacy and authenticity.

Clean up your language and pay attention to the words you use. Be more precise. Stay away from jargon or catch phrases and develop a broader vocabulary. I catch myself when I respond to someone relating an experience with a shallow "great" or even the popular phrase of the moment "awesome." Everything is "wonderful" lately. Have you noticed? I know I'm just being lazy when I resort to this kind of speech and don't really participate fully in the conversation.

Watch what happens around you when you make the change to more careful speech, even in a small way. Living simply is about living consciously. Plain speaking is about the same thing. In an age of disingenuous and downright dishonest speech in so many areas of our lives, honest, thoughtful speech is always refreshing and contributes to everyone's sense of simple well being.

Quiet has a way of putting us in the present like nothing else. As Ram Dass said, "Be, here, now." It's hard to do that when we're constantly chattering, recounting stories from the past, or sharing future plans. There's a place for these, of course, but being in the precious present is easier when we seek silence daily.

Simple Wisdom

"Let go of wasteful speech and idle gossip."

—Duane Elgin, *Voluntary Simplicity*

Quick Starts

One way you can enjoy nature is to start gardening. Spending time outside planning, planting, weeding, and harvesting your own home-grown vegetables provides the perfect excuse to spend time communing with the natural world. For many people, gardening is the perfect form of meditation, too!

Nature School: Lessons from Mom

One of the spiritual concepts that first comes to mind when people think of simple living is being closer to nature. We think of Thoreau trotting off to live in the Massachusetts woods or the old-fashioned simplicity of nineteenth-century farm life. But we don't have to pack up and live in a cabin without electricity like Thoreau or move off to a farm in the country; we can become more at home with our natural surroundings right where we stand.

Mother Nature is full of simple living lessons and wisdom if we just pay attention. Remember that quiet time we talked about a few moments ago? Why not use some of it to tune into the regular cycles of your natural environment? What flowers are blooming right now? Have you any idea? What are their names? What stars are in tonight's sky? Notice the days of longer and shorter light. What is a solstice? What's an equinox? Which is the longest day of the year? The shortest? Learn to enjoy the darkness as well as the light.

Living in the city might make it a little more difficult to notice nature, but you can if you make a little effort. Where are the spots in your city that you can observe nature? Instead of looking at the carefully planted areas, notice what's growing in a vacant lot or in between the cracks in the sidewalk. What kinds of birds do you see in the park? Celebrate the seasons. Take note in your dress, in your home, in your mind's eye, in your heart.

If you keep a journal (which I highly recommend!), include your observations of nature when you write. Some people find they actually like working the other way around—their nature journal becomes their personal journal.

Consider using a sketch book for your journal so you're encouraged to draw as well as write. Park yourself in front of a window or take a walk to a more natural setting. Observe, try to capture what you see, and then describe your feelings and their meaning for you right now. Engage your senses, look for details like tracks in the snow, bring items back with you and examine them more closely, and then try to draw them or describe them in detail. Use your nature journal as a vehicle for learning more about your local environment and the living things that inhabit it.

As you observe the natural world, you'll start to notice the cycles of birth, life, death, and rebirth. You'll become conscious of a rhythm that underlies all things. Once you notice the rhythm of life, your own simple life will begin to take shape.

Finding Gratitude

The simple life is one of gratitude by its very nature. You can't have a reverence for basic, simple things without being grateful. Yet we seem to need

Quick Starts

To help you get started with your nature journal, you might enjoy reading *Nature Journaling: Learning to Observe and Connect with the World Around You,* by Clare Walker Leslie and Charles E. Roth, or *A Trail Through Leaves: The Journal As a Path to Place,* by Hannah Hinchman.

Beyond Basics

A beautiful and inspiring example of a contemplative nature journal and exploration of the soul is Annie Dillard's *Pilgrim at Tinker Creek.*

to remind ourselves of our blessings. Why is that? Could it be that so much of what we see and hear daily is calculated to tell us what we lack? Our daily media diet tells us how buying this or that product will make us better looking, sexier, happier, smarter, or more successful and that, without these things, we will somehow fall short. The messages we get so often are about what we don't have. Is it any wonder we fail to notice how much we do have?

Simple Wisdom

"Gratitude unlocks the fullness of life. It turns what we have into enough, and more. It turns denial into acceptance, chaos to order, confusion to clarity. It can turn a meal into a feast, a house into a home, a stranger into a friend. Gratitude makes sense of our past, brings peace for today, and creates a vision for tomorrow."

—Melody Beattie

Avoidance Techniques

No fair listing the same things every day in your journal, even if it's true! Stretch yourself when you think about your blessings. Tune yourself in to the changing face of your abundance.

If we begin to revamp our thinking from scarcity to abundance, we begin to see that we already have all we need to be happy. This allows us to work from a position of strength and power as we change other areas of our lives. Now we're attuned to our resources, our skills, the knowledge gained from our experience, and all the life-sustaining things that are ours every day—and they're free. As in "no cost."

What are your blessings? Ask yourself this question every day. Look at what you have, not what you lack, when you answer. In her best-selling book *Simple Abundance*, Sarah Ban Breathnach recommends keeping a gratitude journal. Instead, why not make this a part of the nature journal you've already begun? Start today by making a list of everything you can think of in your life right now that you have to be grateful for. Let's shoot for 25 things. How about 50? Try to include the things you are as well as the things you have, emotional and spiritual things as well as material ones. Include other people and what they give to you. Concentrate on feelings, too.

Make a commitment to get into the gratitude habit. In the morning when you take your quiet time, mentally list three things you're grateful for today. At night before you go to bed, list three things you noticed or that happened during the day that you're grateful for. I know it sounds a little hokey, but do it anyway and then tell me after a week of doing this daily that you don't notice a shift in your perspective, a change in your attitude, a growing contentment. I dare you!

Pervasive consumerism lowers self-esteem through a feeling of scarcity. We're always falling short somehow; we're never enough. There's always someone with more than us—more glitz, more stuff, more of "the good life"—and we'll never be at the top of the heap. The pursuit of material things keeps us from paying attention to our inner spirit. Instead of developing ourselves from within, we're preoccupied with the material world and are constantly diverted from our own inner work and workings. Coming from a base of gratitude and abundance counteracts the sense of lacking that the consumer culture works to build.

The Simple Life Is a Creative Life

The last spiritual element I'd like you to consider as you take steps to simplify your life is creativity. "But," you say, "I'm just not the creative type." Hogwash! We are all artists since we create our lives anew each day. So paint! Sculpt! Dance! Sing!

Owning your own creative spirit will take you a long way towards creating a simpler life. You'll need to be resourceful as you work to pare down and streamline your home and your workplace. That's creativity! You'll need to work with other people in your life to have them support you in what you're doing. *That's* creativity! You'll be searching for ways to get out of debt and spend less money while having a richer life. That takes creativity for sure! Of course, I'll be helping you along the way, but in the end, the solutions you come up with will be uniquely yours. The more you acknowledge and develop your innate creativity, the more fun you'll have along the way.

You'll discover that the road to creativity is play. Yes, I said play. Just watch a child and look for the "artist." You used to be one, too. Start playing again and you'll recover your creative self once more.

The consumer society buries and stifles our creativity. Instead of using our ingenuity to solve problems and to answer questions in our own unique way, we purchase something readymade, one-size-fits-all, and then wait a week for it to be "new and improved." Simple living fosters creativity and helps it thrive. As you live more consciously, your creative side will blossom. You'll find yourself playing more, trying things just to see whether they work, adding your own personal touches to what you do. When you slow down, your creative juices have time to flow. When you challenge yourself to "make do," your creative skills will shine.

Beyond Basics

I highly recommend that you take a close look at the book *The Artist's Way: A Spiritual Path to Higher Creativity,* by Julia Cameron. It's actually a course in creativity, and it's not just for "artists," although, when you're done, you may discover there's been one living inside you all along.

Simple Wisdom

"Our creative dreams and yearnings come from a divine source. As we move toward our dreams, we move toward our divinity."

—Julia Cameron

23

Simple Wisdom

"Why should we all use our creative power ...? Because there is nothing that makes people so generous, joyful, lively, bold and compassionate, so indifferent to fighting and the accumulations of objects and money."

—Brenda Ueland

The ultimate goal of simple living, in my opinion, is to enrich the spirit. We can be frugal, help save the planet, volunteer in our community, and live a life that seems to be simple on the surface, and it can be a chore and a drudgery or even a compulsive thing we attempt to foist on others. To live simply is a spiritual choice first and a personal one. In the long run, simple living is about our own personal contentment, or it will never be a lasting lifestyle change. Simplicity is not something in the distance that we're striving to achieve; it's all around us and within ourselves.

The Least You Need to Know

➤ Simple living can be a spiritual journey that's totally unique to you.

➤ Thinking more about your freedom of choice and exercising it more completely is an important part of the simple living path.

➤ Seeking silence, nature, and gratitude will help you create a more lasting move to simplicity in your life.

➤ By simplifying your life, you'll learn to rely more on your own creativity and will have more fun.

Chapter 3

What's Old Is New Again

In This Chapter

➤ Discovering how ideas about simplicity from the past hold lessons for us today

➤ Revisiting Henry David Thoreau's *Walden* to learn about his philosophy of simple living and the details of how he lived

➤ Learning about a couple who chose simplicity in the midst of the Depression and never went back

Simple living is not a new idea. Ancient civilizations had proponents of keeping "stuff" to a minimum and concentrating on the more lofty and satisfying things in life. From the Greeks and Romans to Eastern cultures and the Judeo-Christian tradition, there were cautions against loving "things" too much and losing sight of the riches of the heart and spirit.

Plato advocated a "Golden Mean" between poverty and wealth. Aristotle told us to live a life of equal balance between the mental, physical, spiritual, and material aspects of existence. Jesus called for a life of voluntary simplicity. The *I Ching* advocates limitation, self-limitation or restraint, as a way to enlightenment and true happiness. More recently, the British poet William Wordsworth called for "plain living and high thinking."

In the United States, there is a strong simple living thread that runs through the entire history of this young nation. It is what author David Shi calls "a rich tradition of enlightened material restraint."

Although some saw only raw opportunity waiting in the New World, others came to escape what they regarded as the corruption of the established order. They hoped to live plainly in what they knew would be a harsh environment and felt that hard work and adversity would help keep them godly. The Puritans and the Quakers, for example, both began their journey with these goals but soon found that through hard work and diligence they prospered, and they continually struggled to maintain their spiritual equilibrium.

The founding fathers struggled with these same issues as they forged a revolution from an oppressive and, to some, luxury-loving and corrupt mother country. Men like Samuel Adams hoped the new republic would become an agrarian paradise of simple living and high ideals. Others, like Alexander Hamilton, spoke for the ideals of prosperity and wealth.

The main hallmarks of the American simple living philosophy throughout its history, according to Shi, are "a hostility toward luxury and a suspicion of riches, a reverence for nature and a preference for rural over urban ways of life and work, a desire for personal self-reliance through frugality and diligence, a nostalgia for the past and a skepticism toward the claims of modernity, conscientious rather than conspicuous consumption, and an aesthetic taste for the plain and functional."

For many of the founding fathers, the belief that the pursuit of money and material things shouldn't take precedence over the spirit, mental growth and stimulation, a strong family, or the good of country was a basic principle of freedom and democracy.

It's beyond the scope of this book to cover even a small portion of simplicity's roots in our history, but in this chapter, we'll examine two examples that I think you will enjoy learning about and will find have many lessons still pertinent to us today.

Simple Wisdom

"For the prosperity of fools shall destroy them."

—Proverbs 1:32

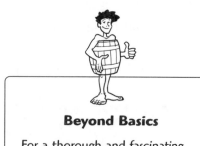

Beyond Basics

For a thorough and fascinating history of the simple living movement in America, read *The Simple Life: Plain Living and High Thinking in American Culture*, by David Shi. It will give you a well-grounded perspective of both the challenges and the rewards of the simple way of life in the midst of changing times.

Transcendence and Choice

Perhaps the best known of all the American proponents of simple living is Henry David Thoreau. The story of his experiment in the woods to learn how little he could live on and to discover what was important to his own soul lives on as an example for others to follow. If you haven't read *Walden* or perhaps read it a long time ago, try picking it up again and reading or rereading it.

Of course, not many of us can even entertain the idea of walking off into the woods with a borrowed axe, clearing some land, building a shelter, and living there alone for two years as Thoreau did, but we can take a mental trip along with him and see where it leads us.

From Harvard to a Cabin in the Woods

Thoreau was born in 1817 in Concord, Massachusetts. After graduating from Harvard in 1837, where he studied the classics, science, history, and several foreign languages, he returned to Concord and taught school. But Thoreau favored writing over teaching, and so in 1841, he accepted an offer from neighbor Ralph Waldo Emerson to stay with the family and work as a handyman and gardener while he worked on his writing.

Thoreau kept extensive journals, which form the foundation of his writing. But he soon learned that writing wasn't going to earn him a living, so he taught himself various skills that would later sustain him throughout his life. He taught himself surveying and carpentry and worked part-time in the family pencil-making business. He was an inventor and something of a natural engineer.

Answering a request from a Harvard classmate to describe his employment, Thoreau said, "I am a Schoolmaster—a private Tutor, a Surveyor—a Gardener, a Farmer—a Painter, I mean a House Painter, a Carpenter, a Mason, a Day-Laborer, a Pencil-Maker, a Glass-paper Maker, a Writer, and sometimes a Poetaster." With this variety of skills, Thoreau made enough money to take care of his needs and still allow time for study and writing.

Thoreau was not a joiner, and although he had an eminent circle of friends in Concord, the center of the transcendental movement, he was considered something of a rebel and an individualist. Thoreau believed in the right to dissent and exercised that right regularly in his own life. He felt strongly that each person should think for himself and pursue his own way, "not his father's or his mother's or his neighbor's instead."

Simple Wisdom

"If a man does not keep pace with his companions, perhaps it is because he hears a different drummer. Let him step to the music which he hears, however measured or far away."

—Henry David Thoreau, *Walden*

Thoreau had an insatiable curiosity and was a keen observer. He was a naturalist and one of the early environmentalists, forever exploring the world around him as well as surveying the world within him and taking notes on what he observed.

On Walden Pond

Thoreau moved to the woods a mile from the town of Concord on July 4, 1845. He considered the two years he spent in the small house he built by hand near Walden Pond to be an experiment. He did not intend to live in the woods permanently but to find out how little he needed to survive and then live simply from then on. He decided, "Most of the luxuries, and many of the so called comforts of life, are not only not indispensable, but positive hindrances to the elevation of mankind.

> "I went to the woods because I wished to live deliberately," he said, "to front only the essential facts of life, and see if I could not learn what it had to teach, and not, when I came to die, discover that I had not lived."

While at Waldon Pond, Thoreau grew some of his own food, foraged in the woods, fished, and on one occasion killed a woodchuck that had been destroying his garden. He managed his time so he had to work very little to maintain himself and used the rest of the time for his nature studies, contemplation, reading, writing (he kept extensive journals and wrote the book *A Week on the Concord and Merrimack Rivers*), and just thinking.

While he enjoyed his solitude, Thoreau wasn't a hermit. He had frequent visitors and made regular visits to town. And he began to spark a great deal of curiosity. To answer the questions of the inquisitive, he wrote lectures, which he delivered in town while still living in the woods. These lectures, plus his journal entries, became the notes for *Walden*. He left Walden on September 6, 1847.

After Walden

Thoreau never married and died in 1862. *Walden* was moderately successful in Thoreau's lifetime but became even more so after he died. Perhaps as a symbol of the issues we face today of shrinking wilderness and less opportunity for solitude and contemplation, the site of Thoreau's small cabin on Walden Pond has been one of controversy and conflicting interests. Some wanted to preserve it as a memorial in its natural state. Others wanted to open it to the public for recreation. Still others wanted to develop it. Over time, a compromise has been reached, but it took a tremendous amount of organizing and publicity to raise the funds to save Walden Pond from development.

Simple Wisdom

"I learned this, at least, by my experiment; that if one advances confidently in the direction of his dreams, and endeavors to live the life which he has imagined, he will meet with a success unexpected in common hours. He will put some things behind, will pass an invisible boundary; new, universal, and more liberal laws will begin to establish themselves around and within him; or the old laws be expanded, and interpreted in his favor in a more liberal sense, and he will live with the license of a higher order of beings. In proportion as he simplifies his life, the laws of the universe will appear less complex, and solitude will not be solitude, nor poverty poverty, nor weakness weakness. If you have built castles in the air, your work need not be lost; that is where they should be. Now put the foundations under them."

—Henry David Thoreau, *Walden*

Lessons from Walden

Thoreau speaks to us now, perhaps as much or even more than he did to his contemporaries. What can we learn from his two-year stay in Walden woods? Here are some points that have stuck with me:

➤ We tend to interpret the phrase "freedom from want" as having everything we want. To Thoreau, real freedom meant wanting little: "A man is rich in proportion to the number of things which he can afford to let alone."

➤ Solitude is an important part of everyday life. According to Thoreau, "The man who goes alone can start today; but he who travels with another must wait till that other is ready."

➤ Simple living is not an end in itself but a means to knowing oneself and living a happy life through the pursuit of deeper and more spiritual things. People can live simply and be base and spiritless as well. It's the vision and purpose behind our living choices that count most.

➤ Technology, though exciting, distracts us from the important questions in life and isn't worth the price if it destroys nature. Thoreau argued, "Our inventions are wont to be pretty toys, which distract our attention from serious things. They are but improved means to an unimproved end, an end which it was already but too easy to arrive at …"

Quick Starts

If you'd like to get a flavor for what Thoreau was like, his writings, and his experiment at Walden Pond, point your browser to //miso.wwa.com/~jej/1thorea.html for a quick overview and introduction with lots of links.

➤ Nature is one of our most important teachers. We need to learn about it—the names of the plants, the constellations, the habits of animals—if we are to understand the universe, both without and within. We need to become careful observers to understand Nature's secrets, as well.

➤ If we reduce our wants to our true needs, we'll be able to work less and spend more time doing the things we enjoy most and find most fulfilling.

These are just a few of the simple living principles I have gleaned from reading *Walden*. You'll surely find your own and can incorporate them into your own personal philosophy of simplicity.

Maple Sugaring in Vermont

A second example of simple living in practice is that of Helen and Scott Nearing, who left New York City in the 1930s to take up maple sugaring and the simple life in the Green Mountains of Vermont. Unlike Thoreau, the Nearings left city life and never returned, preferring a rural lifestyle as their pathway to simple living.

Who Were the Nearings?

For the Nearings, life in the big city as economic depression and unemployment spread, the political scene became increasingly unstable, and technology encroached on individual freedom, was simply untenable. They decided that "the good life" in rural Vermont was a permanent solution and one best attempted, they felt, by a couple or a group of like-minded people.

The Nearings were self-described pacifists, vegetarians, and collectivists. They felt they were leaving a "dying social order" and were, like Thoreau, creating an experiment in another, more "workable social system." They also chose to have no children, which meant they were free from the concerns of child rearing or education, although they later concluded that their lifestyle could easily accommodate the raising of a family.

Making a Simple Life in Vermont

Regardless of your political leanings, there is much to learn from the Nearings' experiments in the woods of Vermont and then Maine. They were, in essence, very practical people who questioned the old ways if they didn't seem to work but relied on them when they did.

What they found living in New York and other cities, both in the United States and abroad, was that the obstacles to their idea of simple living were too great. The obstacles included "complexity, tension, strain, artificiality, and heavy overhead costs. These costs were payable only in cash, which had to be earned under conditions imposed upon one by the city—for its benefit and advantage."

They left for three main reasons: economic (financial independence), health (organic food, less stress, and close contact with nature), and social/ethical (environmental, political). Right from the start, the Nearings knew why they were choosing a new life and what they wanted that new life to represent. Keep this in mind as you read the later chapters in this section because this is exactly what I will be encouraging you to do as you develop your own simple living plan.

Because the Nearings were so clear as to what they wanted to do with their time and energies, as well as what their beliefs were, they were able to structure their lives in Vermont according to a set of principles, a constant "reality check." For the whole story of their enterprise, I strongly suggest you read their book, *Living the Good Life*, but here I will tell you some of the basics.

First, the Nearings needed a cash crop that they could use to make a living but that would be in line with their environmental concerns and would not require the keeping of animals. They chose maple sugaring and learned everything they could about doing it well. They chose not to keep any domestic animals, partially because it was against their principles but also because, on a purely practical level, it meant less work and expense plus they needed less land. They adjusted their diet accordingly and were vegetarians, at first trading for milk and eggs and then later choosing to eat no animal products at all.

Since they ate mostly raw foods that they grew themselves, they were able to control quality and freshness, eat completely free of pesticides or artificial fertilizers, and keep cooking to a minimum. In the wintertime, they had extensive root cellars to store produce.

The Nearings built their own house and out buildings by hand from materials cleared from their own property, using mostly native stone and some wood. They had a 10-year plan based on 12 points, which included not making a profit or hiring employees, paying cash for everything, and carrying no debt. Rather than repair buildings that were nearly falling down on the new property, they tore them down and replaced them only when they had an actual need for the space. The first structure was a place to house green lumber while it aged for construction.

Beyond Basics

If you want to learn more about the Nearings' diet and philosophy concerning food, read *Simple Food for the Good Life: Random Acts of Cooking and Pithy Quotations*, by Helen Nearing.

As did Thoreau, the Nearings combined the manual labor necessary to sustain themselves with intellectual pursuits. They worked on the land only four hours a day with four hours set aside daily for study, contemplation, and what they called their "avocations" or hobbies. On Sundays, they took the day off completely. Yet their enterprise flourished enough to make them a "good life," which they enjoyed in Vermont for 20 years. One area of the "good life" they had hoped to achieve, but found difficult, was creating a cooperative system with the surrounding community. In some small ways, their efforts at community involvement were successful, but mostly they found they had to rely on themselves. I venture to say that today, perhaps, conditions might be more favorable.

Moving to Maine

The Nearings moved from Vermont to Harborside, Maine, in 1952 and took over another derelict farm. Both Vermont and Maine were dedicated to the same goals: "building and maintaining a solvent family economy amid the wreckage and drift of a society that was disintegrating in accordance with the laws of its own self-destructive being."

Again, we do not have to share the same pessimistic view of our current society, but if we're choosing to simplify our lives, we need to determine why and what we hope to create, just as the Nearings provided their own answers.

By the time the Nearings moved to Maine, they were no longer novices and had developed chosen professions: music for Helen, social science for Scott. They traveled, wrote, and lectured where opportunities arose and when time permitted, but their rural lifestyle with no domestic animals to tie them down afforded them a fair amount of freedom.

Visitors would wonder what they did with their "spare time." The answer was that they had none; they were constantly busy. The next question was "What do you do for pleasure?" The answer was "Anything and everything we do yields satisfaction. If we didn't enjoy it, we would do something else or approach our jobs in a way that made more sense."

In Maine, as in Vermont, the Nearings started every day with a plan, an agreed-upon list of activities for the day. They worked with the weather and the seasons. When a job was completed to the best of their abilities, they moved on to the next. Their philosophy on work was clear: "There is a tendency nowadays to elbow a way through the mazes of a complicated life. Wisely and slowly is good advice. If you are running a relay race, it is not decided in the first few laps. Take your time. Ration your energies. Plan your operation carefully. Take one step at a time. Then prepare carefully for the next step. It pays in the long run."

Final Years

Scott Nearing died at the age of 100 in 1982, when Helen was in her 80s. She continued on without Scott until the age of 92, all the while living the life they had held so dear. She said, "I keep open house at our Forest Farm on the coast of Maine to help others see that a good life can still be maintained by a woman alone in her eighties."

Her own idea of her legacy lives on: "When we are long gone, may the search for the good life go on in the lives of our fellow countrymen and country women and may our efforts in buildings and books remain for a while to help others along the way."

The Nearings' Simple Living Lessons

There is so much practical information in the Nearings' books, both for those seeking a real change to a rural lifestyle or those simply looking for a new way of doing things right where they're planted. Here are some of the basic principles I drew from my readings. You will undoubtedly find a great many more:

➤ Know what you believe and set up your living plan according to those beliefs. Write down your beliefs and plans. Refer to them daily. Revise as the need arises.

➤ Have a clear plan every day as to what you want to accomplish. Spend time each morning mapping out the day and adjust for circumstances.

➤ Prepare yourself for each major project or change. Do your homework, decide on a method, take your time, and evaluate as you go along.

➤ Decide on what your essentials are and get rid of the rest. Simplify the basic areas of existence: food, clothing, and shelter. Do you really need to cook every meal? How would a partially raw diet affect the time it takes to prepare meals?

➤ Choose work that is a pleasure. Downsize so that you can support your lifestyle with work you enjoy.

➤ Wherever possible, work cooperatively with neighbors and friends. Trade, share, borrow, and lend. Learn from each other.

Simple Wisdom

"A market economy seeks by ballyhoo to bamboozle consumers into buying things they neither need nor want, thus compelling them to sell their labor power as a means of paying for their purchases."

—Helen and Scott Nearing

The Nearings' "experiment" lasted for some 60 years. Theirs was an economic, political, and spiritual decision. But it was also a love story. If you have never read *Living the Good Life* and its follow-up volume *Continuing the Good Life* (available in a single volume entitled *The Good Life: Helen and Scott Nearing's Sixty Years of Self-Sufficient Living*), please do, even if you have no intention of moving to the country and living off the land. You'll be rewarded for it. And if you want to read a poignant story about love and dignity in dying, read *Loving and Leaving the Good Life,* by Helen Nearing. You'll be better for it, I promise!

The Least You Need to Know

➤ There are many lessons to be learned from history, not the least of which are from our own nation's past.

➤ Like Thoreau, we can create our own experiments to get in touch with the aspects of simple living that most speak to us.

➤ Although we may not want to relocate to the country and live off the land, we can learn from people like the Nearings who have.

➤ Through study of past examples, we can develop our own simple living plan and gather inspiration as well.

Chapter 4

Culture Shock: Lessons from Alternative Living

In This Chapter

➤ How learning about existing communities and cultures different from our own can help us create our own simple living principles and plans

➤ Questions to ask when studying another culture to gain the greatest insight

➤ Two widely different examples of groups living in America according to their own simple living ideals

---

In the preceding chapter, we looked at the historical foundations of voluntary simplicity and at some useful examples from the past that can help us formulate our own simple living philosophy and plan.

But there are communities or "cultures" that exist amidst our modern world that operate outside of what we in America consider the mainstream. Some have actually chosen to opt out of what they see as a destructive world order. They have very different reasons and have organized themselves in very different ways with varying degrees of success. However, we can observe these subcultures as living examples of simple living experiments, each with strengths and weaknesses, and we can learn some practical lessons. Studying these groups can help us decide whether anything in their alternative lifestyle applies to us. In some cases, we can even visit and observe day-to-day life firsthand.

In this chapter, we're going to examine two "intentional communities": one unified by a strict religious belief, the other an ever-changing group of widely diverse people flowing with the times with very little to unite them except some loose political and spiritual concepts. Both are struggling to survive and to retain their original vision. Both reveal many of the challenges and benefits to simple living. Studying each raises questions we may likely need to answer on our own simple living path.

What to Ask When Looking At Other Cultures

It's easy to be judgmental when examining cultures or ways of life significantly different from our own. Their ways may be so outside the norm that we find them peculiar or even shocking. Or their beliefs might be so far from ours that we have difficulty imagining living under their rules (or lack of them). What I'd like to ask you to do as you read this chapter is to suspend judgment. Listen and learn. Ask questions. See what value these alternative ways of life might have for you. Hopefully, you'll ultimately have your own set of principles and ideas. But by examining those of others, it's sometimes easier to see our own by comparison or contrast.

As you learn about alternative cultures that practice simple living, keep some questions in mind. Ask yourself what the communities' underlying principles are, how they view the role of work in their lives, and how they provide basic needs such as food, health care, childcare, clothing, and housing. Keep tab on what you consider to be their successes and their failures. Be on the lookout for strategies and approaches in these other cultures that might be useful to you.

Beyond Basics

A wonderful book of essays on plain and simple living from *Plain Magazine* is *The Plain Reader*, edited by Scott Savage. These personal essays will take you on many different paths and introduce you to a wide variety of simple living "cultures."

➤ What are the underlying principles of this culture?

➤ How do they see work? How does work get done?

➤ How are they governed?

➤ How are children raised? Educated? What are the roles of parents, children and the family in this culture?

➤ What are this group's attitudes toward the land? The larger environment?

➤ How do they provide food for themselves and their families? What are their beliefs and rituals surrounding food?

➤ How is shelter provided for members of the community? What do their living arrangements say about their values?

➤ What are their attitudes toward dress? Household decoration?

➤ How do they handle celebrations? Special occasions? Passages?

➤ How do they allow for individual expression? Privacy?

➤ How is health care handled? What are attitudes toward aging? Mental illness?

➤ What seem to be the successes in this culture? What do they do well? What are the problems?

➤ What are the good points of this particular culture in your estimation? What are the bad points?

➤ How does a particular culture fit into a global world view? How does your own plan? Is that important to you or not?

➤ How does the culture interact with its various communities? Amongst themselves? With their surrounding locality? With their larger community, say, at a state level? Nationally?

➤ Imagine yourself living in one of these groups or cultures. Would it work for you? Why or why not?

➤ Imagine your own life in the ideal. What would it look like? Are there any concepts from the communities we're going to examine in this chapter you would incorporate into your ideal vision? Are there any other groups you find intriguing? How might you find out more about them?

➤ From what sources do you gather your ideas of "the good life"? What do you consider "the good life" to be?

There are all kinds of examples of communities and cultures whose goal is to be simpler than our own—some in other countries, some right under our noses. People are experimenting with all kinds of alternatives in housing, food production and preparation, work, energy, transportation, and just about any aspect of daily existence. Although the two examples presented in this chapter are rather extreme, my intention is to get you to think "out of the box" you're used to.

Quick Starts

In looking at other cultures, ask what their values are. Look for principles, even though religious or political beliefs might be different from your own or a group's lifestyle might not be practical for you or me. What can we learn from them? What's a typical day in the life of an Amish woman, for example? Man? Youngster? What about it could you incorporate into your own simple living vision? What would you not want to embrace? Why, do you think, have such groups remained relatively intact despite the pressures from our modern world? Where have challenges arisen and how have they coped with or adapted to these challenges? Why did the back-to-the-land movement take hold when it did and why did so few communal and coop experiments survive? Are such communities still viable today?

A Visit with the "Plain People"

One thing that stands out about the Amish community, as well as other similar groups like the Mennonites and the Hutterites, is just that—community. Part of what allows the Amish to live so differently from the rest of the world is the fact that they are self-contained and get their practical and personal needs met in the strong support group they have built around themselves. Probably the most important component of this support group is family.

Beyond Basics

A wonderful pictorial look at the Amish way of life is captured in *Amish Home,* by Raymond Bial. For an interesting portrait of the Amish taken from writings published in an Amish magazine and edited for adults, *The Amish In Their Own Words,* compiled by Brad Igou, is an excellent choice.

Lifestyle and Beliefs

If you ever visit an Amish community, you won't be able to take pictures of any of the people since the Amish believe that the Bible directs them against making "graven images," which they include to mean photographs, and because they consider it prideful. But there is no injunction against taking pictures of material possessions since they are of little importance in the Amish scheme of things. I find this distinction between people and things interesting.

One of the most obvious differences between the Amish way of life and "the English" (or nonbelievers) is the horse and buggy used for transportation, perhaps the most visible symbol of their rejection of much of modern technology including the radio and television. Their emphasis, instead, is on family, community, an agrarian way of life, and spirituality. This mode of transportation keeps the Amish world small and close to home. It also keeps life much slower.

Unlike the staunch individualism of people like Thoreau or the Nearings, amongst the Amish there is far less emphasis on individual freedoms. Members of the community are willing to give up some personal freedom for the sake of the whole. The fact that they often speak German amongst themselves, both in everyday life and in their religious meetings, reserving English only for outsiders, keeps them apart from the world, which is their objective. They consider themselves "nonconformists" in relation to the modern world around them, but within their society, there is great pressure to conform.

Young people are not baptized into the Amish faith until they are have reached adulthood (age 16) and have had a chance to decide for themselves whether they wish to adopt the Amish way throughout their lifetime.

Instead of using modern machinery, the Amish use horses for field work. By using animals, which "replace themselves," there is no need to update equipment, plus the cost of feed is less than that of equipment, maintenance, and fuel.

No electricity is allowed in the house, although electricity and a phone are sometimes found in Amish barns. This is a relatively new concession. Electricity is only used to operate a minimum of machinery, and the phone is used strictly to call out for selling produce to the outside world and for obtaining vital information. In some Amish communities, phones are still frowned upon. One of the main reasons for keeping electricity out of the house is to keep television and radio out of family life. The mass media is considered the enemy. Another relatively recent change has been to allow the use of gas-powered refrigerators and water heaters.

Children are educated through the eighth grade, usually in Amish-run one-room schoolhouses. After they leave school, however, young people are encouraged to learn practical skills, and there is much emphasis on self-education through reading and experience.

Like Thoreau and Helen and Scott Nearing did, the Amish work close to nature, but theirs is a cultivated nature. They feel that working the land brings them closer to God. The more you read their words, the more you sense the same self-reliant spirit that drove the Nearings to work the land and provide for themselves. Their prime directive is to keep themselves, according to their interpretation of the Bible, as "unspotted from the world" and to live "in this world, but not of it."

Although men and women have clearly defined roles, with men firmly implanted as the head of the household, they are considered in equal partnership, and wives co-own their farms with their husbands. Women usually manage the finances.

The Amish grow most of their own food and raise and slaughter their own meat. They buy only a few

Quick Starts

If you live in one of the many states that has an Amish community, try to arrange a visit. In Pennsylvania, check out the Pennsylvania Dutch Web site at www.800padutch.com/mem-cat.shtml. For Ohio, go to www.amish-heartland.com. If you can't actually get up and go, visit a Web site that's the next best thing—Discovery's delightful visit with an Amish family at www.discovery.com/area/exploration/amish/amish1.html.

Simple Wisdom

"America's current love affair with technology is partly based on the notion that hard work is a bad thing. If you are the smart guy, you'll think of a faster, easier way to do things than by manual labor. The cleaner one's hands are from the grime of hard work, the more highly esteemed and highly paid."

—David and Elizabeth Vendley in *The Plain Reader*

Simple Wisdom

"Some families are just so many individuals with the same last name, living in the same house .... These sad little groups of lonely individuals are not families at all. They are failures. They are missing out on one of the greatest challenges on this earth—building a meaningful family relationship where work, possessions, and even feelings can be shared in love and trust."

—E. Stoll, 11/77, *Family Life Magazine*

staples at local stores. Handcrafted quilts are sold by Amish women to supplement their income, and quilt-making is a large part of their social life apart from their families. Other ways various communities earn money are by making furniture and toys and by selling produce and prepared foods.

The Amish are pacifists. They no longer pay social security tax because they refused the benefits even when they did. They don't have insurance, and they take care of their old, so have no need of nursing homes. They do avail themselves of modern medical care, however. The Amish community has its own magazines and newspapers, providing reading material that it feels reflect its own values.

The Amish people are plagued with some of the same problems as modern society. There are instances of sexual misconduct, alcoholism, suicide, and crimes committed both within the order and outside. Young people often leave when they are old enough to decide; some return but many do not. But these problems are being dealt with openly, sometimes within the pages of their own publications, which can be subscribed to by "the English."

Lessons from the Amish

Very few of us would want to live as the Amish live, even if at times it might seem romantic. Yet there are lessons to be learned from their way of life that might be useful to us. Here are a few that surfaced for me:

➤ Having a support group makes it easier to stick to choices that may not be followed by the majority.

➤ Restricting or even eliminating mass media, especially television, can greatly enhance family life and personal growth.

➤ Spirituality is often a good foundation for simple living, whatever the source of that spirituality might be.

➤ Couples who share the same vision and treat each other with respect and love can have an abundant simple life together.

➤ Children may not share the simple life vision when they are older. They need to be allowed to choose for themselves, although teaching them the value of simplicity can contribute to their future happiness and contentment.

➤ Self-sufficiency from government services is possible if there is a commitment to taking care of the elderly, the infirm, or the less fortunate within families and groups of people with shared beliefs.

➤ What you feed your mind and heart will determine your direction. The Amish reinforce their beliefs with individual worship, group worship, and devotional reading. This doesn't have to be applied only to a religious faith; it can apply to any direction in which an individual is trying to discipline him- or herself. Lowering influences that are contrary to your goals and surrounding yourself with those that inspire and reinforce your goals will help you achieve them.

➤ Community is sometimes a tradeoff between support and personal freedom. How much and to what degree is up to us, but are there some worthwhile compromises to build community rather than maintain a lonely freedom?

1960s Holdovers or Pioneers?

In the 1960s, there were lots of "back-to-the-land" communities and communes that formed and faded away. One of the few to survive into the new millennium is Twin Oaks Community in Louisa, Virginia. I actually looked into Twin Oaks as a possibility in the 1970s but decided communal living wasn't for me. But what does this community have to teach us about simple living today?

Twin Oaks was founded in 1967 by a woman named Kat Kincade, along with her then husband, daughter, and five others. It was based on *Walden Two*, the controversial Utopian novel by B. F. Skinner that was first published in 1948. Skinner was the father of behavioral psychology and believed that, through social and behavioral engineering, people could learn to live in ideal communities of 1,000 people without poverty, conflict, or crime.

Although the title refers back to Thoreau's *Walden,* Skinner draws on many other sources for his ideas. He even borrows from the Nearings, advocating a four-hour workday, which Twin Oaks was never able to achieve. Work was to be based on free choice, with each person doing some manual work but basically doing the work he or she enjoyed most. Although work should be chosen, some work that was considered more unpleasant got higher credits, and other work that was more fun got less in Skinner's system.

Beyond Basics

Yet another community that bears study and offers us lessons about simple living is the Shakers. For a fascinating account of one woman's summer at one of America's last Shaker communities, read June Sprigg's *Simple Gifts: Lessons in Living From a Shaker Village.*

The original idea for Twin Oaks was to base the community on income-sharing and group parenting with no real political philosophy, although some would call these first two ideas decidedly socialist or even communist. They strive to be nonsexist and nonracist, yet the makeup of the community has been and is currently mostly white. Starting with 100 acres in rural Virginia, the group's land holdings have grown to more than 450 acres held in a land trust.

Founder Kat Kincade is now 69. She is the only original member still there, and even she left at one time and came back. Community members live in eight residences and eat together in a main dining hall. There are currently (according to their Web site) 80 people in the community, 67 adults and 13 children. Shared values stated are "cooperation, sharing, nonviolence, equality, and ecology." Instead of being a true *Walden Two* community, they now acknowledge that they are not actually based on the novel, saying that it is just one of "many influences that have helped shape Twin Oaks' character."

The Twin Oaks Community has three income-producing activities: a hammock and casual furniture business, selling soy products (especially tofu), and indexing books. They say they are "economically self-supporting and partly self-sufficient."

Each summer they host a Women's Gathering and a Communities Conference, plus there are weekly tours on Saturdays from March through October and alternating Saturdays from November through February from 2 to 5 P.M. The charge is $3. There is also a three-week visitor program for people considering joining the community or for those who are just interested in learning more.

Working at Twin Oaks

Individuals can choose the work they want to do (from what needs to be done) except dishwashing, which everyone is expected to share. Each adult individual is expected to work 45.5 hours a week, but this includes childcare, cooking, cleaning, laundry, and other regular household chores. There is a labor credit system with one credit equaling one hour of work. The quota is lowered as people age or for special circumstances. One member estimates that about two thirds of the work of each individual goes toward maintaining the community and one third goes toward earning money for expenses. Each person gets around three weeks of vacation time a year but can earn more if he or she works extra hours. Vacations are taken whenever members want.

Instead of earning money, members of the community earn time. They feel this is better than "the pointless and harmful accumulation of excess wealth." They've found that the credit system, although criticized by some residents on a regular basis, keeps things friendly. The system runs on the honor system, and residents say people are less inclined to cheat because they'd be stealing from each other in the community and would have to face that person every day.

Twin Oaks has a four-acre garden that provides most of the community's food, plus they produce fresh cheese, yogurt, and milk from their own cows.

The community originally attempted to home-school their children, but that fell by the wayside. Parents are basically responsible for raising their children, but arrangements can be made with others for childcare on occasion.

Twin Oaks is self-governed, and everything is decided collectively, although there are three "planners" who "carry out executive functions and help focus the community's attention on issues and the long-range effects." These planners rotate every 18 months. Opinions and objections are posted on a 3×5 card on the community bulletin board located in the dining hall.

People can keep personal resources outside the community, but they can't "benefit from their use while a member." There are no private vehicles, but several shared cars and vans are available for members' use. All articles kept in members' rooms are considered personal and not shared.

As with the Amish and many other groups I've examined, television isn't allowed because the members of the community feel it "would be too big a pipeline for just those values and products we are trying to avoid." There are videos and 16mm movies available plus a darkroom and a woodshop for personal use as well as radio, newspapers, and magazines. Various activity groups form depending on interests.

Beyond Basics

To contact Twin Oaks Community, to learn more about it, or to make reservations for the Saturday tours, call 520-894-5126. The community's address is 138 Twin Oaks Road, Louisa, VA 23093 (fax: 540-894-4112; e-mail: twinoaks@ic.org; Web site: www.twinoaks.org).

Twin Oaks calls itself an "eco-village," promoting recycling, organic gardening, and responsible consumption. Yet some argue that their hammocks and chairs are made in part from old-growth white oak trees and are sold to Pier 1 Imports, a symbol, perhaps, of consummate yuppiedom. The material they weave their hammocks from is plastic and nonbiodegradable.

Community buildings are mostly heated by solar energy and/or wood. They are not off the grid, and another irony is that their electricity is obtained from a nuclear power plant, which in their philosophical system might be considered unecological.

Children born on the commune and those who came at an early age with a parent usually leave and don't come back. There have been disagreements over the years that have led to mass exoduses, suicides, and other problems, just as in any community.

Difficulties are handled collectively with a voting procedure determining how final decisions are made.

The Lessons of Twin Oaks

Although intentional communities aren't for everybody, there's much to be learned from them. Some of the lessons I took away from reading about the Twin Oaks experience are:

➤ The amount of work it takes to support a large family or a small community simply and ecologically is still considerable, but the work may be more meaningful and diversified.

Beyond Basics

Is it Utopia Yet? is a book by Twin Oaks founder Kat Kincade on the community's first 25 years. It gives both a specific view of this particular community and a view of the challenges of any communal living arrangement.

➤ It's difficult to allow for diversity and then be consistent. Procedures need to be highly fluid when personalities and beliefs within the group are constantly changing.

➤ Removing television seems to spawn more creative and community-oriented ways of entertainment and recreation.

➤ Choosing income-producing work that's totally ecological can be difficult.

Is Twin Oaks viable for more than a relatively small group of people? Is the communal way of living workable for you? Some believe there is a new back-to-the-land movement but that this one is being fueled by people who've made their money in mainstream ways and then invested it and retired early, downscaling and simplifying. Is this any less valid?

The Least You Need to Know

➤ By studying other cultures and definitions of "simple living," we can enrich our understanding.

➤ Basing communities on simplicity has benefits and challenges.

➤ Joining together with people who share your beliefs and principles can make sticking to your plan easier.

➤ People with diverse beliefs can also join together and share resources if certain basic principles are also shared.

Finding Your Own Simple Living Way

So far, you've had a chance to examine the nature of consumerism, how other cultures exist simply today, and past examples of simple living. You've gotten in touch with your spiritual side and spent some time thinking about what simple living is. Now you can begin to create a tailor-made plan just for you. This completes what I call the "brain, heart, and soul work" of this book—the part where you have some conversations with yourself about exactly where you are right now and where you want to go from here. After this chapter, we'll be looking at specific actions you can take right now and in the future in each of the important areas of your life.

By the end of this chapter, I hope you will be armed with a list of goals in order of priority and a clear idea of where you want to go next. The rest of this book is organized by areas of concentration. After you've created your plan, you may want to move immediately into revamping your home, getting out of debt, or changing the way you buy, store, and cook your food. Skip around if you want to. Work according to your plan and make this book work for you. Start where you are and take it step-by-step according to the choices you feel most compelled to make.

Beyond Basics

One of my favorite books on goal-setting and knowing what you really want is Barbara Sher's *Wishcraft: How to Get What You Really Want*. You'll learn how to discover your strengths and weaknesses, how to use your negative feelings, how to create a support network for what you want to do and much, much more.

Quick Starts

Using your journal or a notebook, try considering these questions separately and thoroughly, one at a time. You might even spend a day on each, reading the question in the morning and thinking on it during the day, then writing your answers before you retire for the night. Give yourself plenty of time to reflect on these questions, since the answers will be important as we move on to consider specific areas of your life you may want to simplify.

In Chapter 2, "Simplicity and the Spirit," we talked about choice. This is the chapter where you start exercising your choice muscles. This is where you begin to define what simple living means for you. For one person, it may mean getting rid of most of their possessions and living in a small cabin in the woods like Thoreau. For other people, it may mean staying right where they are and rethinking how they use their space, what they do with their time, and how they spend their money. It's about "conscious" choice, what Thoreau called "living deliberately," and the choice is completely yours.

Getting to Know "You"

To tailor a simpler life meant just for you, you have to know who "you" is. That's why I put the chapter on spirituality before this one. One way to know yourself better is the same way you get to know anyone—ask questions! Seek others who will challenge you by asking questions, and you'll both get to know you better.

So what kinds of questions do you need to ask yourself when it comes to simple living? I've come up with a few that I hope will suggest others to you. Sit back with your beverage of choice and have an intimate conversation with the person in charge—you! Have a pad of paper or notebook handy and write these down. The answers will become the foundation of what simple living means to you:

1. What area do you feel is most out of control in your life right now? The most complicated? If you could change them, how would they look?

2. If you had your finances completely in order, how big an impact would that have? Do you have a budget? Do you know how much you owe? How much you bring in?

3. What issues are most important to the other people you share your life with? Have you asked them? If not, why not? Of all the people in your life right now, which ones would you consider to be part of a circle of no more than 10 vital people in your life?

4. If you needed more information about your situation, in which areas would that information be most helpful? Do you need to have a better idea of your debt and income? Do you know how efficient your home is? Your car? Do you need to know more about employment options? Community services? Other people who are living simply and how they're doing it?

5. How is your health? Is health an issue? Would it restrict certain simple living choices you might make? How do you envision a simpler life benefiting your health? How do you currently pay for health care?

6. How much clutter is in your life? Can you find things when you need them? Do you have enough storage? Are you storing things you never use? Does your life feel orderly or scattered?

7. How do you feel about the time available to you? Do you feel like you have enough time? Are you always pressed for time? Are you spending time doing the things you really care about?

8. How satisfied are you with your job? If you're not satisfied, is it the job or the occupation? If you could be engaged in your ideal work, what would it be? (Give yourself some time to think here and don't censor yourself.) If you are not sure, what would it take to find out?

9. What kind of shape are your relationships in? Look at each one of your most important relationships and evaluate them. If you could change or improve your relationships, what areas would you concentrate on? (Again, look at each one.)

10. How much time each week are you willing to commit to simplifying your life?

For each of us, the process of creating a plan for anything is generally the same. What do we really want? Where are we right now? What changes are we willing to make to have what we want? What are the steps we need to take to get there?

One of the things that can guide us in creating a life plan is to have a mission statement. What, you don't have one? You don't even know what one is, you say? Well, many human enterprises—corporations, schools, clubs, and organizations—come up with a mission statement. This helps existing and potential members of the group know what they're getting into, and it keeps them on track, giving them a measuring stick for future decisions.

Simple Wisdom

"The first step in any kind of change is getting a realistic picture of what is really going on."

—Cecile Andrews

Quick Starts

Not sure how to write a mission statement? A book to get you off to a great start is *The Path: Creating Your Mission Statement for Work and for Life,* by Laurie Beth Jones.

Simple Wisdom

"The degree of simplification is a matter for each individual to settle for himself."

—Richard Gregg

Basically, a mission statement is a statement of purpose—what you're about. It can be as simple as one sentence or can run much longer than that. Simpler is usually better. Work on a mission statement for your life, one that takes into account the answers you gave to the questions above. Write one today and then let it sit for a day or two. Revise it, work with it, try it on for size, repeat it regularly, and see if it continues to fit. Take however long you need to write one you truly feel comfortable with. Hopefully, you will come up with something that Stephen Covey in *The 7 Habits of Highly Effective People* calls "your constitution, the solid expression of your vision and values. It becomes the criterion by which you measure everything else in your life."

Make sure your mission statement expresses *your* purpose, not someone else's. Put aside other people's expectations for you or what you think you *should* be doing. In the end, you're the one you need to satisfy, to please, to respect.

The next thing I'd like you to do is daydream. Well, sort of. You're going to do a visualization, which is nothing more than closing your eyes and imagining something according to a guided path or a specific subject. Close your eyes and imagine yourself living "the simple life." Where are you? Who's there with you? What are you doing? How does it look? Add lots of details—a home, furniture, sights, sounds, smells, feelings. Allow yourself to stay in the place for a while. In fact, allow yourself to change places several times if need be and then go back to the ones you like the best.

Write down everything you can remember as soon as you complete this exercise. Note similarities. Note differences. Notice any difficulties you had imagining certain areas. Pay attention to conflicts or uneasy feelings, any attempts to judge or censor what you were trying to create. Take the time to write whatever comes into your head about what you've just "seen." This is important; you'll be building on this information. Repeat this exercise as often as you'd like in the months ahead. You'll most likely obtain new information and clearer details every time.

In coming up with a simple living plan that's tailored to you, resist giving over your power to experts. Instead, trust your own experience and intuition. There's nothing wrong with reading what other people have done or even what so-called "experts" have to say, but in the end, it's your life and your plan, and it may not end up looking anything like what authorities or experts describe.

If simple living is living consciously, then it is highly individual. If simple living is getting rid of the superficial and living life more in the essence, then, again, it is highly individual since only the individual can determine what is superficial in his or her own life and what is essential. Trust yourself and know yourself. You can't go wrong.

Also be skeptical about the media's take on the simple living movement. It's a lot more diverse than you may see presented. Some people complain, in fact, that the simple living movement seems to have been taken up by yuppies who've made their money and are now heading off to the woods to simplify in custom-made log homes with spas in the backyard. Sure, there are many people who've embraced the simple life who put time in the "rat race" and left early after they'd made a comfortable nest egg, and I don't think that's invalid. But there are as many stories as there are people.

There are kids coming out of college who are opting out altogether and are starting out simple. There are single parents who want to spend more time with their kids and are looking to simplifying and downsizing to help them do it. There are displaced caregivers, the elderly, or blue-collar workers seeking a better way. We need to be careful about the media image, which tends to focus on extremes, because in reality, simple living is being embraced in all kinds of circumstances and in all sorts of ways.

Taking Care of #1 ... That's You!

Whenever you make changes in your life or change is thrust upon you (isn't that *every* day?), it's important to care for yourself, to nurture the person who's going to be coping with these changes. I can't emphasize enough the importance of self care—getting good nourishment, uninterrupted and adequate sleep, plenty of privacy,

Simple Wisdom

"The clues to your life path are not lost. They are just scattered and hidden—some of them right under your nose, in plain sight. They need to be gathered together and carefully examined before you can begin to know how to design a life that truly fits you, a life that will make you feel like jumping out of bed in the morning to meet the world, a little scared at times, but fully alive."

—Barbara Sher

Avoidance Techniques

Be wary of trendy new magazines that focus on "simplicity." While it is certainly worth taking a look at anything that might help you simplify your life, keep some questions in mind before you fork over any money: Does the magazine accept paid advertisements? If so, what kind of products and services are featured? Do the lifestyles promoted mesh with the type of lifestyle you desire?

Avoidance Techniques

Refrain from judging yourself (and those around you, for that matter). If you're going to be making fundamental changes in your way of living, there are bound to be fits and starts, blunders and bloopers. These are blessings given to us for our education and enlightenment.

peace and quiet. Make a list of your favorite ways of indulging yourself with the emphasis on free or low cost. Concentrate on sensual pleasures, renewing experiences, and things that bring you joy. Name your list "Simple Pleasures" and add to it whenever you think of something that applies.

If nothing else, simple living gives you a space where you can attend to your needs, care for yourself, and check in with yourself regularly. As you develop your own plan, begin with this. Time spent caring for yourself keeps you on track and nourishes your relationships. Don't ignore its importance or its power.

Oh, and always have a good breakfast! Hey, if things get rough, you can live on one good meal if you have to. Make that meal a hearty, healthy, enjoyable breakfast, no matter where you're running off to.

Clearing the Decks

In tailoring a simple living plan to yourself and your unique situation, one of the first things to do is clear away the clutter, both physical and mental. Clear the decks by physically cleaning out, passing on, and decluttering your living space. If you're not sure where to start, start small—one drawer, one closet, one corner of a room you use every day. Or choose the area that would have the greatest impact on your life if it were put into order. Use my book, *The Complete Idiot's Guide to Organizing Your Life,* if you know you need to do a complete overhaul or you just need some help with specific areas. Or use your own ruthless common sense. Take time to rid yourself of excess baggage and then organize what's left.

I contend there are three absolutely key areas in any house that need to be kept clear and orderly for any kind of inner or outer peace. These are first, where we sleep; second, where we nourish ourselves and prepare food; and third, where we care for ourselves and keep ourselves clean. The bedroom, kitchen, and bathroom are, to me, the key rooms to make uncluttered, physically comfortable, pleasing, and functional. Create an oasis from which to operate every day and then branch out.

The next step is to stop. Once you've unstuffed your space, don't bring any more into it! Declare a moratorium on spending and shopping. If you think you must have something, write it down and then delay the purchase until you've spent more time planning your simplification strategy. You may decide you don't need it.

Withdrawal symptoms are highly likely. As you let go of clutter and refrain from spending, you may experience some real discomfort. Take it slow. Turn off the messages to consume whenever you can. Give yourself time to think, to reconnect, to ponder, and to plan. Scale down right where you are. Lower your outside commitments. Schedule blocks of time to spend with yourself on this. Read materials that will help you stay on track. Associate with people that are on the same road. We'll talk about actually starting a simplicity circle later on, but for now, just seek out others of like mind.

Quick Starts

Create an area in your living space for managing your life. Even if there's chaos everywhere else, clear a space, organize it, gather the tools you'll need in this area, and defend it. It can be a card table in the corner or a desk no one is using. Add a file box or cabinet, some basic supplies, and a notebook, and you've got your life management center. You'll find that this simple step will have a profound effect on your initial efforts to simplify your life. You'll create an outward symbol of an inward decision to find the center of your life.

Keep a notebook that includes a list of questions that come to mind and any exercises you may be doing along with this book. That nature journal you started after reading Chapter 2 would work nicely.

In addition to paring down your possessions, consider doing the same with relationships. Stop acquiring new people willy-nilly. For many of us, that's what our relationships are like. We consume people as well as things, and then when we're bored with them, we move on to the next. Assess the people you have in your life. Pare down to those that really contribute to your happiness. Plan to include them in a life balanced with alone time and primary, quality relationships. Be ruthless about defending these relationships and nurturing them and be very selective about who and what you allow to take up your time from here on. Start by saying no to people who make demands on your time that don't fit into the mission statement you wrote earlier in this chapter. Be conscious about your relationships.

Time's a Wastin'

Another important step in tailoring your simple living plan to you, the individual, is to identify your time and energy wasters and begin eliminating them. Do you spend a lot of time handling junk mail and reading it? How about junk e-mails (and I include

Beyond Basics

The classic book on time management is *How to Get Control of Your Time and Your Life,* by Alan Lakein. If you've never read it, do. If you have, read it again.

Simple Wisdom

"When we're in a hurry, or recuperating from being in a hurry, we don't have time to take note of the minute changes and fluctuations of daily life. It is awareness of these minutiae that make for a deep meaningful life."

—Janet Luhrs

chain letters, jokes, and unverified virus warnings among these!)? How well do you handle the phone? The TV? Making small talk? Shuffling stuff around? Keeping up with current events? Shopping?

Now, each of these activities has its place (well, maybe some you could eliminate altogether—we won't say which ones!), but how much time would you have if you cut them down to the bare minimum? A lot, right?

How do you feel about time in your life? Are you always "catching up?" Do you feel pressured for time? Do you take time to thoroughly be engaged when you do things you enjoy? Are you really "present" when you're involved in each activity or are you thinking ahead to the next thing you have to do with your time? Your relationship with time is a key component of simple living. Start noticing how you feel about it, how you use it, where you waste it, and how you'd most like to be spending it.

Make a list of your time and energy wasters and post them somewhere you can see them. Glance at them every day. Remind yourself. Create new habits from new consciousness.

When people first start thinking about simple living, they often complain that "simple living takes more time!" But that's not necessarily true. We need to look at the true cost of things, both in money and in time. One example is a food processor. Unless you're doing bulk cooking, it may well not be worth the time it takes to use and clean one, the time it took to earn the money to buy it, and the storage space it takes up. If you do cook in bulk, perhaps you could go in together with several people and share it once a month. When you're evaluating whether to keep or buy something, always look at the true cost. Besides the cost in time and money, you may also be robbing yourself of the tactile pleasure and fun of sharing tasks like chopping vegetables. All these things need to be factored in.

All the mental and emotional preparation we've been doing in these first chapters of this book may seem like a lot at first, but once you do the "brain, heart, and soul work" up front and settle these issues with yourself, the rest will go ever so much smoother.

The Least You Need to Know

➤ For a simple living plan to really work for you, you have to know yourself, what you really want, and your life's purpose.

➤ Taking care of yourself is a key step to simplifying your life.

➤ Ridding key areas of your home of clutter and choosing your personal relationships according to how they fit with your personal goals are essential to creating the necessary space for a simpler life.

➤ By examining your ideas and beliefs about time, you can reclaim more of it to do what really matters to you.

➤ Whenever you evaluate whether to get rid of something you already have or to acquire something new, consider its true cost.

Part 2

Your Money IS Your Life!

What could possibly be complicated about money? It's simple: There's never enough! If that's how it seems to you, then this part may surprise you.

These next five chapters will help you come to terms with the meaning of money in your life and will explain how debt is actually "the enemy," not money. You'll learn how to keep track of where your money goes and create a plan for true financial freedom. And if you're thinking that relocating or changing jobs is the answer, you'll have the information you need to decide.

While it may seem on the surface that you will be denying yourself pleasures and material goods as you get on the right financial track, you'll see how living with less is actually more abundant, more fulfilling, and an ultimately freer lifestyle that's better in every way.

Chapter 6

Going Debtless: How to Gain Your Freedom

In This Chapter

➤ Understanding the nature of debt and how it inhibits freedom, limits choices, and lowers self-esteem

➤ Learning the important steps to getting out of debt

➤ Living with new strategies to remain debt-free and work toward financial independence

---

What does debt have to do with simple living? The simple answer is everything! Living debt-free is actually the foundation of a simple life.

Let me ask you the following:

➤ How much time do you spend working simply to pay interest on purchases bought on time? Do you know?

➤ How much satisfaction and pleasure have those purchases really brought you? Can you even remember what they were?

➤ How often do you lose sleep worrying about bills?

➤ How much money do you have in savings?

➤ If you were to lose your job tomorrow or for some reason be unable to work, how long could you survive?

➤ What kind of retirement do you expect to have?

➤ How would your life be different if you didn't owe any money to anybody?

Simple Wisdom

"Ya load Sixteen Tons, whadaya get? Another day older and deeper in debt. Saint Peter don't you call me 'cause I can't go I owe my soul to the company store."

—"Sixteen Tons" by Tennessee Ernie Ford

Now, if you own everything outright and have no debt, this chapter may not apply to you. Still, skim it over to see if there's anything you might learn, then move on to the next chapter. But if you're anything like millions of Americans, you're carrying three to five credit cards in your wallet, some charged up to the limit, and you're paying interest on several of them. You're probably carrying a minimum of around $2,000 in credit-card debt monthly. You may also have a car loan and a mortgage, possibly even a second mortgage or a "bill consolidation" loan that was supposed to get you out of this mess some time ago. Sounds like you? Or perhaps you may fall somewhere in between debt-free and debt-burdened.

"But," you say, "everyone has debt! That's how the world works these days. Heck, even the government does it! That's how you manage to have the best things in life for yourself and your family." I say that's what crazy sounds like—for people and for nations.

What's Crazy? This Is!

You may not think your life is insane, but if you could get a more distant view, a different perspective, you just might change your mind. Not that you're alone. Every morning on the freeway, there are lots of other people just like you engaged in the same insanity. Once upon a time, I was there, too.

Consider this scenario:

The alarm clock jolts you out of a troubled sleep just in time to shower and throw on your "work" clothes. (You know the clothes. The ones you only wear when you're not having fun. The ones you pay to have dry-cleaned.) You grab a convenience breakfast or stop at the fast-food drive-up or maybe you skip breakfast altogether. On the road at rush hour, you drive a car you don't own, paying a premium on your auto insurance policy because you drive it every day to work. Meanwhile, as you sit in traffic burning gas, you're paying to heat, light, and insure an empty house, perhaps even paying a security company to monitor it while you're away so no one breaks in and steals all the things you've managed to accumulate.

Maybe you hire a cleaning company to do the housework you never seem to get to. Someone might even come in to walk the dog. If you have kids and they're in school, they may come home to either a baby-sitter or an empty house, or they may stay at an after-school program or daycare center until you can pick them up. All the while, you're working at a job you might not even like to pay for the car, clothes, house, child care, and services that allow you to go to the job you don't like that pays for ... (Get the picture?)

Then, when you finally get home in the evening, you're so exhausted and stressed out that all you have energy for is watching TV, complaining about your job, spending some limited time with family and friends, and catching up on the personal stuff you didn't have time to do during the week. And you wonder why you need a weekly massage, can't wait until the next vacation, often have trouble sleeping, and seem to come down with the flu a lot lately.

And this isn't crazy? What keeps it all going? Spending and debt. Debt and spending. The work, spend, debt, work, spend, debt merry-go-round is a trap, and the first step toward getting off the maddening cycle is getting out of debt.

What's Debt Ever Done for You?

What exactly is debt? According to the dictionary, it's "something owed to another," but read on; it's something deeper than that. It's also "the condition of owing." What does it mean to be in "the condition of owing?" Doesn't sound free or self-reliant or dignified, does it? Sounds demoralizing, tied down, dependent, limited.

So what are the benefits of getting out of debt?

➤ **Choice.** When you owe nothing, you can make new choices. You can adjust your life to meet new opportunities and can accept unexpected challenges.

➤ **Freedom.** The freedom is both physical and emotional. It means freedom of choice and freedom from the world of worry.

➤ **Security.** Real security is being able to take care of yourself and your family, not surrounding yourself with things. No debt means your resources are freed up to create real security.

➤ **Self-esteem.** Debt-free living feels good. It's living in integrity. It's relying on your own resources rather than borrowing from others.

➤ **Self-reliance.** Life has its ups and downs. So does the economy. Being without debt means there are bumps in the road, not catastrophes.

Beyond Basics

The best book I've ever read on getting out of debt, indeed, about our relationship with money and how to get straight with it, is *Your Money or Your Life*, by Joe Dominguez and Vicki Robin. Read it and do everything it says. Don't skip anything. I guarantee it will change your life.

The Meaning of Money

We tend to have all sorts of misconceptions about money. In a society that can talk freely about sex, we're pretty darn ignorant about money and finances, and we don't want to talk about it! Money means lots of different things to different people;

sometimes it has many conflicting meanings for one individual. We may think of money as "dirty" or "nonspiritual" or even "evil" (as in "the root of all ..."). We may think of it as the ultimate problem solver ("just throw some money at it") or the answer to all our dreams ("the best of everything"). Witness the new wave of money game shows and their high ratings.

Before I chose to simplify my life, money was something I feared. In my experience, it caused arguments and was used by people to control other people; only inferior, "worldly" people quested after money. If you were rich, you had to be bad. If you were struggling and found it difficult to make ends meet, you were somehow "nobler." I alternated between feeling righteous in my scarcity and envious of those whose lives were financially abundant.

So what does money mean to you? Try these formulas on for size:

Money = Freedom

Money = Bondage

Money = Happiness

Money = Security

Money = Evil

Money = Greed

Money = Success

Money = Repression

Money = Discrimination

Recognize yourself? Take out a piece of paper and write "MONEY" in big green letters across the top. Add a few fat dollar signs if you like. Then take a deep breath and, without stopping, write for a full minute (use a timer or ask a friend to time you) everything that pops in your head when you hear the word "money." Does what you've written reveal anything to you? What might your "formulas" be?

The truth is, money isn't anything by itself. It's completely inert, without value except what we assign to it. Money is a necessary "store of value" used to navigate in the world as it is today.

What are your money fears? Are you afraid of not having enough? Of making the wrong choices? Of being without? Are you afraid being financially solvent or even financially independent might leave you without friends? Does misery love company in your life? Are you afraid having money will corrupt you?

Facing our attitudes about money brings with it the need to face other things we might not want to face like death, disability, loss of loved ones, illness, old age, paying taxes, or what we really want for the future.

Money isn't the enemy, but our perception of it may be. And spending more of it than we have is definitely an enemy to what we say we want—simplicity and peace of mind. Debt is the enemy. I like the analogy that Vicki Robin and Joe Dominquez use in *Your Money or Your Life*. They present the concept that money is a symbol of life energy. It's what we get paid in exchange for expending our life energy at some kind of task valued by others. So when we spend it, we're spending our life energy, limited by our time on earth, the length of which is unknown.

A Twelve-Step Program for Getting Out of Debt

The more you spend, the more you have to work. The more you spend money you don't have (debt), the more you work with nothing to show, and the more life energy you give away with no return. Getting out of debt is a top priority if you're going to simplify your life and make the most of your life energy.

Step 1: Stop Spending Now!

Stop spending now. We talked about it in Chapter 1, "Consuming Passions: How the World Got Un-Simple." Well, if you didn't do it then, do it now. Try a day without spending one penny. Now stretch it to a week. See if you can do it. To keep from feeling denied, keep a gratitude journal like I described in Chapter 2, "Simplicity and the Spirit." Keep a list handy of things to do besides spending and of substitutes for things you would normally have spent money on.

While you've imposed a moratorium on spending, use the extra time not spent shopping to look for dollars you may have hidden that you can start applying to paying down your debt. Here are some to get your started:

➤ Do you have medical insurance claims you haven't sent it?

➤ How about rebates you forgot to redeem?

➤ Can you shop for lower rates on your car, home, or medical insurance? Can you afford a higher deductible?

➤ Can you lower existing credit card rates or consolidate all your cards onto the one with the lowest rate?

➤ Maybe you could go through your belongings (you know, the ones you're in debt for) and sell some that you really don't use. If you have a lot of clutter, get rid of it and make some money at the same time by holding a tag sale. Besides, it'll keep you at home so you won't be tempted to spend!

How many more can you find?

Step 2: No More Credit

Stop spending money you don't have. Don't use your credit cards, don't purchase items like televisions or cars on payment plans, don't borrow money from family and friends.

Quick Starts

One of the first things to do is cut up your credit cards. All except one, which you don't carry with you. Ever. This card is strictly for dire emergencies, renting a car, or guaranteeing a hotel room. If you can't manage to keep your hands off it, cut that one up, too, and find another way to handle travel and emergencies. Do whatever it takes to stop creating more debt.

Beyond Basics

A good book to teach you the fundamentals about money and debt is *The 9 Steps to Financial Freedom: Practical and Spiritual Steps So You Can Stop Worrying,* by Suze Orman. She explains the emotional traps that our attitudes about money can get us into as well as providing lots of basic financial concepts and terms.

If you have to, go on a completely cash system including closing your checking account if you can't stop using it as a loan-a-matic. You know, you make loans to yourself against the money that's going to be there, and if you don't get it there on time, you pay a fee, sometimes one that's higher than the cost of the loan. (Ever bounce a $5 check?) In some circles, they call this gambling. Credit allows us to indulge in the "quick fix" of spending to solve every problem or to escape from the ones we can't solve.

Step 3: Face the Truth

I call this the day of reckoning. What is a reckoning? It's a "count or computation; the settlement of an account." It's not a judgment but a tallying up, an honest appraisal. Set aside a weekend for your personal financial reckoning. Get comfortable. Organize your finances. Set up files if you've never done them. Do a complete inventory. Get all your credit reports or at least request them. This is like going to the doctor and getting a complete checkup to determine the state of your physical health. Only this is a financial health checkup. It doesn't help to ignore disease. If we know what we're facing, we can look for a cure. If your finances aren't exactly "diseased," then look at this as preventative medicine. You're getting an accurate handle on exactly where you are so you can point your financial life in the direction you choose.

Get out your calculator. Determine how much you owe, how much you have in fixed expenses, and how much you have coming in. Want a wakeup call? Figure out how much of your total expenditures goes specifically to pay off debt—interest.

We need to face our fears, get the facts, and create new truths based on accurate information, honesty, and integrity. Know that there are lean times and fat times. Learn to understand the nature of money as it ebbs and flows through life and begin to prepare for the changing tides.

Step 4: Keep Track of Expenses

Record all your ins and outs. Everything. If you want a really good system for doing this, read *Your Money or Your Life* (see the sidebar earlier in this chapter). Essentially, starting tomorrow morning, keep a notebook and pencil with you at all times and write down absolutely everything that goes through your hands, both income and outlay, down to the last penny. Give lots of detail and break down expenditures into categories if they're grouped together from one store. You'll be doing this for some time, so find a system that really works for you.

You'll need to balance your checkbook every month, too. If you have access to a computer, it may (notice the word "may") be worth your while to use financial software to keep track of some of your finances. Since I'm a professional writer, I use a computer every day, and having my finances on Quicken software is a natural. Before I used Quicken, I never balanced my checkbook. Since I've been using Quicken (some 11 years now), I've never *not* balanced my checkbook. There are other good software programs out there such as Managing Your Money. Set a regular time weekly to update and tally up your expenses, too.

Quick Starts

If you're one of the many people who can't live without a Palm Pilot, this could be the perfect tool for tracking all of your expenses. You can enter the information into the Palm Pilot as you spend the money and later download it into your home computer.

Step 5: Cut Everything in Half

Eat half of what you do now. Use half the toothpaste. See if you can cut your electric bill in half as well as your fuel bill. If not half, challenge yourself to at least a third. What can you cut or eliminate altogether? Expensive haircuts? (Learn to do it yourself or trade with a friend.) Restaurant meals? Can you cut gasoline by a third or half? (Cut consumption by grouping errands, parking downtown and walking to several locations, staying home for pleasure, and car pooling.) What else can you slash in half?

To keep from feeling deprived, decide in advance what you'll substitute instead. Give to yourself in place of buying something. How about candlelight dinners instead of having all the lights on (turn off the TV, too)? Turn off the tube and go to bed early,

Quick Starts

Here's an eye-opener: If you brew your own coffee and take it to work in a thermos, it'll cost you maybe 8¢ a cup. Compare that to $1 or more to buy your "cuppa java" at the corner coffee shop (not counting the tip). How many other places can you find daily where this kind of action is going on?

then lay in the dark with your spouse and talk. What a concept! You may even end up doing more than talking ....

Throughout this book we'll be looking at ways to simplify, which in many instances are also ways to cut expenses. You'll want to pay special attention to the chapters on food, clothing, shelter, transportation, recreation, and celebrations; they will give lots of strategies for cutting down and saving money while being more satisfied. Pick an area and revamp it. Devise your "living on less" strategy. (There's more help in Chapter 9, "How Living with Less Can Mean More.") It'll make life simpler, will get you in touch with deeper values, will tap your creativity, and will help you get out of debt.

Avoidance Techniques

Don't let your debt woes keep you from getting started on simplifying your life! Being in debt may mean you have to take smaller steps toward simplifying—can't quit that job just yet, for example—but keep in mind that simplifying your life will also help you get out of debt more quickly because you'll be spending less on unnecessary stuff!

Step 6: Get Help If You Need It

There's lots of help out there if you want to jump-start your debt-reduction program. You may just need some accurate information to help you assess things. There are several publications and Web sites out there that may be just the ticket.

Try Mary Hunt's "The Cheapskate Monthly," with the promise of "bringing dignity to the art of living within one's means." Her book, *Debt-Proof Living,* is also worth a look. Mary's Web site is at www. cheapskatemonthly.com, and you can get both an online and a print version of her newsletter.

Step 7: Contact Your Creditors

Beyond Basics

If things are really bad, you may need CPR. There are organizations that can set up a plan for you and hold you to it. Contact the Consumer Credit Counseling Service at 1-888-GO2-CCCS (1-888-462-2227) or www. credit.org, and they'll help you get on track.

Don't hide. Call your creditors if you've been avoiding them. Even if you're not behind in your payments, call your credit-card companies and see if you can lower your interest rate. They may say "no," but then again, they may say "yes." Know each and every one of your creditors. How much interest are you actually paying? What are the other fees involved—for late payments, for example, or annual fees? What is their billing date and when must payment be received to be considered "on time"? Don't cut it too close, though, or you'll end up paying. Keep these all in one place and keep track. Pay bills as soon as they come in if at all possible. Weekly, at least.

When I finally took a look at my own credit cards, I found a wide difference in annual percentage rates, from a low of 11.97 percent to a high of 23.49 percent! And two different cards from the same bank varied as much as 7 percent! You can't know where you're going if you don't know where you are. Read over your credit-card agreements. Call the customer service department if there's anything you don't understand and ask them to explain it to you. Check your bills every month; make sure they're accurate and that you understand the charges.

Avoidance Techniques

Beware of bill-consolidation or debt-consolidation loans. These can be very dangerous, especially if you don't take any other steps to stop racking up debt.

Step 8: Create a Plan

Decide what course you're going to follow to get out of debt. Create a plan. Read up on the subject. Set some goals and time limits. When would you like to retire? Would you like to work less and spend more time with your family now? How about your job—would you like to be doing something else or doing your job in a different context? If you share your financial life with someone else, share the information you've gathered and devise a plan together. You need to be allies, not adversaries.

Make things visual whenever possible. Make a graph, a list, a chart, whatever will help you appreciate where you are and visually illustrate your progress. Post your goals where you can see them, too.

Avoidance Techniques

Don't let occasional blunders cause you to give up on your new financial plan. Instead of giving up after you slip up—and unless you're perfect, you will—use these times as opportunities to learn from your mistakes. Consider anything you spend beyond what you've budgeted to be "loans" you make to yourself and then find ways to earn extra money to pay off the loan.

Step 9: Pay Yourself First

The majority of Americans have little or no savings. Imagine your peace of mind if you had six months worth of living expenses in the bank. Or how about a year's worth? Why, you could actually take some time to figure out what you really want to do with your life, survive a layoff, or start your own business. See what I mean about debt and freedom? Without debt you can save. With savings you create choices.

Quick Starts

Create a timeline for getting out of debt based on your budget. Set aside time each week to compare your actual progress to the goals you set in your timeline. Use this time as an opportunity to evaluate how well your plan works for you and what kinds of adjustments you may need to make to your lifestyle or your plan in order to make them work.

Avoidance Techniques

Avoid savings accounts that you can access through cash machines. This makes it too easy to take money out of your account when you don't really need to.

Don't touch your savings. Make it difficult to get at them. Get on an automatic savings plan at work if one is available. Put the money in a bank that's inconvenient—one that's not the same as your regular bank. Put it in a money market account and put the checks in a safety deposit box or some other inconvenient place.

Find ways to interrupt your instant gratification pattern. Whatever it takes. If you have a 401(k) plan at work, take the maximum deduction as soon as possible. If you get a raise, only use it to pay off debt. As soon as you're debt-free, bank the raise or have it taken out of your paycheck. Keep the same "standard of living" no matter how much more money you make.

Step 10: Join with Others

If you've started to create a simplicity support network around yourself (see Chapter 19, "Circle of Community: You Can't Do It Alone,") perhaps the first things you should tackle together are attitudes toward money and getting out of debt. Share resources and experiences, approach someone who's done it, and ask him or her to work with you.

Hang around people of like mind and shun "the Joneses." You're not keeping up with them anymore anyway. Your new group may provide a social outlet that won't be another leak in the money dam.

Step 11: Shift Your Consciousness

Change your mindset when it comes to money. Find out what your money consciousness is, decide what you want it to be, and begin reprogramming yourself.

Getting out of debt will help you "do the right thing" in other areas of your life. Perhaps you've put off doing responsible things like making out a will, getting life insurance or long-term care insurance, estate planning, or starting a college fund for your kids. Respect money and you respect yourself. Shifting your consciousness and getting straight with your money attitudes will lead to greater confidence and self-trust. Abundance thinking about money will spill over to other areas of your life.

Step 12: Consider More Drastic Measures

Now, I'm not asking you to sublet your apartment and go live in your car (although some people have successfully taken similar drastic measures to save themselves from bankruptcy), but there may be some big sacrifices you'd be willing to make to effect a big impact on your finances in a short period of time. This willingness is a test of how serious you really are about living debt-free and moving on to other aspects of simplifying your life.

Could you move out of your house or apartment and live in a tent or travel trailer for a few months? This may sound nuts, but I know someone who did it and got a handle on his finances in less than six months. Could you move into your basement and rent out the upstairs? Could you work a second job for a few months to get a head-start? Do you have something valuable to sell? Do you have some space you can rent out like an extra bedroom, a basement, shop space, or a garage?

Do you need everything you're indebted to? Is there a cheaper substitute? Could you sell the car you have the loan on, pay it off, and pay cash for a gently used car? Could you downsize your house so you have no mortgage or a much smaller one? Do you really need a boat? A motor home? A vacation house? Show me the money!

Take a look at *all* your resources and see if you can turn any of them into cash. Try some "blue sky" thinking and don't censor yourself. Be a little out-rageous. You may actually stumble on a solution you hadn't thought of that could move you forward faster than you ever dreamed possible.

You may be so behind that you're thinking about declaring bankruptcy, and that may be an option for some people. In my opinion, bankruptcy is not the way to go. It just doesn't seem "in integrity" no matter how I look at it. This is your name, your reputation, and what you stand for on the line here. Unless there's absolutely no other way out, I think bankruptcy shouldn't be an option.

Quick Starts

A quick way to start saving some money is to cancel extras like cable TV or newspaper and magazine subscriptions, at least until your debt is paid off. You may find that after living without these for a few months, you're happier that way!

Staying Debt–Free for Life

No Debt + Savings = Choices, Freedom, Peace of Mind

Living debt-free is contrary to our culture—it's actually "counter-culture." Resisting the impulse to buy on credit takes some real willpower if you're to exist day-to-day in mainstream America. But people do it and so can you.

To first live within your means and then live below your means and save—that's financial independence. We'll talk more about how to achieve financial independence in Chapter 10, "In the Independent Republic of Finances," but I can tell you that you can't get there and be in debt.

Here are five things to keep in mind to help you stay on track once you've killed the debt virus:

1. Continue to keep track of expenses and work on a cash basis whenever possible.

2. Resist rationalization by recognizing it for what it is. Squash the little voice that says, "I'll save after I've bought the whatamahingus that I really need," and pay yourself first. If you still need the whatamahingus, save for it.

3. Tune out messages from the consumer culture by turning them off or at least analyzing them. If you limit your exposure to advertising and always approach it critically, you'll lower your vulnerability.

4. Surround yourself with others who are committed to living debt-free. This can be done both in your actual day-to-day contacts and in your reading material.

5. Keep your goals in mind. Remind yourself regularly why you're doing this.

What Have You Got to Lose?

If you think living debt-free is too difficult to attain, think of the alternative. If you have no money now, what will you have in 10 years? In 20? If you think it's too late, it's not. Teach your children the value of living debt-free, compound interest, and simple living and to start saving now.

The Least You Need to Know

➤ Debt keeps you from simplifying your life and having peace of mind.

➤ There are specific steps you can take to rid yourself of debt and focus your resources toward the life you want.

➤ Once you eliminate debt, you can begin to save and provide security and freedom for yourself and your loved ones.

Earning a Life, not Just a Living

When someone mentions the word "work," what pops into your mind? If you're like most people, you think of your 9-to-5 job or some kind of unpleasant task you generally try to avoid.

What if I told you that "work" was the essence of life—the key to happiness? How we think of work and the role it plays in our lives has everything to do with fulfillment and happiness. And it's something we have to settle with ourselves to create a simpler life. As you read through this chapter, hopefully you'll be able to come up with a new, more useful definition of the word "work" and create a working life for yourself that allows you to be all you want to be.

Reworking "Work"

Have you ever heard someone say "I'd do this even if I didn't get paid!" or "I'm having so much fun I can't believe they're paying me!"? Can you imagine feeling that way about what you do to provide a wage for yourself and your family? It's certainly possible and, in my estimation, is a central goal of simple living.

But before we can redefine work or figure out what the best course for the future might be, we need to define where we are now. Let's look at the here and now. Ask yourself the following questions about your current job:

➤ How do you feel when you get up to go to work in the morning?

➤ How does your job leave you feeling at the end of the day?

➤ What does your job say about you (and what do you say about your job)?

➤ How does what you do for a paycheck reflect your values?

➤ If you weren't doing this, what would you rather be doing?

➤ When someone asks you what you do, what do you say? How do you feel when you say it? Do you answer with your paid employment or a broader description of what you really do with your life energy?

➤ What did you want to be when you grew up? How close have you come? What did you want to be *doing* when you grew up? Notice the difference.

➤ Besides financial compensation, what benefits do you get from your work? Be sure to include emotional benefits as well as financial ones.

➤ What would you do first if you lost your job tomorrow? What kind of provisions have you made in case this happens?

Now, imagine what you would be doing if you didn't have to work at a conventional job at all. Let's say you were financially independent and could provide for all your basic needs without working. Not rich, mind you, but able to comfortably provide for your basic food, clothing, shelter, health care, and so on. Would you rock in a hammock all day? Play golf? Go fishing?

That might be fun for a while, but it might get old. What would you do with your time if all your basic needs were taken care of? The answer to this question is at the core of redefining work because we all need some sort of "occupation" to make our time meaningful; to spend our life energy on that would give us fulfillment, satisfaction, even joy. Once you begin to understand what your real life's work would be if you took control, you can begin to create the working life you'll love.

If we go back to Joe Dominguez and Vicki Robin's equation that money is life energy (refer to Chapter 6, "Going Debtless: How to Gain Your Freedom"), then paid work is the giving of life energy in exchange for money. Of course, we give our life energy in other tasks for other rewards. Money is only one manifestation of where and how we are "spending" our life energy. So our pay represents the life energy we've put into our job, and somehow it should be compatible with the preciousness of what it represents.

Quick Starts

Joe Dominguez and Vicki Robin, in their book *Your Money or Your Life,* ask the reader to reflect how expenditures might change if he or she didn't have to work for a living. Now that you're keeping track of your expenses after reading Chapter 6, make a list of which ones would be lowered or increased if you didn't go to a job every day. Changing your definition of work and the way you think of your work life might open up some new choices you didn't see before. How would expenses like gasoline (maybe even the need for a car), insurance, clothing, food, housing, vacations, and escape entertainment change if you didn't commute to a job every day? Indeed, how would the very fabric of your life change if your entire approach to work were to change?

Working for Yourself

In time past, people worked just for survival. And they worked less! From what we know about simpler, so-called "primitive" societies, working three or four hours a day to provide the basics was enough, and members of the tribe or community spent the rest of their time socializing with family and friends, playing, and engaging in ritual and celebration. So what we learned in Chapter 3, "What's Old Is New Again," about the Nearings' idea that they should only need to do physical work four hours a day is not much different than what ancient people actually did. Maybe if we focused our efforts on the basics, we could do the same thing.

Our current economic philosophy and work ethic tells us that "full employment" is highly desirable. The more people work more hours, the stronger the economy is supposed to be. This philosophy is based also on "full consumption," the idea that the economy only benefits from the work, spend, work, spend cycle. We'll talk more about whether this concept is really all it's cracked up to be later on in this book, but for now, suffice it to say many of us have bought into the idea and are living it out as we speak. The result is that we increasingly identify with our work. Our jobs or careers in many cases *become* our identity.

Instead of working for a living, what if you started working for yourself? Now, I don't necessarily mean starting your own business or becoming a

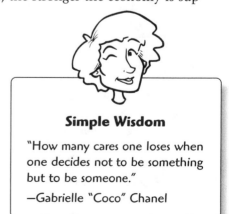

Simple Wisdom

"How many cares one loses when one decides not to be something but to be someone."

—Gabrielle "Coco" Chanel

freelancer, although that's a possibility we'll explore later in this chapter. In any job you can work for yourself including the one you're in right now. When you decide to *always* work for yourself, you can change your attitude, perhaps even reinvent your job. How do you "show up" at your current job? Are you just putting in time, watching the clock until you can leave for home? How well do you treat yourself on the job? How do you treat others? How do you honor the life energy you're trading for a paycheck each week? Wherever you are, whatever you're doing, look for ways to make things more pleasurable. Create a pleasing workspace within the limitations imposed on you. Ask. Maybe you can do more than you realize.

As you know by now, I believe in taking stock before embarking on a new direction. If you know where you are, you can make better choices about where you're going. I also believe in being in the present and looking at the possibilities within existing parameters. There may be different ways of configuring what you already have, and even if you want to move on, while you're preparing your game plan you can improve the situation right where you're standing.

Perhaps working for yourself actually means changing jobs altogether. If that's what you decide is warranted, take the time to look at all the choices you have. And if you haven't handled your debt, brought your spending down to within or below your means, and put money away in savings, consider how your choices would be different if you'd accomplished that and consider taking the time to do it before you move on.

Evaluate how you got where you are in the first place. Why do you work at your current job? Is it the money? The security? Are you carrying on a family tradition or fulfilling someone else's plan for you? Are you there out of a sense of duty? Does it provide you with prestige? Does it just keep you busy? Or do you get things like pleasure and satisfaction, constant learning and challenge, personal growth, a creative outlet, spiritual fulfillment, a real sense of service to others, or positive feedback from others? What motivates you?

If you don't get these things at work, where do you get them? Dominguez and Robin bring up another interesting point—all the benefits we get from paid

Quick Starts

While you're thinking about improving your current situation, ask for a raise or do some research to find out what other people are being paid for the same work you do. You may be surprised. What are all the possible job configurations in your current field, perhaps even within your own company? What can you do to make the absolute most of what you have right now?

Simple Wisdom

"Breaking the link between work and wages has as much power in our lives as the recognition that money is simply 'something we trade our life energy for.'"

—Joe Dominguez and Vicki Robin, *Your Money or Your Life*

employment other than money can be gotten from unpaid activities. They emphasize the need to distinguish between "work" and "paid employment." Work is any productive or useful activity. Paid employment is what we do for money.

By making this simple shift in how we view work, we now create more choices, can make our work more in line with our inner direction, and integrate the different parts of our lives into a more harmonious whole. In the simplest terms, what counts is that you earn the money you really need and use your time to work at the things you really love. How you put that together can be as unique as you are!

Working at Home

One option that can simplify life immensely or can complicate it unwittingly is moving your paid employment to your home. The contributions such a move can make toward simplifying your life are fairly obvious. You can save money on expenses like gasoline and clothing, you have more time to spend on other things because you're not commuting, and you can control your working environment.

Yet all these benefits can also create problems if you don't know yourself, don't have clear goals, and haven't thought through what it means to be without the structure of a conventional job. You can end up spending more money on things you never dreamed of out of boredom or a need to make yourself feel validated without a full-time job working for someone else. You can end up watching daytime TV, feeding the birds, and catching up with the neighbors instead of earning a living. You can spend more time decorating your office and less time concentrating on creating business or meeting deadlines. And you can find yourself spending all day at the beach and then being too tired to get your work done when you get home.

Simple Wisdom

"To live with simplicity is by its very nature a 'life-serving' intention. Yet, in serving life, we serve ourselves as well. We are each an inseparable part of the life whose well-being we are serving. In participating in life in this manner, we do not disperse our energy frivolously, but employ our unique capacities in ways that are helpful to the rest of life."

—Duane Elgin, *Voluntary Simplicity*

Avoidance Techniques

Keep in mind that working at home takes a lot of self-discipline and willpower for it to be beneficial. If you're the kind of person who needs the structure of an office and a boss looking over your shoulder for you to get any work done, then working at home probably isn't right for you.

Beyond Basics

If you're thinking of working at home, but you're not sure it's for you, I highly recommend that you read two books. First is the now–classic *Working from Home: Everything You Need to Know About Living and Working Under the Same Roof,* by Paul and Sarah Edwards. This book covers every aspect of making a living where you live from the nuts and bolts to the emotional and psychological. The second book is called *Working Alone: Making the Most of Self-Employment,* by Murray Felsher. I don't always agree with Murray, but this book makes me think and is full of interesting ideas from an independent consultant who knows what he's about and knows how to get paid what his work is worth.

Take a look at what you enjoy doing and see if it might be adaptable to a home-based situation. Could you continue to work for the same company if you truly enjoy what you do, but work part of the time from your home? Is there such a thing as telecommuting in your company or field? Would learning how to make use of certain technology create this option for you?

Are You an Entrepreneur?

Although working at home may mean for some people starting their own business as well, that may not be the case. Nor does starting your own business necessarily mean working at home *or* simplifying your life. As with everything, owning your own business has pluses and minuses. As you go through the process of redefining work for yourself, consider the self-employment option in all its versions but know all the upsides and downsides in each one.

Because my husband and I have created the scenario we talked about in Chapter 6 of having no debt (except our mortgage and we're working on it!), lowering our expenses, and having enough in savings and investments to take care of our basic needs, being in our businesses has a completely different context. The freedom of being financially independent allows us to choose carefully what we take on, how big we allow our businesses to get, and what direction we want them to take. We are in control. We need to work at our businesses to be "comfortable" but not to survive, and that makes all the difference. In our case, owning our own businesses is the simple life.

But some people give themselves over completely to their business, and it becomes their life. They become more driven than they ever would have been in a job in which they worked for someone else. Their identity is far more wrapped up in their business than it ever would have been in paid employment. Everything else takes a back seat to "the business," and it permeates every corner of their life.

The simple living version of owning your own business is one in which you control *it,* not the other way around. You can run your business the way you want in line with your deeper principles and greater goals. You keep it the size you want. You decide how you want your business to fit into your life, how much you want to make, how much time you want to put in.

If your business fits into your life in a balanced way, with little or no money pressures and a cushion of savings, you have much more control over whom you work with. You can actually pick and choose the jobs you take, the clients you work with, or the products you sell, based on what's enjoyable, creative, challenging, and has a low aggravation factor.

Consider the option of making your business a part-time business. A stay-at-home parent, for example, might arrange his or her business to be conducted on weekends or in the evenings, while the other parent is home to take on childcare. A business can be as big or as small as you allow it to be, and it doesn't have to be full-time.

Quick Starts

Start a work notebook or folder. Clip quotations or write down ideas about what you think work is for you. Imagine yourself doing various kinds of work, complete with all the surroundings, tools, education, and whatever you'd need. How does it feel? What would you need that you don't have now? What's stopping you? What would you be doing now if you didn't have to work for a living but could work for your life? Who could you interview that has redefined work for themselves? Use these tools to revise your own definitions. Let those creative juices flow!

Finding a "Calling"

I have a friend whose real job is rescuing hybrid wolves from almost certain death as they're abandoned or taken to shelters by people who were unprepared for the special considerations of caring for a part wolf, part dog. The marketplace doesn't reward the

Avoidance Techniques

Beware of making your calling your means of paid employment. It can work sometimes, but it can also become twisted as we try to turn it into a moneymaking proposition. We might be more true to ourselves to work at something else, creating the freedom to do what we love in the best way possible, not dependent on money.

work that Bill feels called to do, so he has arranged his life around his calling, has found part-time work to provide for his basic needs, and has lowered his expenses to fit.

You might have such a calling but think it's impossible for you to listen to its call. Think again. How can you use what you've learned so far in this book to rethink your position and to begin follow your calling? You may not be ready yet, but put the idea in your work notebook, keep it, and let it grow.

How do you know you've found your calling? Well, if you asked Bill he'd say that, although it's a lot of work, it feels a lot like play. His entire life is built around it, and now that he's found a partner who shares his calling, his relationship is inextricably bound to it as well. Not everyone finds a calling in life, some of us have several, and others simply strive to create a balanced, satisfied, whole life. In a simple living philosophy about work, all of these are possible. In fact, they're preferable!

New Work Choices

Hopefully, by now you're beginning to think of work in different terms, and maybe you're even thinking about changing your own terms of employment. But before you do anything drastic, let's explore still more options. By the time we're done, your work folder or notebook should be filled with entries, sketches, question marks, pieces of this and that. When you tackle this "job thing," you'll have the clearest possible idea of what the options are for you.

Working for yourself actually means that, no matter what you're doing, you're working for *yourself*—your vision of your life's purpose. When you start working for yourself, everything you do is part of the picture of your life. Some new choices that might fit into the bigger picture of working for yourself are

➤ **Downsizing your job and working less.** Consider working part-time at your current job or finding a higher paid part-time job for paid employment, using the rest of your time or life energy working at your life's work, for which you may or may not get paid. You may need some training or education, but with this option, you might get the most money for the least amount of time spent.

➤ **Asking about job sharing.** Is there someone else at your current employment that might like to cut down on hours, too? Can you propose this idea to them and go together to your employer?

➤ **Working in cycles or with the seasons.**
Seasonal or cyclical jobs such as tax preparer,
gardener, freelance writer, teacher, tour
leader, and a host of others can mean working part of the year and having part of the
year off. There might be a period of intensive
activity making money and then intensive
activity doing the rest of what you care
about. You'll need to be very careful about
how you save money while you're earning it
to make it last for the whole year.

➤ **Combining jobs.** For some people, the best
kind of working life is one made up of several
things they care about, combined to make
enough money to live simply. None of their
occupations may earn a high wage, but combined they produce enough and make an integrated, meaningful life.

➤ **Sprinting to the finish line.** Some people
would rather work full-time for a limited pe-
riod of time at something that's very lucrative but not what they want to be
doing forever. They save a lot, invest, and retire early.

> **Simple Wisdom**
>
> "This is the true joy in life, the
> being used for a purpose recog-
> nized by yourself as a mighty
> one; the being thoroughly worn
> out before you are thrown on
> the scrap heap; the being a force
> of nature instead of a feverish
> selfish little clod of ailments and
> grievances complaining that the
> world will not devote itself to
> making you happy."
>
> —George Bernard Shaw

➤ **Temporary solutions.** Perhaps taking temporary jobs when you need the
money works best for your lifestyle. Again, this approach requires that you bank
what you earn when you're earning so that you have funds when you're not.

➤ **Those who can, teach.** Can you teach what you love? This might allow you to
pursue your calling and share your enthusiasm with others, while getting paid
for it. An additional benefit is learning still more from your students.

➤ **Volunteering your way into a new career.** Sometimes when you pursue what
you love without pay, it turns into a way of earning money because you do it so
well or because opportunities you never thought existed present themselves. If
you don't know of a job doing what you want to do, volunteer and be open to
the possibilities.

➤ **Take a sabbatical.** Perhaps your job is what you love, but you simply need time
off to take it to some new level or renew yourself. Does your employer provide
for a leave of absence or sabbatical? It can't hurt to ask. You can take advantage
of this option only if you have savings, low expenses, and no debt. See how it
keeps coming back to that!

Making Your Life Work

Being unemployed can be a devastating experience or a time of discovery. It can set you back or push you forward on your road to the simple life. If you have savings to fall back on, you can redesign your work life instead of frantically looking for the next job that doesn't truly suit you. You're not really "out of work" if you're not working for wages alone but "working for yourself."

Prepare now for this possibility and you can be preparing for a better future this time. If you're not yet ready to take some of the steps we've described so far toward self-reliant, independent, and simpler living, but you feel you need to get a new job at this point, how can you find a new job that better fits your life's purpose and that brings you closer to your simple living goals?

➤ **Know your purpose.** Know what your life's purpose is and be able to clearly define it to yourself. If you use this as a constant yardstick of intent, your next job will likely be more satisfying and rewarding.

➤ **Let go of your fears.** Identify your greatest fears about being unemployed and see if you can take care of them now before you're confronted with the situation. Knowing your demons and putting them in their place ahead of time will serve whatever you decide to do in the future, near or far.

➤ **Roll up your sleeves.** Be willing to really work and be active, not passive. Let people know what kind of job you're after. Talk it up. Be willing to do "whatever it takes."

➤ **Pay attention to opportunities.** Beware of self-limited talk and thinking. Don't only look at the obvious and use the methods you've always used. Look carefully for openings and reshaping what exists to what you want.

➤ **Commit yourself to lifelong learning.** Do you do only the bare minimum required for your job? Are there related skills you could gain but haven't made the time or focused your energy? Educate yourself and learn new skills continually, and you'll both enhance your current work situation and create opportunities for the future.

➤ **Give yourself the power.** Expect the best from your next job—getting paid a high wage is simply your own self-respect for what you do. Being paid well for good work is not greed or competitiveness. If you give your life energy, the best of you, you should be well compensated. Give yourself the power to do well.

As you navigate your way through the rest of this book, you'll learn lots of other ways to rethink your daily life, some of which will open up new options in regard to work. Keep adding to your notebook as we go along and work well!

The Least You Need to Know

➤ Old definitions of work are fragmenting and limiting.

➤ We can reinvent the way we spend our life energy in any number of ways, keyed to our purpose, our calling, and our financial independence.

➤ Working for yourself means more than having your own business. We can be working for ourselves in whatever we do.

➤ If we choose to remain in a conventional full-time job for the time being, we can improve our situation and prepare for a better, more simple living–compatible job in the future.

Chapter 8

Location, Location! The Simple Truth About Where You Live

In This Chapter

➤ Determining whether your current location is the best place for you to simplify your life

➤ Choosing a new location based on your own best lifestyle

➤ Deciding when and how to relocate

➤ Making the move, simplified

When some people think of simple living, the first thing they envision is a place in the country. If you're not already in a rural environment, that's certainly a possibility, but is it for you? Do you even need to relocate to enjoy the simple life? And should you decide moving is the best choice for you, how do you decide where to go?

These are the issues we'll be considering in this chapter. Although you may not be pulling up stakes tomorrow, you'll be equipped to evaluate your current location and pick the best relocation if that fits your own simple living plan.

Start Where You Are

Part of deciding whether you're in the right location is getting a good fix on the one you're in. How well do you know your community? How does the cost of living

compare to other regions of the United States? Are you making the most of the resources right where you live to start you on your simple living path? If you're thinking of relocating, would you be running *from* something or going to a better way of
life? How much of your dissatisfaction with your current location has to do with *you?*

To evaluate where you are now (and, indeed, any place you might be considering
moving to), you'll need to start a list. Actually, two lists. One will keep track of advantages, the other of disadvantages. Some of what you put on your list will be subjective, but some will require you to do some research. Here are some things for you
to look at and decide if your current location is positive or negative in each category:

➤ **Cost of living.** You'll need to determine the cost of living for where you live and
   compare it to other parts of the country to get a picture of where you are. A trip
   to your local Chamber of Commerce will yield lots of helpful free information.
   Approach your information gathering as if you were new to the area or were considering moving there and setting up business. Some good clues are cost of real
   estate per square foot, salaries, food prices, gasoline prices, and tax rates.

Beyond Basics

The quickest way to do this is to get online (ask a friend or check out your library's
Internet access if you don't have your own) and go to the Web site of the Economic
Research Institute at www.erieri.com. Take a look at their home page and some of
the free information they provide as well as their paid services. Then go to www.
salariesreview.com/surveys/national_costofliving.cfm to put in your zip code, and for $38,
you can get a complete breakdown of your area's cost of living. Check their sources list as
well since there might be free information provided at one of the links listed there. By
clicking on the Arizona Department of Commerce link, for example, I was able to find a
community profile for where I live and obtain quite a bit of cost of living information for
my area for free.

➤ **Safety, crime, and law enforcement.** Take a good look at the crime rate in your
   community. Do you know what your area's crime profile is like? Do you feel safe
   walking the streets at night? Do you feel safe in your home? What is your stand
   on self-defense and are your community's laws (and state laws) supportive of
   that stand? How reliable is your local police department?

Besides crime, what other safety issues might there be? Are you near an airport, a toxic waste area, a highway heavily traveled by vehicles carrying toxic substances?

Having a safe place to live is a fundamental need and right, in my opinion. It's hard even to contemplate a simple life when you're in constant danger or worry about your safety.

➤ **Weather.** What's the climate like in your region and what kind of climate do you like? What threats are there to life, limb, and property due to weather where you are? Do you need to be concerned about hurricanes, tornadoes, earthquakes, severe winter storms, or drought? Is your location conducive to growing your own food if that's what you want to do? How does climate affect heating and cooling costs?

➤ **Health.** When evaluating the healthiness of your current location, look at all the factors: mental, emotional, spiritual, and physical. What kind of health care is available to you and how do costs compare? Are there any diseases that seem to occur disproportionately in your area? Why might that be? Look around you—how healthy are your friends, the people you work with, your neighbors? Does health seem to be a concern in your community? If alternative health care is important to you, what kinds of options are available where you live?

Quick Starts

Want a quick picture of the weather in your town or any other? Visit GO Weather at weather.go.com for records and averages, current forecasts and even severe weather tips.

➤ **Environment.** Environmental quality includes the quality of the air we breathe and the water we drink; whether our soil, rivers, and streams are contaminated; the substances in our building materials; how good and pure our food is; how much noise we have to deal with every day; and even light pollution. Try to be objective and then analyze the environmental quality of your community. Even if some of these things aren't particularly important to you, at least know what you have and what compromises you're willing to make.

What is the city or town's infrastructure like? Is it old and crumbling or being revitalized? Do essential services like public transportation, electricity, water, or waste disposal often have problems? Are the recreational areas environmentally protected and managed to stay that way?

➤ **Character.** This is a more subjective evaluation, but let's look at it nevertheless. Sometimes a town's character is what keeps us there more than anything else. Maybe it's quaint and cozy, maybe it's full of "movers and shakers," maybe it's the history or the scenery or a particular cultural influence. See if you can come up with a paragraph to describe your community's character.

➤ **Education.** If you have children in the school system, how happy are you with the quality of their education? If you're home-schooling, what kind of support is there locally for your efforts? What higher education opportunities are there in your area and what are their costs? How about adult and continuing education programs?

➤ **Natural resources.** Are there any serious issues surrounding natural resources in your area? Here in Arizona, for example, a key issue is water, and it will likely become even more so in the very near future. What do these issues mean for future growth (putting a lid on it might not be all bad!), future availability of natural resources, and the local economy? If you're considering staying where you are and living more simply, what availability is there for alternative fuels, for example, or would you be allowed to put a windmill or turbine on your property? What would the practicality be of converting to solar energy in your area?

➤ **Transportation.** What are the realities of transportation in your locale? Must you own a car to get around, perhaps two? Is there public transportation and how effective is it? How far away is the nearest airport and is this a consideration? What provisions are there for alternative transportation such as bike paths? Is your area pedestrian friendly? Can you park at one location downtown and walk to most of your errands or must you drive from place to place?

➤ **Culture and entertainment.** What cultural events do you enjoy and how important are they to you? Are there substitutes you might enjoy as much? Take a look at the past year and honestly record the number of times you took advantage of them. If this is a high priority for you, then it will be a substantial advantage for you if you live near a cultural center. I find I truly enjoy the events I'm able to take in when visiting the New York area or my daughters in Chicago and Boston, but I don't need to live near a major metropolitan area. It just isn't that important to me. You need to decide if it is for you.

As you begin filling out your lists, you may find yourself thinking of other areas I haven't mentioned. Add them to these evaluation questions (come up with questions of your own) because you'll be using them again when and if you decide to consider relocating.

To further get to know your community, pretend you're a tourist or a person considering relocating there and do the things they might do. If you don't already, read your local paper. Try to see your existing home with a new perspective. You may surprise yourself and decide it's *exactly* where you want to be or surprise yourself in the other direction and wonder why you're still there!

The second part of "starting where you are" is to begin actually putting into place your own simple living plan right now, not putting it off. This will also help you decide whether where you are is where you still want to be. Regardless of where you finally end up, starting your simple living plan in motion now will …

➤ Help you gain the skills you need to simplify your life wherever you end up.

➤ Help you decide where you want to go by seeing where you are thwarted in your current location in your simple living efforts.

➤ Make the transition easier if you decide to relocate and help you fully appreciate your new home.

Once you've carefully evaluated your existing community, you may discover yet another option. Perhaps it's not the community but the specific home or neighborhood you live in that needs a change. Could you move but stay in the same place? If you've determined you like where you are and the advantages are considerable, the next thing to decide is whether relocation in the same area would be to your advantage. Evaluate other areas within the same location the same way you did your existing one.

So You've Decided to Go!

If after a closer, deliberate look you decide you just don't want to pursue your simple living plan in the place you live now, what are your options? Well, they're considerable, as you might have guessed. You can move to an urban environment, the "burbs," or head for the hills and a more rural community. Which is the best for you will be based on who you are, what your goals are, and how you define simple living. Let's take a look at each.

Hot for the City

Now, some people would say you simply can't live simply in the big city, and it could spark a pretty heated argument. (I've seen many of them in online discussion groups!) I don't see it that way, although city living would definitely not be my choice. Part of the picture is *which* city, and a second part of the picture is what being in the city would contribute to your simple living plan as you've designed it.

On the one hand, it's hardly necessary to have a car in an urban area; in fact, it's a liability. So right there you've eliminated the cost of a car, maintenance, and insurance. You no longer need to find a place to park it or shelter it either. Depending on what kind of an urban community you live in, most of what you need to sustain yourself is within walking distance of where you live.

Beyond Basics

If you doubt that cities can be great places to live, read *Cities Back from the Edge: New Life for Downtown* by Roberta Brandes Gratz with Norman Mintz for lots of real-life examples of cities that are renewing and revitalizing their communities.

You have available to you just about every employment option, all the technology you'd need to work from your own home, plus a client or customer base that's concentrated and large. There's the cultural environment we talked about earlier and the intermixing of people from all walks of life and all parts of the world.

There's also a large variety of goods available, and herein may lie the problem for some on the simple living path. With so many choices and so many messages aimed at you every day (billboards, circulars, storefronts, and so on), it's hard to control spending for some people. Yet there's also strength in numbers when it comes to consumption. Groups can join together to form cooperative arrangements for buying food, sharing housing or childcare, trading services, or sharing tools and resources.

Beyond Basics

Didn't think you could compost in the city? Well, you can! Get your hands on a copy of *The Urban/Suburban Composter: The Complete Guide to Backyard, Balcony, and Apartment Composting*, by Mark Cullen and Lorraine Johnson. It's out of print, but try your local library or a used-book-finding service. Also check out the University of Florida's Online Composting Center at www.compostinfo.com.

Depending on the city, there may be all sorts of simple living tools available like community gardens, city composting, and recycling. If you want to see one city's efforts, check out the Green City Project of San Francisco. Their Web site is at www.green-city.org. Just following the links is an urban eye-opener. A new book by Timothy Beatley called *Green Urbanism: Learning From European Cities* is an exploration, using some successful European models, of how we can live more sustainably in our cities. There are even "city farmers" growing their own food on rooftops and in courtyards, even hydroponically, composting in their apartments.

Now on the negative side of the equation are the things like pollution of all kinds, high crime, issues surrounding the raising of children, the high cost of living, rampant consumerism, crowding, and stress. Plus there's the overall consideration of what impact cities in general have on the earth and the ecosystem. These are all factors to take into account as you decide on your "home base."

Suburban Scene

The burbs have some of the advantages and disadvantages of both city and country. You can lose the convenience of public transportation, for example, and spend a great deal of time in the car, yet fail to gain a lot of the small town atmosphere and lower expenses of living in the country.

There's the convenience of being able to go into the city for cultural events, but you need to evaluate how often you use these things and how truly important they are to you. There are lots of jobs and entrepreneurial opportunities in the suburbs that take advantage of the nearby city, and the infrastructure is usually very supportive of home-based workers and entrepreneurs.

One question to ask is whether you could still pursue these activities even if you were in a less crowded, less expensive area through electronics, mail, and perhaps some travel. Another disadvantage is that the consumer culture is also a very strong influence in the suburbs, perhaps even more so than in the city. Keeping up with the Joneses can be a major pastime in some suburban communities.

Schools are often better, but there can be other problems for kids, especially teenagers. You'll need to take a careful look at things like drug use and alcoholism in the community of your choice.

A great thing about suburbs is you can really explore and accomplish many aspects of your simple living plan in relative comfort and with lots of conveniences and resources around you. If you have even a small amount of property, you can grow enough food to feed a family of four, or at least supplement your groceries, should that be something you'd like to do. You can work on your money/debt reduction/savings/spending plan and produce more things for yourself. That's always a good question to ask yourself, regardless of where you are or how far along with your plan you've gotten: "What can I provide for myself that someone else is now providing?"

You can make your suburban home more energy efficient, can practice and experiment with sustainable and self-reliant alternatives, and can take advantage of the availability of tools and information to help you make the transition from a consumer lifestyle to a simpler one.

Country Mouse

Some of the advantages of living in the country are lower cost of living, more basic values and lifestyle, a greater sense of community and neighborliness, safety and relative freedom from crime, privacy (but not anonymity!), high environmental quality, slower pace, and well, just plain beauty.

Quick Starts

A great way to get a quick handle on a community to which you're considering moving is to check out the town's Web site if it has one. Even small towns are putting up Web sites these days. Check out the calendars, business listings, governmental pages, and Chamber of Commerce link. You'll also want to subscribe to the local paper and any regional publications that might apply.

Beyond Basics

Two excellent resources for someone considering a move to the country are Marilyn and Tom Ross's *Country Bound! Trade Your Business Suit for Blue Jean Dreams*, which covers all the nuts and bolts of finding a rural paradise, and *The Encyclopedia of Country Living*, by Carla Emery, "an old fashioned recipe book" with tons of practical advice to get you started on your country skills.

Simple Wisdom

"The country has its charms—cheapness for one."

—Robert Smith Surtees

Beyond Basics

If you're sure you want the country life and all you need to do is find your homestead, make sure you read the "bible" of rural real estate *Finding and Buying Your Place in the Country*, by Les and Carol Scher before you see the realtor.

In the minus column, you may experience a sense of isolation. You'll find some things hard to get. Sometimes the phone lines aren't so good, and your online connection may suffer. You'll likely have to travel longer distances to shop, but this can be compensated for by grouping shopping needs together and buying in bulk. You may be separated from family and friends, something we make up for by weekly phone calls and almost daily e-mails. You'll need a car, most likely. Public transportation is almost nonexistent in most rural towns, and even taxis are a rarity. You may have reduced choices in health care, or facilities may be some distance away.

If you're not used to entertaining yourself, you may find rural life decidedly "unhip." There may be few of the cultural activities you were used to if you lived in the city, but you can find enjoyment in your own hobbies and outdoor activities. Plus, there are usually video stores and libraries as well as lots of community entertainment events and continuing education classes at the high school and area colleges. Activities tend to more home-centered and community-oriented in the country.

It's also harder to hide. Now that can be both a positive and a negative. If you like getting recognition and having people stop you on the street to talk, then a small town is for you. If you like anonymity and can't be bothered with your neighbors, then small town living may not be for you. There's a give and take that's part of country.

Movin' On!

If you've decided a change is on the horizon, you'll want to start getting ready for your move. Even if you haven't pinpointed the area exactly, you can certainly make preparations now that will serve when the time has come.

You've thoroughly researched the area and have made lots of personal visits, perhaps even spending an extended period of time there, so you should be familiar with the climate and major features of the area.

Armed with information and firsthand experience, give yourself time before you move to pare down; get rid of things you no longer use and don't see yourself bringing into your new life. Why bring your down jackets and ski gear if you're going to the desert and don't see yourself jetting somewhere to ski? If you're going to be homesteading or farming, you probably won't need your business suits. If you won't have a lawn, don't take the lawnmower!

Acquire many of the new skills you might need in your new endeavor before you leave. If you're buying a bed-and-breakfast, learn everything there is to know about the business before you take the plunge. If you're starting a home-based business that's not geographically dependent, start it before you leave. It's easier to work out the kinks on familiar ground and make fewer changes all at once. To learn about whether starting a bed-and-breakfast is for you, go visit some and ask the owners lots of questions about how they got started, what they like about it, what they don't like about it—anything and everything. And read the book How to Start and Operate Your Own Bed-and-Breakfast/Down-to-Earth Advice from an Award-Winning B&B Owner, by Martha Watson Murphy!

Try to establish ties in the new area before you actually move in. We had some referrals from friends who had friends living in our new community. We looked them up, they introduced us to their friends, and … our first contact happened to be actively involved in the town's Chamber of Commerce. He was both a gold mine of information and someone who knew just about everybody.

Set up ways to keep in touch with your old community. We have found e-mail and fairly frequent visits back to our former home have done that for us. We have a guest room that's easy to get ready for last-minute arrivals and plenty of home-cooked food in the freezer. We supplement our e-mails with weekly phone calls to family and close friends. Because our family is quite spread out,

Avoidance Techniques

Don't make a major change without trying it on for size first. If you're thinking of raising a lot of your own food in the country, try it first—you may find you really *hate* gardening! The same goes for buying a bed-and-breakfast or campground. This may sound like something obvious, but one of the most common mistakes people make is taking on something new without really knowing what they're getting into.

Avoidance Techniques

There's nothing more offensive than someone who moves into a new area and complains that things just aren't like they were at "home." This is your new home; you chose it for what it is, now learn to fit in. Take the time to learn the local customs and try them on for size.

we've had to make an effort to stay close, but we have and we do. You can, too, if you prepare for it and figure out how you're going to make it work.

Whether you decide to pursue the simple life right where you are or make a major location change, giving yourself lots of time to make the right decision and preparing thoroughly for any changes will make the whole process a positive one. Know yourself, gather the information you need, think on it a while, and experience the location firsthand. And remember, simple living is a "way," not a place!

The Least You Need to Know

➤ Before making a move, you can make a lot of progress toward your simple living lifestyle right where you are.

➤ After researching your own community, you may realize you're better off staying put.

➤ City, suburb, or country—each has its own set of advantages, opportunities, and challenges.

➤ You'll make an easier transition to a new community if you spend plenty of time there in advance, get involved right away, and learn to adapt to the way things are done.

Chapter 9

How Living With Less Can Mean More

In This Chapter

➤ Understanding "The 10 Laws of Stuff" and how to use them to help you recognize the stuff you don't need

➤ Sorting your stuff, paring down, and organizing what you have left

➤ Living more with less: six simple principles

➤ Unstuffing more than just your stuff

The comedian George Carlin had a comedy routine that I'll never forget. I believe he named it "Just a Little Place for My Stuff." He made us laugh with lines like "If I didn't have any stuff, I could just walk around all day" and "A house is just a pile of stuff with a cover on it!" He observed that thieves only took "the good stuff" and noted how, every time we go on vacation, we take a smaller version of our stuff and then spread it around our hotel room to feel at home.

Sure, it made us laugh, but it also pointed out how much of our lives, our very psyche, revolves around things or "stuff." The goal of this chapter is to help you recognize the useless stuff in your life and clear it out, then keep it from coming back in.

How Needy Are You?

As you begin to look through your house, your car, your office, and beyond, one of the first things you'll need to distinguish is the difference between needs and wants.

How often do you say, out loud or silently, "I need that!" when what it's really about is want? We have very few bona fide needs, but our wants are endless. And as we've seen in earlier chapters, our wants are often created by outside messages, manipulated emotions, and faulty thinking. What is enough? What is your bottom line when it comes to needs? This is the constant challenge I put before you, indeed, before us all.

When we acquire stuff, we may actually be attempting to fill a need that has absolutely no relationship to what we're buying. There may be a need to alleviate boredom (a new toy will do that for a while, but wouldn't it be better to learn what truly excites us?), to be accepted in our peer group (who needs friends who love you for what you own?), or to exhibit our prosperity, success, and achievement (perhaps our values and definitions need revamping?). What needs are you fulfilling by having too much? What are better ways to meet those needs?

With these thought-provoking questions tucked in the backs of our minds, let's tackle the task of getting rid of some of the stuff in your life!

Beyond Basics

For a thought-provoking study of the difference between needs and wants, read Alan Durning's *How Much is Enough?* and Timothy Miller's *How to Want What You Have: Discovering the Magic and Grandeur of Ordinary Existence.* Knowing what our real needs are can liberate us from the tyranny of wants and lead us to a simpler life.

Quick Starts

Even the most stuff-loving people can feel bloated with stuff after the holiday gift-giving seasons. In an effort to stop stuff at its source, try something new this year: Propose to your family and friends that you celebrate without gifts this year. Or suggest that you pool the money you would have spent on something you can all share and use.

Principles for Cutting Down

In my book, *The Complete Idiot's Guide to Organizing Your Life,* I developed what I called "The 10 Laws of Stuff." Keeping these in mind will help you understand the nature of stuff and how we all seem to get so much of it.

The 10 Laws of Stuff

Law #1: Stuff breeds. The more you have, the more you need. It's almost as if you give stuff a dark corner and some time and, before you know it, there's more! You know how it works—the new whatzeymahingit you just bought needs a special cover and it's very own cleaner with specially shaped brush! After you've cleaned it once or twice you realize it's too damned much trouble after all or you can't find that danged brush! So you get back to doing it the old fashioned way—by hand—and the whatzeymahingit and all it's cousins sit in a corner in the garage.

Law #2: The useless stuff crowds out the good stuff. If you have a lot of stuff you don't need, you have trouble finding the stuff you do. Or you spend more time shifting the good-for-nothing stuff around, and you have no time left to do the things you really enjoy and care about.

Law #3: Dust, bugs, rodents, and moisture all love stuff. Stuff you don't use regularly usually gets relegated to places like the garage, the basement, the attic, or the back porch. By the time you ever get around to using it, one of "the destroyers" has gotten to it and rendered it useless anyway!

Law #4: Stuff tends to stay where it lands. Ever notice that stuff has inertia? It just begs to land somewhere, and when it does, it doesn't *move!* Like the kitchen table, the coffee table—any flat surface, come to think of it. Then there's the knick-knack caddy and the thingamajig holder and, oh glory, the junk drawer! If we toss things without making a decision to keep or to trash or to put something in its place, it'll just lie there!

Law #5: Stuff expands to fit the space available. The more room you have, the more stuff you can buy to fill it. Just because the space is there, it doesn't mean we *have* to fill it! And once it's full, then we rent a storage facility with a monthly fee. Nuts, isn't it?

Law #6: Over time, stuff becomes invisible. After we live with clutter for a while, we don't see it. I once thought I was being clever by tacking some airline tickets on the bulletin board in my office "so I'd know where to find them." Well, the day of the trip comes, and I'm frantically looking for the "lost" tickets. They were right in front of me all the time, but over time, they'd become part of the scenery! Try to see your surroundings with new eyes.

Law #7: Stuff costs you money more than once. Not only did you have to give your life energy or essence to earn the money to buy the stuff, there are lots of hidden costs you may not have thought about that continually sap money and time. There's the cost to maintain and insure the item. Then there's the cost of the space you have to provide to store it—both monetary and in time.

Quick Starts

Take a tour of the house as if you were seeing it for the first time, as if you were a guest. Write down the items you see that add nothing to your everyday life and could easily be termed clutter or junk, then set a time to get rid of them.

Avoidance Techniques

Be careful about bulletin boards and other catch-alls. Unless you're very disciplined about it, they tend to just become another clutter center. And besides, after a while you don't even *see* what's there!

Quick Starts

Think about the cost each month per square foot of your home. Don't leave out things like heating, lighting, homeowner's insurance, and cleaning. If you look at the true cost of the real estate you live in, you have a better idea of the cost of keeping useless stuff.

Law #8: Stuff has a powerful effect on your state of mind. Useless stuff is a burden. It weighs us down. A lot of clutter can make us feel irritable and depressed. We feel so much better in a room that's open and airy, where everything seems to fit and have a purpose. Now, we can't always keep things uncluttered—I know I can't—but keeping clutter at bay gives us a sense of control and well-being that may be hard to measure, but it's for real.

Law #9: Stuff takes on value only when it's used. If something sits in a corner gathering dust, it has no value, at least not to you. The same item might be a daily tool for somebody else, but for you it's a lead weight. The more something is used, the more value it has. So when's the last time you used that hot dog cooker? Do you really want so many valueless things in your life?

Law #10: Stuff doesn't make you happy; you do! We know this in our hearts, but to look at our houses, who would guess? We have to learn to distinguish needs from wants, decide what is "enough," value our life's essence and spend it wisely, and make ourselves truly happy through our work, our relationships, and discovering our inner joy. No, money doesn't buy happiness, and neither does stuff!

Simple Wisdom

"Actually, this is just a place for my stuff .... That's all I want, that's all you need in life, is a little place for your stuff .... Everybody's got a little place for their stuff. This is my stuff, that's your stuff. That'll be his stuff over there. That's all you need in life is a little place for your stuff."

—George Carlin

So, how do we start sorting it all out? If it seems like a mammoth task, start small and work from there. Different methods work for different folks or for the same folks at different times. One way is to work in timed increments. Set aside an hour a day or work in 15-minute chunks, if that's all you have. Take one small area and work until it's done. Or, if you're feeling ambitious and bigger changes help keep you motivated, take a weekend and tackle a whole room or do a closet in a day. Before we actually get to the sorting process, though, let's talk about a few more principles that will help you decide what's of value and what needs to go.

Quality, Not Quantity

Instead of six knives that won't hold an edge and feel funny in your hand, have one superb knife that sharpens like a dream and feels like it was made for you. Rather than a closet full of trendy clothes that don't really fit well and aren't well made, have a simple wardrobe of durable, beautifully crafted garments that never go out of style. Dress them up with accessories. If you're going to spend your life energy on an item you need, why not spend it once on something that does the job perfectly and will last a lifetime?

Abundance, not Excess

Paring down and living simply doesn't mean being poor. The simple life is abundant; you have everything you truly need and the time to satisfy your true, inner wants. This isn't deprivation! This is true abundance. Excess, clutter, and useless stuff are the true deprivers.

The Less You Have, the Less You Have to Organize!

It's true. The more gadgets and gizmos we have, the more we have to deal with. It means storing it, stacking it, moving it out of the way to get to something else, cleaning it, packing it when we move, and just plain *handling* it. You'll see later in this chapter how to sort things so you can see the duplicates and items you don't use, get rid of the excess, and put the rest away so you can make the most of it. But remember—the more you get rid of up front, the easier your job will be at the other end!

Quick Starts

Challenge yourself to see how much you can reduce clutter in just 15 minutes. While you're waiting for the coffee to brew, clean off a counter. While you're on hold, sort some papers: Throw out most of them and then file the rest. There's a lot of power in just 15 minutes!

Multi-Use, Not Single Use

Whenever possible, don't buy a tool or appliance that only does one thing. A food processor, for example, is a multi-use appliance. Some people buy them and they gather dust. I use mine almost every day for chopping, blending, grating, and pureeing. Now the pasta machine I bought is going out! Once I finally learned how easy it is to make pasta by hand, the few times a year I do it aren't worth dragging out that monstrosity.

Stop It at the Source!

Don't take that brochure or flier! Don't bring home that souvenir! Get off those mailing lists! Don't buy any more stuff you don't need! If you stop it at the source, the stuff never has to be handled because it didn't find its way past the door. The more you can keep it that way, the easier it will be to get and stay organized.

Is It Worth Your Essence?

When you're thinking of buying something, ask yourself this question—"Is it worth my essence?" We're not talking about just the life energy it took to make the money to buy it, but the energy it will take to dust it, move it around, and take care of it. Even the energy it takes each month to pay for the space it's going to occupy is part of the cost. Ask the same question when you give someone a gift and then ask if it's worth it to him or her. Don't take up other people's essence with useless gifts. Give something of yourself like a luscious batch of homemade cookies or an experience they'll never forget. Give something that will become a treasured memory, not a burden.

Beyond Basics

Join the Stop Junk Mail Association and keep that clutter from coming! For $20, they'll delete your name from a variety of sources and will lobby for you to protect your postal privacy. Call or write to Stop Junk Mail Association c/o 3020 Bridgeway, Suite 150, Sausalito, CA 94965 (1-800-827-5549).

Quick Starts

Having trouble deciding whether to get rid of that special appliance or a particular piece of clothing? Ask yourself how long it has been since you last used the appliance or wore the clothing. If it has been over a year, chances are you don't need it. Give it to someone who might.

Unstuff Your Life

So how do you get rid of it all? Even if you've put a lid on spending and have stopped bringing home all those free goodies and stupid souvenirs, what do you do with what you have?

Sort, decide, and move it. The best method I've found for this is the "box" method or, if you prefer, the "pile" method. I prefer to use a set of boxes that are labeled and reuse them each time I declutter. There are lots of variations on this system, but these are the categories I've found most useful: Trash, Put Away, Pass On, Mystery, and Fix.

Some people like to have a Put Away box for each person in the household. I prefer to have one box and ask everyone to come get his or her stuff. If they don't, it goes to the Halfway House. (That's the garage, on its way out!) If they still don't come and get it, it goes to charity or the garbage man. The Pass On box is stuff that needs to either go to charity or be recycled. (You'll probably want some permanent place to sort and gather recycling in the kitchen pantry, garage, or breezeway.) The Mystery box is for things you just can't decide what to do with. (These should be few because you're going to discipline yourself to decide now!) It can go to the Halfway House for a limited time. The Fix box is for things that are perfectly good and that you think you'll use once they're repaired. These last two should have time limits put on them.

This should get your started with paring down and "unstuffing" each area of your life. The system can be applied to every room. An adaptation of the system can even work with filing cabinets or stacks of paper cluttering your desk.

Organize the Rest

Once you've gotten the clutter under control, the next task is to put things where they'll be most useful and store them in a way that they'll stay usable and you can find them. First you'll need to group things that are alike in one place so you can see how many of the same things you actually have. The "group like things together" rule is a very important step. This allows you to get rid of duplicates, keep the best-quality item, and get rid of the rest. It also lets you provide the most efficient storage, pick the best container, and put the item in the place where it is used most. You may find you have 16 cans of tomato soup and only one AAA battery. When everything was all spread around, it was hard to tell!

Two other important concepts in organizing what you have are learning to distinguish between short and long term and understanding the concept of *prime real estate*. Prime real estate is the space closest to where you do most of your daily living. This refers to places like the kitchen cabinets and drawers, the storage area under the sink in the bathroom, your dresser drawers, and the hall closet. The things you use daily, or at least regularly, should be in these spaces for them to be the most useful. So get those skis out of the hall closet and hang them in the garage. Use your prime real estate; put stuff where you use it most. If you peel potatoes next to the sink, put the potato peeler in the drawer next to the sink.

Short term and *long term* refer to storage priorities. If it's not in prime real estate, it's in storage. But not all stored items are created equal. There's a difference between extra toilet tissue that will be used over the course of a month and Christmas ornaments that only get displayed once a year. Put short-term items in the easiest-to-get-at spaces and long-term items in the more remote storage areas.

Next, put it where you can find it. If you have to, create a list of where things are or label the insides of cabinets with a list of what's in them so you don't have to wonder.

Another thing to remember is the importance of labeling and alphabetizing. Make labels for everything so you don't have to waste time looking in boxes or drawers. And whenever it makes sense, put stuff in alphabetical order. You might also considering making up "kits" for particular activities. Find a box or a basket and make a sewing kit with

Avoidance Techniques

Neat is not necessarily organized. Completely spartan isn't either. If you have to go out every time you do a project because you don't have any supplies in the house, that's not efficient. Keep what you need and get rid of the rest!

everything you need to put on a button or tack up a hem. Make a shoe-shine kit, a bike-repair kit, a car-washing kit. Label the kit and put it where you do the task. This saves time when assembling the tools and makes you more likely to actually *do* the task.

There are lots of other ways to organize better. Some you'll discover as you go along for yourself. Some you'll learn from others. Keep your eyes and ears open. Look for systems, not just temporary solutions. Do your very best job and then hire a professional organizer to see if you can do better or can solve a difficult problem. Commit yourself to living with less and making the best of what's left.

It's Not Just Your Stuff You Need to Unstuff!

While you're looking to unstuff your stuff, how about taking it further? We can have junk in lots of other areas of our lives as well. There's junk food and junk clothes, junk information and junk noise. And there are junk relationships. Don't just look at clutter in your space; also look at clutter in your time and in how you expend your precious emotional and physical energy. How many relationships in your life right now are unsatisfying or even aggravating? How much time do you really spend with the people you care about most? Do you give them your full attention?

I like to think of my relationships as a quality circle. I surround myself with people that I love, that share my values, that make me laugh, that make me think, that give me encouragement and support. These are my people of quality, and I take care of them first. If you think about it, how many people do you really have time and energy for? Six? Ten? That's even a lot. Identify your quality circle and see that they get the best of you. If there's time for any more, great, but there's little time for people who drain you, belittle you, bring negativity with them wherever they go. Oh, and don't forget to include yourself in your quality circle. Without taking care of you, there's nothing for anybody or anything else.

> **Quick Starts**
>
> Take a look at how you spent your time this past week. Who got your time? Did you have lunch with that colleague you never did really like? Did you spend time with someone who belittled you or others? Did you do something with someone not because you wanted to but because they cajoled you into doing it? Analyze the importance of these relationships and consider ridding your life of them.

The Least You Need to Know

➤ Learning to tell the difference between needs and wants will help make "un-stuffing" easier and will simplify your life ever after.

➤ The first step is to pare down what you have to the things you really use and those that have value.

➤ After you've gotten rid of the clutter, concentrate on organizing what you have so you can find it and so it's located where you use it most.

➤ Not only can we have junk in our space, we can also have "junk" relationships that need to be pared down so we can give our precious time and energy to those we care about most.

Chapter 10

In the Independent Republic of Finances

In This Chapter

➤ Getting your finances in order

➤ Covering yourself for emergencies

➤ What to do now that you've lowered spending and expenses, gotten out of debt, and accumulated a "cushion" of savings

➤ Insights into investing and making yourself bullet-proof

If you followed the advice in Chapters 6 through 9, you're well on your way to a freer, simpler life. In fact, the next step is financial independence! In Chapter 6, "Going Debtless: How to Gain Your Freedom," you learned why reducing, and eventually eliminating, debt is so important. It's the foundation of simple living. In Chapter 7, "Earning a Life, Not Just a Living," you discovered that work is more than what you do to make money and that, by eliminating debt, lowering spending, and creating a surplus, your freedom to work as you choose is greatly enhanced. In Chapter 8, "Location, Location! The Simple Truth About Where You Live," you carefully evaluated your current location and made a decision as to whether relocating might make sense. And finally, in Chapter 9, "How Living With Less Can Mean More," you learned about paring down your "stuff" and organizing what's left. In fact, you may have unstuffed so well, you could move to a smaller house!

These are the necessary preliminaries to the step you're going to take in this chapter—moving into financial independence.

Organizing Your Finances

If you're still working on the ideas contained in this book so far, that's okay. This part of Chapter 10 is still for you.

Another crucial part of simplifying your life around finances is to organize them. Do you know where your statements are? Could you put your hands on your medical records in a flash? Do you know how much you spend on each category? Does it take you weeks to get ready for tax time?

Well, you're going to fix that. Regardless of where you are on the path to financial simplicity, integrity, and independence, getting your records in order is an important step to knowing where you are on the path and staying there.

My first recommendation is to establish what I call a life management center. This is central command, operations, or the bridge of your Starship, if you will. You're in control, and you need the tools to manage. All you may need is a calendar or date book, a desk, and a file cabinet. For myself, since I take care of all the finances in our household, I've integrated my life management center into my home office. I have one entire two-drawer file cabinet devoted to it, a computer program, and my small Dayrunner. You may prefer a rolling file that you can tuck away and a spiral notebook. It doesn't matter as long as it does what you need it to do. You're creating *systems* that you'll revise and refine as time goes on.

While you're creating this system, I'd like to reiterate my advice from Chapter 6. Know where you are! As you organize, get any missing information. What do your utility bills average? What are the months of highest and lowest usage? When was the last time you looked at your credit report? Do you know your total debt? Do you know the interest rates on your credit cards? Do you have adequate insurance coverage? Do you even know?

Don't feel bad if the answers to most of these questions is "no" or "I don't know!" We're going to fix that.

Quick Starts

Get all your materials together before you begin your financial organization blitz and set aside a weekend to get this done! Make labels that are bold and in large print. (I used a computer label program.) Do both hanging and manila folders so that, if you take one out, you'll know immediately where it goes when you want to put it back; if it's missing, you'll see it right away.

Filing So You Can Find It

The major categories in your filing system should match your specific needs and what you'll need at the end of the year for taxes. Here are some categories that you might consider including in your file cabinet:

- ➤ Automobile
- ➤ Bank statements
- ➤ Birth and death records
- ➤ Budget
- ➤ Contributions
- ➤ Computer expenses
- ➤ Credit-card statements
- ➤ Education
- ➤ Emergency information
- ➤ Entertainment expenses
- ➤ Food expenses
- ➤ Home inventory

- ➤ Household equipment records and warranties
- ➤ House repairs and maintenance records
- ➤ Insurance documents
- ➤ Legal and professional services
- ➤ Medical and dental records
- ➤ Mortgage
- ➤ Office equipment and expenses
- ➤ Social security info
- ➤ Taxes
- ➤ Travel documents and expenses
- ➤ Utilities

Beyond Basics

If you haven't seen your credit reports in some time, you should probably get them. It's all part of "facing the facts," and there may be some things you need to correct or amend. Arrange to get a copy of your credit report. It should be free if you've recently been denied credit.

These are the three major credit bureaus:

Equifax, P.O. Box 105496, Atlanta, GA 30348-54961; 1-800-997-2493 www.econsumer.equifax.com/equifax.app/Welcome

Experian, National Consumer Assistance Center, P.O. Box 2104, Allen, TX 75013-2104; 1-888-397-3742; www.experian.com/customer/mail.html

Trans Union Corporation, P.O. Box 2000, Chester, PA 19022; 1-800-888-4213; www.tuc.com

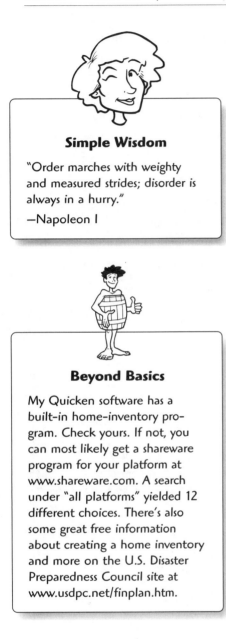

Simple Wisdom

"Order marches with weighty and measured strides; disorder is always in a hurry."

—Napoleon I

Beyond Basics

My Quicken software has a built-in home-inventory program. Check yours. If not, you can most likely get a shareware program for your platform at www.shareware.com. A search under "all platforms" yielded 12 different choices. There's also some great free information about creating a home inventory and more on the U.S. Disaster Preparedness Council site at www.usdpc.net/finplan.htm.

Other categories you may have could be childcare, credit reports, homeowners association, savings, and investments. For the last category, I have a separate file drawer since we have several investments and have recently done our estate planning, which creates a fair amount of paperwork. Sort your stuff and see what you have. You'll add some categories and eliminate others, most likely. The idea is for your system to be logical, clear, and easily used by someone else in your absence.

This is an important concept. Could someone walk into your life if you were incapacitated and take over for you? What would happen if your house were devastated by fire? What steps would you be able to take to pick up the pieces? If you had to evacuate on a moments notice, what would you need to take with you and could you lay your hands on it? We'll talk more about emergency preparation later in this book and even in this chapter because being prepared for an emergency is an important piece of financial (and emotional) independence and self-reliant thinking.

Paying Bills on Automatic Pilot

Do you have a system for paying bills or do they get done haphazardly, often because you're in denial or avoiding confronting the truth? Well, that certainly doesn't solve anything! What would it take to have your bills paid on a schedule, almost on automatic pilot?

I believe in the value of scheduling and creating habits. Pick a day (doing the bills weekly helps you keep on top of things better, but you may not want to do them this often) and do it the same day each time. Set up a ritual. (Mine is a cup of tea, some soothing music, a comfortable chair, and my laptop.) Put the tools you need in one place. You may decide on a box, a drawer, a rolling cart, a basket—whatever suits your fancy and *works!* Whenever you can standardize a task, make a system to handle it, and create rituals to make it more pleasant or to trigger positive involvement, you're simplifying your life.

Electronic Helpers

Financial matters really lend themselves to computerization. I think computers can often sap time and energy, and we have to be very careful in analyzing whether a particular application is *really* easier or timesaving. But at least for me, computerizing my finances has made a huge difference.

The two areas that have helped me most have been money-management software and electronic bill paying. I personally use Quicken software by Intuit and have for 10 years or more. There are other good programs out there as well, so be sure to look around, try out demos, and see what program is recommended for your particular platform. It takes a little work up front to enter each check I write and put in information about categories, but in the end (especially at tax time) I save tons of time. I also have a searchable record of expenses, which has come in handy more times than I can tell you. I can put together a profit-and-loss statement or an income statement in nothing flat, can tell you how much I've spent on electricity so far this year, and can reconcile my checking account statement (every time, honest!) in nothing flat.

Electronic bill paying may not be for everyone, but for us it's a real time saver, plus it saves money on checks, postage, and envelopes. We do travel quite a bit, and this service allows me to pay bills from a hotel room. A backup copy, which I keep up-to-date, of our file allows me to handle most anything from the road as well. Make sure you have adequate security on your laptop so that no one can access your financial information if it's stolen. Quicken's system for electronic bill paying is pretty simple, and the only problems I've ever had were either my error or an error on the part of the payee, never the service, and these have been few and far between.

However you elect to organize your financial records and your bill-paying procedures, your goals are to know what's going on, to be able to access

Beyond Basics

You may want to use a pre–designed medical-records book to keep track of your information. A good one is *Healthmate Medical Planner: A Practical Guide for Taking Control of Your Health and Having Your Medical Records Always Available—Even When Your Doctor Isn't* by Kathleen Deremer. There's also software available for the Windows platform called Health-Minder. Check it out at www. health-minder.com.

Avoidance Techniques

If you do decide to go the electronic route with your financial stuff, keep a backup that you update *every time you make changes!* I keep two backups. One resides on my laptop, and I have a second on disk that I keep in our home safe.

your information quickly and efficiently, to be able to turn things over to someone else in a crisis, and to stay on track with your long-term financial plans. The up-front work is quickly repaid in time and energy savings forever after.

When All Else Fails

Whether or not you decided to prepare for the changeover into the new century, what we came to call Y2K, there was a message in it that I think was terribly important: There are no certainties in life. We may hope for the best, but perhaps it's also a good idea to prepare for the worst.

An emergency can come from almost any source. It could be a natural disaster like a hurricane, a blizzard, or an earthquake. It could be a man-made disaster like a chemical spill, a nuclear power plant failure, or a terrorist act. Or it could just be that "life happens." We might become ill or have an accident and need some time to recover. We could lose our jobs or have some other setback that might make it difficult to pay our bills for a time. Now, if you've paid off your debt, have a savings cushion, and have other income apart from your wages to cover the basics, you're way far ahead of the game. We talked about the incredible freedom of creating this scenario for yourself earlier.

Simple Wisdom

"There are no emergencies for those who are truly prepared."

—James Talmage Stevens, *Making the Best of Basics*

But there are some emergencies where you need more than money to get you through. Consider stocking up on a three-month supply of canned goods and drinking water and keeping an emergency medical kit in your house where it is easily accessible. Just think of the peace of mind you'll have knowing that, if you suddenly lose your job or are unable to get to town for food, you'll be able to rely on your emergency storage and preparation for some time to come!

Whatever comes along, you've got a three-month grace period to tide you over, even if for some crazy reason there's nothing coming in the door financially. You're self-reliant, which in an emergency frees you to think clearly, gives you a foundation from which to work, saves you money, and offers comfort and a sense of well-being, confidence, and competence.

Making Your Money Make Money

Okay, let's review. You've learned how to get on an even financial keel, and if you're not there yet, you're on your way to financial soundness. You've "faced the music" about your spending habits, your debt, and your disorganization, and now your records are in order. You've plugged your spending holes, and you've made things right with all your creditors. Hopefully, you've got money in savings and may have even been able to rethink your work and what you do for a living. Now, if everything's working as planned, you have some money to invest. So what do you do with the money you're saving that will ensure your financial independence in the future?

The object is to have enough money coming in without working to cover your most basic expenses for housing, energy, food, clothing, health care, and transportation. The lower these expenses, the less it takes to earn the money you need to subsist. Having enough money coming in for the basics frees you up to work for the extras or to do without, to work for less, to volunteer, to work part-time, to take time off, whatever serves you best. Imagine how simple your life would be if this were the case.

Once you've taken the steps we've already talked about and are creating a surplus that's going into the bank as savings, you'll need to decide where to put that money so it can work the hardest for you. It will also need to be in a safe place since your whole plan hinges on it producing a certain amount of income.

So where do you put your nest egg? Joe Dominguez and Vicki Robin recommend long-term U.S. Treasury and U.S. government agency bonds. They have a long list of criteria and a very thorough explanation why they feel this is the perfect investment vehicle, along with resources to help you get started and instructions on how to purchase them for yourself. I like the idea that you need only become an expert in one specific segment of the investment market and that it's a safe, liquid investment. Part of our investments are in this vehicle, but we feel we have the ability to take just a bit more risk, so have invested some money in the stock market.

The ideal, it seems to me, would be to have most of your money invested in treasury and agency bonds, covering your absolute rock-bottom expenses. Then, if you have a little more to invest or will have at some later date, you could put some in a higher yield, slightly higher risk vehicle like blue-chip stocks and then reinvest the dividends. This becomes your backup in case you need some special help or would like to help someone else. Having more than just enough allows you to be generous. The idea is not to accumulate wealth, but you may find, as the Quakers and Puritans did, that being frugal and working well brought them prosperity. You can use that prosperity to help fund the things and people you believe in.

Avoidance Techniques

Don't save haphazardly and expect to have enough to invest. You know what will happen to it! Remember to "pay yourself first." Put money into savings before you do anything else, even if it's only $10, even less if that's all you can manage. Then pay your bills and live off what's left.

Janet Luhrs, author of *The Simple Living Guide*, recommends having an "emergency reserve account" with enough money to cover living expenses for three to six months. I agree with this strategy. Add to that about one month's expenses in cash at your fingertips and three months or more hard goods to tide you over, and you've got a redundant emergency system that should tide you

Beyond Basics

If you want to learn more about investing in the stock market, consider joining the National Association of Investors Corporation (NAIC), P.O. Box 220, Royal Oak, MI 48068. The organization's toll-free phone number is 1-877-ASK-NAIC (1-877-275-6242), or you can go to their Web site at www.better-investing.org. This organization also helps people for investment clubs, which is another way to learn how to invest on your own.

over longer if need be. She also advises putting your long-term savings into something that's difficult to get at, just in case you might be tempted to return to your evil ways and spend it!

Learn something about simple investing and the various choices open to you. But don't wait for your store of knowledge to increase to start saving. At the very least, open a basic bank account, but I'd suggest an interest-bearing money market account as a better alternative. Pay yourself first each pay period or each time you get a check, and sock it away until you can figure out what's best for you. Give the checkbook to a trusted friend if you can't trust yourself to keep your hands off it. But really, you've got to get a hold of yourself! Make saving a habit and start learning about how to make the most of your savings.

By the way, you can invest with your conscience and still work toward your financial independence. We have invested in socially-conscious mutual funds for years, and our return has been quite satisfactory. Since the goal isn't to be rich but to create the funds to live comfortably and to pursue your life's purpose, these funds might be worth your consideration.

Bullet-Proofing Yourself

As part of your plan, you'll need to give thought to the worst that could happen. This exercise will further "bullet-proof" your financial independence plan. One of the primary areas you'll need to address is health care.

The best medical insurance is to stay healthy—get adequate rest, eat a balanced and nutritious diet, engage in regular exercise, greatly reduce stress, and remove the health destroyers from your life. (Stop smoking or abusing alcohol and lose weight if you're not in a healthy range.) Yet, sometimes we do all these things and still get sick.

You'll need to get major medical insurance. If you're providing this for yourself, it can be quite costly, so shop around and make comparisons. Since you have a good financial cushion, you can live with a fairly high deductible, which is what we do.

Comparison-shop as well for drugs and medical supplies. Use the phone and your on-line connection, if you have one, to get the best price.

Long-term care is another concern. If one partner ends up needing convalescent or nursing-home care it can be a major blip in your otherwise smooth financial plans.

We have long-term care insurance. It costs us about $130 a month (for both of us) and comes automatically out of our investment income. We never see a bill.

Think about life now! Talk about simple living! You've got everything you need and don't have to worry about your future. You have rewarding and fulfilling work to do, but your survival is not dependent on it. You're prepared for emergencies, and even an economic downturn won't upset your apple cart. You're taking care of your health, and if for some reason you do get sick, you're covered. Wow! What a way to *live*. Now go do your stuff! Have fun, follow your dreams, find your creativity, and do good.

The Least You Need to Know

➤ Once you've lowered spending, eliminated debt, and started saving, you'll need to invest to provide lasting financial independence.

➤ Organizing your financial life is an important step toward financial self-sufficiency.

➤ By preparing for emergencies, you add yet another key element to self-reliance and simple, low-stress living.

➤ Health care is a major consideration to help "bullet-proof" your financial independence plan.

Part 3

Simple Living Basics: Food, Clothing, and Shelter

Food, clothing, and shelter—the most basic stuff of human survival. You can't get any simpler than that! Yet providing our daily bread, keeping up with the costs of fashion, and finding affordable, comfortable housing isn't so simple.

In these next five chapters, you'll examine these most basic elements of your existence to see how they contribute to the simple life or create complications. You'll discover alternatives that are healthier, more friendly to the environment, and less expensive in the bargain.

If you've ever thought of saying goodbye to the utility company, you'll learn more about what's involved, and we'll look at another basic of modern existence—transportation—and how it can get in the way of a simpler life.

Chapter 11

Food Fancy: You *Are* What You Eat!

In This Chapter

➤ How to understand and rethink our relationship with food

➤ Simple and delicious ways to prepare food and save time

➤ Understanding the advantages of growing your own

I'm studying to be a kitchen goddess. Don't laugh! My idea of a dining divinity is someone who whips up healthful, nourishing meals in minutes, sustains herself and her family through health and sickness with her kitchen wizardry, and spends very little time fussing and cleaning. Sound impossible? Well, read on!

Over years of changing my eating patterns, fighting a tendency to be overweight, and more recently, learning to work with a food allergy, I've found kitchen gods and goddesses of my own aplenty, some of whom you'll meet in this chapter. There's Helen Nearing, Francis Moore Lappé, Ellen Ewald, Cait Johnson, and a few other heroes and heroines. I'll be sprinkling this chapter with references to their particular brand of culinary magic.

Food, the Sustainer

As we seek to make our lives simpler, spend less, and live better, food is one of the easiest areas in which to take charge of our lives and to make changes wherever we happen to be. Just change one small thing, and you'll notice an immediate impact. Every day you get new opportunities to try something different. Taking charge of our food is

Quick Starts

Keep a list of everything you eat for a day. Notice when you were hungry or if you were hungry when you ate. Then try fasting for a day, having only water, herb teas, and small amounts of juice. Next try a day with only raw vegetables and fruit. Introduce some whole grains and see what that feels like. Next, try going without meat for a week. Introduce meat back into your diet and see what kind of difference it makes. Experiment.

Simple Wisdom

"The food I prepare and serve is meant to build healthy bodies, not to cater to corrupted taste buds that urge one to eat unhealthy things long after the claims of hunger have been satisfied. Enough is as good as a feast: better, in fact, because if you don't overeat, you don't get sick or fat."

—Helen Nearing

taking charge of our bodies, and that's an incredibly empowering thing. Rethinking the role of food in our daily routines, our social lives, and even our unconscious emotions can make a huge difference.

Food offers us a feast of the senses if we truly take time to experience it. A meal doesn't need to be elaborate or require a lot of time or effort to prepare to be nourishing and tasty. Instead, we can take time appreciating the textures, forms, and smells.

Whether you're religious or not, there is much to be grateful for each time you sit down to partake of the earth's bounty. In addition, there's a sense of gratitude for our own ability to provide. So slow down. Turn off the TV when you sit down to a meal. Eat at the table with a pretty plate or a pleasing ceramic or wooden bowl. Take it all in. Eat slowly and chew each mouthful. Commune with yourself, the food, and the people sharing a meal with you. Perhaps you can put on some soothing music, but keep it low and encourage uplifting conversation.

Mealtime can be an important transition from the "world out there" to home and hearth, from labor to relaxation, from chaos to order. Start out simplifying your relationship to food just by paying attention to it. You'll see a difference right away!

Why Waste?

Why is there so much waste in this country surrounding the growing, distribution, preparation, and eating of food? Some of it is just unconscious. We have so much and have had it for so long that we don't realize the enormity of our abundance. We make trips to the grocery store any time of the day or night. And if we don't feel like preparing something for ourselves, there are all-night diners. We stuff food in our mouths without thinking. Where does your food come from? How was it grown? How did it get from there to your table? How many hands or machines touched it before it got on your plate?

As you begin to examine how food fits into your life as it is now, think about how you would like it to be.

Would you like to eat better? Lose weight? Spend less time in the kitchen? Invite people over more often? While you're looking at your eating habits on an individual level, look at how you waste unnecessarily. Do you buy foods only to have them spoil? Do you make frequent trips to the supermarket? How much packaging surrounds the foods you buy? Do you throw away things like vegetable and fruit peels, eggshells, and coffee grounds? Do you leave the water running while you're peeling or preparing? Do you often heat and reheat foods? How often do you eat things raw? Do you use disposable plates, cups, utensils, or napkins?

Eating badly and wastefully costs more money up front when we first make our purchases, it has a huge cost for the environment (energy costs, packaging, transportation, pollution, poor land use), and then we take synthetic vitamins to supplement and drugs to combat the ill effects. Eating badly costs us in every way. We're back to needs versus wants again. When we stick to our most basic needs, things seem to work. When we begin to indulge our ever-increasing, unconscious wants, we get into trouble.

So What's Cooking?

If you were to look at food through the simple living lens, what would it look like? Simple food to me means fresh, unadulterated, and straightforward. It means nourishing and satisfying, not rich, not fancy, just good, honest food.

Well, if that's what simple food means to you, I have good news! It's cheaper, healthier, and often quicker to prepare. It doesn't take a lot of special gadgets, and much of it can grow in your own backyard if you want it to.

First let's look at what might be considered a simple meal. The dishes that come to mind for me are soups, stews, salads, maybe a casserole or meatloaf. Even simpler is a loaf of whole grained

Quick Starts

Waste is one of the first areas we can begin to control and simplify. Look for alternatives that use less packaging. Buy in bulk. Use cloth napkins. (Have a different napkin ring for each person in the family.) Start a compost pile. If you don't garden, does your neighbor? Is there a community compost project? Are there other uses for your waste around the house? Can you recycle?

Quick Starts

Take a food inventory at your house. Carry a pad and a pencil with you and write down what you discover in your pantry, kitchen cabinets, refrigerator, and freezer. What did you learn? Note the dates on canned goods. How long have some foods been there? Toss (or compost) the stuff with the green mold on it. Ask yourself how *that* happened!

Simple Wisdom

"Imagine creating a kitchen that fills you with a sense of your own magical power—whether you spend three minutes a day cooking in it or three hours. Imagine finding a way home to your ancient birthright of soul-nourishment and deep pleasure in food. Imagine cooking like a goddess."

—Cait Johnson in *Cooking Like a Goddess: Bringing Seasonal Magic into the Kitchen*

(maybe even homemade) bread, some good cheese, and some fresh fruit. Not a meal, you say? It is to many the world over! Maybe you need to rethink your "definitions."

The ingredients for these dishes are pretty basic: vegetables, grains and flours, meats and fish, and some spices and herbs. They can generally be prepared ahead of time and, even then, require little time on the part of the cook. Cleanup can be limited to one large pot, bowl, or casserole dish. To those whose diet consists of rich restaurant foods and fancy prepared dishes at home, these old-fashioned staples are now called "comfort foods." I just call them "simple!"

Three cooking methods that have revolutionized my life in the kitchen are "quick cooking," "bulk cooking," and "slow cooking." The first involves taking fresh ingredients and eating them raw or cooking them lightly in one pot, pan, or wok. The second is a plan for cooking large quantities all at once and freezing them in smaller portions so you don't have to cook at other times. The third makes extensive use of a slow cooker or crock-pot.

Quick! Start Cooking

The quick-cooking philosophy is to use a minimum of the freshest ingredients that can be easily assembled, often cooked in one pan or dish, usually taking 20 minutes or less from start to finish. What I had for breakfast this morning is an example of quick cooking: a handful of raw, rolled oats (not the "instant" kind) and another handful of a mixture of dried fruits, nuts, and seeds that I put together myself in a big jar, with a little low-fat soy milk on top. Preparation time: 1 minute. Cooking time: zero. Dirty dishes: one bowl and one spoon. Nutrition: super! And this "meal" was very low in fat.

Bulk Up and Save Time

Busy folks who want to have "fast food" without the cost and poor nutrition have discovered how to make the most of their budgets, their time, and their freezers with bulk cooking. Called "investment cooking," "once-a-month cooking," "frozen assets," and "freezer cooking" by different cookbook authors and other proponents, this method makes the most of money, time, and energy. Now, I don't like to eat only frozen food, so for me, bulk cooking is great for a few days each week, with quick cooking and crock-pot dishes filling in the rest.

Bulk cooking it's a great way to make the most of restaurant sizes at the grocery store, seasonal sales, and an overabundance in the garden. The basic idea is to plan a series of menus, shop for all of them at one time, and then cook all the meals at one time and freeze them. Typically, if you're cooking for a family of four for a month, this will take two to three days for shopping, preparation, and cooking.

What a Load of Crock!

Everybody has a crock-pot gathering dust in the back of a cabinet. Well, get it out, dust it off, and start using it! If you don't have one, you can probably pick one up at a garage sale for a pittance. Slow cooking means

➤ Everything's prepared in one pot for minimum cleanup.

➤ Making use of less expensive cuts of meat.

➤ All the juices and nutrients are kept in.

➤ Conserving energy to prepare a meal.

➤ You can cook a meal while you're doing something else.

Beyond Basics

Want to know more about bulk cooking? There are several good books I've found, but the one that got me started was *Once-a-Month Cooking* by Mimi Wilson and Mary Beth Lagerborg. There's a great bulk Web site, too, at members.aol.com/ OAMCLoop/index.html.

I use my crock-pot extensively when I'm doing bulk cooking as well as for regular meals. I have an extra large one that I use to double up on recipes. We eat one half and freeze the other. This is a really painless way to fill up the freezer. When I'm actually doing a bulk-cooking session, I cook two whole chickens the night before while I'm sleeping, another double dish while I'm shopping the next day, a third double recipe the night before cooking day, and another double dish that day. That's six completed dishes and cooked chicken for several more.

With these three methods—quick cooking, bulk cooking, and slow cooking—there's no reason why you should be spending any more time in the kitchen than you want to! Frankly, I'd rather be playing! Another benefit, not to be undervalued, is that having food prepared ahead of time or utilizing the ability to put a meal on the table quickly allows us to be more hospitable and spontaneous. I think nothing now of saying "How about staying for dinner?" or bringing over a dish to a sick neighbor.

Getting the Best Ingredients

You'll want to get the best ingredients for your efforts and money, and if simple living to you also means "living lightly" on the earth, then how these ingredients are produced and the natural resources used to get them to market will matter to you. Three simple principles will hold you in good stead:

1. **Buy locally.** The advantages of buying locally are that it helps sustain rural communities and lifestyles, it means fewer after-harvest pesticides and other chemical treatments for shipping long distances, and less fuel spent for transportation and packing. Plus, if you get to know the grower, you know how the food was grown—organically or not. It just appeals to our common sense that the shorter the distance food travels from the farm to our table, the better it will be.

2. **Buy organic.** The cost of organic produce is sometimes higher because organic farming is more labor intensive, but you'll be getting better nutrition and fewer unwanted "extras," and you can offset the higher cost with lower meat and dairy-product consumption. If you buy local organic produce, you may not pay any more or even less than nonorganic.

3. **Eat and buy seasonally.** When you buy foods in season, they're usually cheaper and fresher, and somehow the body responds to the seasonal change. During the winter months, if you live in a colder climate, live off the stored (maybe you have a root cellar or might want to think about creating one?), canned, and frozen foods you "put by" from what was in season during the summer and fall.

Avoidance Techniques

Be wary of perfect produce—it often takes heavy pesticide spraying to make the pretty fruits and veggies, and sometimes shiny coatings are added to make them look that way. A few blemishes and imperfections are natural and common with organic produce and what you pick from your own garden.

More Ways to Simplify Your Cooking

There are still more ways to make life easier and to spend less of it in the kitchen. Here are few more to try:

➤ **Rethink what makes a meal.** A fairly large portion of rice or another grain like millet, a small amount of meat, lots of vegetables in a broth over the rice, some bananas or applesauce, and some tea. That's a meal! You'll find yourself full but not overly so.

➤ **Make it from scratch.** You may think it takes longer, but more often than not it doesn't. And what do we honestly save when we buy prepared foods? It took more life energy to pay for them since they're definitely more costly. And by cooking from scratch you have control over what goes in, which includes your own loving energy, a gift to yourself and to your family. Remember to consider the *true* cost of things in terms of money, time, and energy. Many foods that look like a savings really aren't.

➤ **Eat it raw!** The less food is cooked, the more nutrition is passed on to you. The Nearings ate approximately 50 percent of their food raw and recommended that, at the very least, we eat something raw at every meal.

➤ **Play with your food.** Become intimate with vegetables and fruit—eat one variety many ways—raw, sautéed, baked, boiled, mashed, shredded. Then try combining it with other things a little at a time. Ever try apples and onions? Keep heavy sauces to a minimum and let the true flavor come through. Experiment with fruits and vegetables you normally wouldn't eat. Have a love affair with one food at a time.

Beyond Basics

In her delightful cookbook (or should I call it an "uncook" book) *Simple Food for the Good Life*, Helen Nearing also recommends whole grains over breads and pastas, some of them eaten raw as well. The closer a food eaten is to the natural state, says Helen, the better. Not sure how to start adding more raw foods to your diet? *Dining in the Raw*, by Rita Romano will tell you everything you need to know about no-cook cooking.

Beyond Basics

Even if you're not a gardener, you can have fresh greens year round with a minimum of effort by growing sprouts. Varieties of sprouts include lettuce, alfalfa, clover, radish, onion, garlic, sunflower, buckwheat, and mung beans. All you need is a wide-mouth one-quart jar, some rubber bands, and some cheese cloth or plastic hardware cloth roughly the size the mouth of the jar. Everything you ever wanted to know about sprouting, including various sprouting devices, seeds, and ways of using sprouts to their greatest nutritional advantage, can be found at www.sproutpeople.com/.

Avoidance Techniques

So what about eating out? That makes life simple, right? Many restaurants use aluminum cookware because it heats up faster and is cheap and lightweight. Aluminum has been linked to Alzheimer's disease. Some restaurants also microwave food and use less beneficial fats and other additives. The only way to know is to ask (or to work in the kitchen!).

Simple Wisdom

"I like to have a dearth of materials out of which to make things, not an overflowing refrigerator and pantry. It fosters more ingenuity. ... I'm a spur-of-the-moment cook and make do with what materials are at hand in the pantry, cellar or garden, and let my mind and fingers work on them. Something usually emerges which is edible and nutritious. Mine is rough and ready cookery."

—Helen Nearing

➤ **Eat a variety every day.** Getting a variety of foods every day means you'll give your body what it needs and will have more interesting meals! Remember to get foods from all the food groups: Concentrate on fruits and vegetables and then grains and cereals. (These include rice, pasta, and breads.) Eat dairy, meat, fish, poultry, beans, eggs, and nuts in smaller quantities. Fats, oils, and sugars should make up the smallest category.

➤ **Try vegetarianism.** You don't have to stay one, but it's an interesting change, and reducing the amount of meat you eat can help your health, save money, and introduce you to new ingredients and cooking methods.

➤ **Use what you have on hand.** When you run out of something, try to use what you have in the house instead of running out to the grocery store. If you've planned ahead you probably won't have to, but in the event you missed something, make do. You'll save gasoline as well as your own energy and time, and you'll tap into your creativity and maybe invent something new and tasty.

The Well-Equipped Kitchen

Keeping it simple in the kitchen doesn't mean having all sorts of labor-saving appliances and gadgets. Besides, you'll have to find places to store them *and* spend time cleaning them! But there are a few I use all the time. Your choices might be different, but think carefully before you add more clutter to countertop. Here's my short list of indispensable helps in the kitchen:

➤ Crock-pot

➤ Yogurt maker

➤ Food processor

➤ Juicer

➤ A few good knives

➤ A garlic press and pasta machine (nonelectric is best)

Beyond Basics

Get yourself some good basic cookbooks with a simple living slant. Some I'd recommend to start are *Diet for a Small Planet* by Francis Moore Lappé and *Recipes for a Small Planet* by Ellen Buchman Ewald; *The New Laurel's Kitchen* by Laurel Robertson, Carol Flinders, and Brian Ruppenthal; Molly Katzen's *The New Moosewood* and *The Enchanted Broccoli Forest* cookbooks; and *The Tassajara Bread Book* and *Tassajara Cooking* (this one's out of print so look for it at a used book store) by Edward Espe Brown. These, along with some of the others I've mentioned in this chapter, will give you a whole new slant on "getting your daily bread."

Whatever tools you decide you need (note the operative word: *need*), do some research and buy the best quality you can afford. I look for professional quality in tools and utensils I know I'll be using day in and day out. Avoid aluminum cookware and utensils altogether and opt for high-quality stainless steel, enameled cookware, or glass.

Learn the best ways to choose, store, prepare, and cook fruits, vegetables, and grains. Your cooperative extension service is likely to have free information on food storage methods for longest freshness. Or you can check out the Colorado State Cooperative Extension food publications at www.colostate.edu/Depts/CoopExt/PUBS/FOODNUT/ pubfood.html. They're very low cost or even free, and they cover everything you want to know about food storage, safety, and preparation—even high-altitude cooking!

Beyond Basics

To learn more about turning your kitchen into a goddess's (or god's) workshop, check out *The Green Kitchen Handbook: Practical Advice, References, and Sources for Transforming the Center of Your Home into a Healthful, Livable Place,* by Annie Berthold-Bond. Bond talks about a new "green diet," the importance of eating locally grown foods, and how to shop, store and preserve your healthy foods. This book even covers homemade cleaning products to substitute for that chemical waste dump you could have under your sink.

How Simple Is It to Grow Your Own?

You may imagine all the work having a food-supplying garden entails and exclaim, "That's not simple! That's work!" Well, yes and no. It's also exercise (why buy an exercise bike when you can accomplish the same thing and grow fresh lettuce?), fresh air, a religious experience (just about every religious tradition says so!), and fun!

Okay, it's not for everyone, but why not give it a try? Your garden can make a major dent in your food budget or be just a small supplement to your grocery shopping, but there are some things every household can pretty much manage to grow with little experience or expertise. Start with a tomato plant or two, some herbs and healing plants, and maybe some pretty flowers for pleasure. (Why not make them edible, too?) I bet once you get a taste of the convenience and flavor of home-grown basil and tomatoes, you'll never go back!

No land? A sunny windowsill, balcony, or terrace might let you grow a few things. I have a friend who gardens on the roof of her garage! See if there's a coop or community garden in your town. If not, maybe you can start one. Several large cities even have community garden projects. If your area doesn't, try some container gardening. Need help to get started? Begin at your local library and find out what resources might be available from your cooperative extension center or nearby colleges or universities. Start small and work from there.

Food is the sustainer. Food is life. By returning to basics and simplifying your relationship to food, you're making a huge step in simplifying your life.

The Least You Need to Know

➤ Food buying, storing, preparing, and growing is an easy area to make changes toward a simpler lifestyle.

➤ There are lots of ways to save money and cut down on time spent cooking including eating more raw foods and buying in bulk.

➤ No matter where you live and how much space you have, you can grow some of your own food.

Chapter 12

The
LaTest
Thing!
$2000⁰⁰

Fashion: Trends or Tyranny?

In This Chapter

➤ Examining your clothing habits and becoming more conscious about clothes shopping

➤ Finding your own clothing style

➤ How to dress comfortably and well for less

➤ Caring for clothes so they last

"Clothes make the man [or woman]," so the old saying goes. But do they *really?* You'd certainly think so, the way we put such emphasis in our society on how we dress and look in general. Where do we get our ideas about our daily threads? And how does "success dressing" fit into the simple life?

Who Decides Your Clothing Future?

Compared to the fashions of times past, we wear far less restrictive clothing today and have many more choices with regard to dress. Dress on the job for both men and women has relaxed to the point where some corporations have "casual day" or "jeans day" once a week or even all the time. Hair lengths and styles can be found in every extreme for both men and women. There is a myriad of makeup products for both men and women to enhance their best features, to create a particular "look," and even to cover up birthmarks and scars. So what could be bad?

There's no fashion police, that's for sure. You're free to wear whatever you want, right? Or *are* you? If we go back to our original definition of simple living as *conscious* living, we might begin to see things differently. When is what we wear unconscious consumption, mere image imitation, and exploitation of both natural resources and human beings and when is it a matter of self-expression and freedom of choice? That's for you to decide as I raise some issues for you to think about in your own simple living context.

Quick Starts

To become more conscious of the messages underlying the media depiction of fashion, go through a fashion magazine with new and critical eyes. What's being used to sell the clothes? What kind of body image is being presented? What kind of character do they seem to be promoting? What is the overall image of the models in the ads? What is the idea of beauty being presented? Ask the question "If I wear this, I'll get *what?*" For even more eye-opening food for advertising thought, point your browser at the Web site at about-face.org and read on!

So what is clothing in its most basic form? We can probably break the essential elements down into just three simple functions: protection from the elements, comfort, and modesty. We dress to keep ourselves warm or to shelter us from the sun, to protect our bodies from various surfaces and threats from our environment, and because human society has long imposed a certain (although constantly changing) sense of modesty on appearance in public. If we evaluate fashion from these three basic needs—protection, comfort, and modesty—our reactions to certain styles might be quite different.

Besides falling short in the practicality department, most "fashionable" clothing isn't flattering on the majority of people. Many of the styles imply a hidden (or perhaps not so hidden) pressure to be excessively thin and to have a certain shape. The body image promoted is neither healthy nor attainable by the average person. In some cases, advertisers even use children and their immature bodies to sell clothes to women, presenting what some observers feel are unwholesome sexual images.

By constantly changing clothing images and styles, the consumer needs to buy new clothes on a regular basis to keep up. The fashion industry needs to make your wardrobe obsolete on a regular basis, so designers and manufacturers keep changing the rules to create new "needs" that must be satisfied for you to be in fashion.

That's not to say clothing can't also be a means of self-expression. But is it really *self-expression* or what I call "following the fashionazis" when we let others dictate how and what we wear? Self-expression is about looking the way *you* want and feeling good about it rather than pursuing an image someone else hands you so that you'll hand over your hard-earned cash.

Clothing as Consumption

Think about the number of garments we buy, wear for a short time (if at all), and then get rid of. We have, in fact, so many discarded items there's an entire retail industry that has grown up around re-distributing them—thrift and consignment shops.

How much of what's in your closet was con-sciously purchased? How many items were used for only one activity and then rarely after that? How many days could you dress yourself without re-peating the same outfit?

"But," you may argue, "I didn't pay a lot for my clothes! I got them on sale. I can afford to have lots of choices." And why are our clothes relatively inexpensive? Where and how are they made? Are there labor and environmental practices that wouldn't be tolerated under the law in this coun-try, yet are supported unwittingly by us in other distant nations through our clothes consumption decisions? And if we again return to equating money with life energy or essence, how much true cost does our clothes closet represent?

Simple Wisdom

"In many parts of the world a thrift shop movement is unthink-able. To organize a thrift shop or buy there is blessed, but to live so that you have little to donate is an equally high calling."

—Doris Janzen Longacre, *Living More with Less*

Finding Your Own Simple Clothing Style

One way to greatly simplify your clothing life is to find your own simple style and stick to it. If you consciously create a clothing style that suits your needs in terms of the activities you engage in, that fits your body type and figure, and that represents a classic style that's always around, you'll always look nifty without having to think about it very much. Your pocketbook will be less burdened, too, since there will al-ways be a large pool of used clothing around to fit your fashion statement. Even if you do have to "dress for success" or at least have a dress code at your job, there are ways of meeting those requirements simply and economically.

First, let's look at some guiding principles when revamping your closet to fit your conscious clothing style:

1. Dress for comfort, according to the weather, and for the job to be done.
2. Buy or make good-quality clothes of classic style and cut.

125

3. Recycle unused clothing by donating your used items and by buying preowned clothes yourself.

Beyond Basics

Not sure how to find your own personal style and flatter your figure? There are books to help. Although some are written by "image" consultants, the basic concepts are there. Look for the basic principles and you can't go wrong. I would recommend *Looking Good*, by Nancy Nix-Rice and Pati Palmer, *Flatter Your Figure* by Jan Larkey, and *Always in Style*, by Doris Pooser, all of which are currently in print. If you're lucky enough to find Olivia Goldsmith and Amy Fine Collins' book *Simple Isn't Easy: How to Find Your Personal Style and Look Fantastic Every Day* in a used book store or library (it's out of print), grab that one first!

Go through your closet and look at what you wear most often. Why are these your favorites? Look at them critically and analytically? What style are they? What colors? What lines? Take out anything you haven't worn in a year or more. Try on each item. What's wrong with it? If it needs ironing or mending, do it and then put it back in your closet. If it doesn't fit right, ask yourself if it's worth it to alter it yourself or have it done. If it doesn't go with anything, perhaps it's best to pass it on. Acknowledge your mistakes and know you'll be creating a clothing philosophy that will minimize them in the future.

Simple Wisdom

"Do not be anxious about ... what you shall put on. For life is more than food, and the body more than clothing."

—Luke 12:22–23

Look at each area of activity in your life and what your options are. Look at each component—undergarments, shoes, shirts and blouses, pants and skirts, jackets and sweaters, hats, gloves, and accessories. What makes sense for your climate, your location, your line of work, your leisure activities? Is there one style you like that suits you and that can be adapted to most or all of your needs?

Components like jumpers for women allow lots of flexibility in different weather. If made out of a mid-weight fabric in a neutral color, you can add a turtle neck and warm leggings for winter or a T-shirt and sandals for warmer weather. Layering adds flexibility in changing temperatures. A classic, well-made blazer can be used to dress up any outfit, even jeans, and add warmth.

Men can work with simple, but flexible components, as well. Khaki pants can be dressed up or down, and a neutral sports jacket works much the way a blazer does in a woman's wardrobe. The same shirt can be dressed up with a tie or down with a pullover sweater. Again, layering adds flexibility.

One thing I refuse to do is wear clothing with brand advertising. "No logos!" is my motto and no labels on the outside. I just figure there's enough advertising around, I don't need to be a walking billboard! I'm not saying you should agree, but on this one I'm personally pretty stubborn.

So what's your style? Classic? Romantic? Western? Ethnic? Natty? Have fun with it and see if you can pin it down. Notice if what you think you are matches what you have in your closet and what you tend to grab from it on a regular basis.

Clothing Craft: Doing It for Less!

You've made yourself more aware of the fickle finger of fashion; you've done your closet analysis and have found your own personal clothing style. Now, how do you make it all work within your simple living finances?

Here's a list of tips to get you started:

➤ Work from a list. After you've evaluated your existing wardrobe, make a list of only the things you've determined you really need or that will help you stretch what you have. Do the same for other family members. Keep a list of sizes and measurements for each person, too. Stick to the list!

➤ Whether buying new or used, find well-made items at reasonable prices. Check the seams and buttons to make sure they're sewn properly. Pull the fabric in different directions to see if it's strong and durable. Take a white cotton cloth and rub it on the fabric to see if the color comes off. Read the care and fabric content label.

Beyond Basics

For a riveting discussion of the culture of brand names and logos, in fashion as well as more generally, check out Norma Klein's book, *No Logos*.

Avoidance Techniques

There are lots of media messages telling us to use consumption of clothing and beauty products to change our feelings. Sad? Get happy with XYZ chewing gum. Feeling frumpy? Get a new "do" and become a new "you!" Be aware of the messages and question yourself when you hit the mall to feel better.

➤ Don't rely on the size stated on the label. Try it on.

➤ Stay away from "designer" labels. A white T-shirt from Hanes is half the price of a nearly identical white T-shirt from Calvin Klein.

➤ Choose a color palette. Having one basic color for the two main clothing seasons helps make it easy to mix and match. A color palette gives you a foundation to work with and makes serious faux-pas purchases more unlikely.

➤ Make your own. It's not as hard as you think, especially with today's really easy patterns and detailed instructions.

➤ Learn to mend. If you know how to repair a seam, replace a button, and patch a tear, you'll stretch your clothing dollars a mile.

➤ Evaluate special clothing carefully. Do you really need a different outfit for skiing or playing golf?

➤ Choose natural fabrics like cotton and wool. These fabrics are more energy efficient to produce and to wear.

➤ Declare a moratorium on new clothes. Give it a try. Decide not to buy anything new for a whole season.

➤ Trade places. Need a special dress or tuxedo for a wedding or fancy event? See if you know someone who could loan you what you need.

➤ Take care of what you have. If we hang up our clothes, protect them from dirt and wear, remove stains as soon as possible, and keep them clean, we'll have them longer.

➤ Buy really good shoes. Always buy the very best quality shoes you can afford. Your shoes are one item of clothing that can affect your health and how you feel on a daily basis. Find good brands that fit you well and that last a long time and then invest in quality footwear.

> ### Beyond Basics
>
> You *can* remake clothes you already have in your closet or ones you find at yard sales or thrift shops if you know how. I found three guides at used book stores that will help: *Gladrags: Ways and Means to a New Wardrobe*, by Delia Brock, *How to Recycle Old Clothes into New Fashions*, by Fenya Crown and *The Yestermorrow Clothes Book: How to Remodel Secondhand Clothes*, by Diana Funaro. These three books are out of print, but I had no problem finding several copies of each on the used book search engine ABE at www.abebooks.com/.

➤ Check the classifieds. Watch your local paper for yard sales, garage sales, tag sales, barn sales, rummage sales, estate sales, moving sales, flea markets, and swap meets.

➤ Use accessories to expand your wardrobe. Accessories are easy to make or find inexpensively and can completely change the look of an outfit.

➤ Rediscover aprons, smocks, and "mess-up" clothes. A lot of times, good clothes are ruined because of carelessness or just plain absentmindedness.

> ### Simple Wisdom
>
> "Beware of all enterprises that require new clothes."
> —Henry David Thoreau, *Walden*

I'll bet you can think of lots of other ways to dress simply and well for less or to make the clothes you already have last longer. The point is that, when you free yourself from the tyranny of the fashion dictators and express your own personal clothing independence, you're in control of both your fashion sense *and* your dollars and sense.

Watch That Wash Basket

Did you know that part of saving money on your wardrobe and making it last longer is in the suds? The laundry suds, that is. Decisions you make about fabrics at purchase and then how you take care of them from there can determine how long your clothes wear and how well they look.

Machine washing and drying is hard on clothes. Just look at what's left in the lint catcher! So an obvious way to prolong the life of your clothes is not to wash them as often. Could you wear an outfit again if it got a good airing rather than a washing? Just hang your clothes out on a line for a few hours or in a well-ventilated porch and then put them back in the closet for another day. Maybe all a garment needs is a brushing and a little touch-up ironing.

Soap Suds

What you use to wash and dry your clothes can make a big difference as well. The gentler the detergent (or soap), the easier it is on the clothes. The gentler the cycle you can use to wash, the better as well. Try to match the process with the soil. Generally, undergarments are not terribly soiled and can be washed in mild soap and water on a shorter, gentler cycle in the washer. Outer garments that are worn for working in the garden or changing the oil in the car will need a stronger detergent (investigate types and their chemical formulas—some are kinder to the environment than others) and heavier and longer agitation.

Hard water requires extra attention. In soft-water areas, plain laundry soap rather than harsh detergents might be fine for most loads. In hard-water areas, softeners and boosters might be necessary.

Water temperature is also a consideration. Hot water is harder on clothes, but it's necessary to remove some dirt and grime. Adjust the temperature to the fabric and level of soil.

Return of the Clothes Line

Dryers really take a lot of the life out of clothes. Just clean the lint trap for the hard evidence. That's part of your clothes in there! By not overloading or overdrying and by taking your clothes out as soon as the drying cycle is through, you'll do the least amount of damage, but I'm finding myself drying our clothes the old-fashioned way a lot more these days.

Avoidance Techniques

Watch out for fabrics that aren't fire retardant. The U.S. Consumer Product Safety Commission's checklist includes information on how to contact the agency to check on product recalls, bans and safety standards. You can reach them by visiting their web site at www.cpsc.gov. Their Thrift Store Checklist is available online as well or send a postcard to Thrift Store Checklist, CPSC, Washington, DC 20207 to get your free copy.

Quick Starts

Take heavy items like blankets and comforters to the coin-operated laundry to wash and dry. Their larger heavy-duty machines are built to take the load, and you'll add life to your laundry appliances.

At first I thought line drying would take more time, but I'm not really sure it does in the long run. I don't do all my clothes on the line all the time, but whenever I can, I take advantage of the free breeze and sunshine. Besides, it's a great break from work, it gets me out in the fresh air, and I can oversee the bird feeders at the same time!

Good Grooming Simplified

If you want to open your eyes about the cost of keeping clean and well groomed, start making your own personal care products. You may not want to do this as an ongoing thing (I do), but it will amaze you to discover how cheaply these basic products can be made. Cost out your ingredients and imagine the markup on commercial products. And you may be getting all sorts of chemicals and additives that you don't need or that may cause certain allergies or sensitivities besides.

Again, let's get down to the lowest common denominator. If you eliminated all the extra rinses, gels, sprays, and powders and got down to the bare essentials, most likely you'd have just a few simple products: shampoo, soap, moisturizer, toothpaste, deodorant, and possibly a body powder. Most makeup, hair-care products, lotions, and sprays are extras you probably don't need to be clean and well groomed. Not that you should necessarily give them up, mind you, but you might want to examine whether they really add anything to your life or simply complicate matters.

Check out the Appendix, "Resource Guide," for information about how to make your own shampoos, lotions, soaps, deodorants, toothpastes, and just about anything else you can imagine.

You might also want to reconsider your hairstyle. If you find you need to spend a lot of time styling your hair, perhaps it's time for a new, simpler look! And forget about that makeup, too; it just costs money and clogs your pores anyway. Of course, we all like to look and feel special on occasion, but try cutting back on the time and money you spend on personal grooming. You might just find you like the person looking back at you in the mirror!

There are certain things you can do to keep your grooming routine simple. Long or short hair seem to be the easiest to keep. Simple styles that can be air dried save time as well. Keep your nails short and rub in a little vitamin E oil to give them strength and luster. You may not mind the extra time needed to blow dry, set, and curl your hair or the gels and sprays needed to keep it looking good, but we're talking simple here! You decide what you want to spend your time and life energy on. Me? I'd rather be doing something else!

Beyond Basics

My herbalism teacher, Jeanne Rose, has written some great books that contain simple, natural recipes for personal care products. I'd recommend *Jeanne Rose's Herbal Body Book* and *Jeanne Rose's Kitchen Cosmetics* for starters. There are some other books I'll be mentioning in the next chapter for homemade cleaning products that also have personal care product recipes in them as well.

And what about makeup? No makeup is cheaper and saves time, but a little makeup can make a lot of difference to some people. To me, just looking healthy and well-groomed is more attractive, but I admit there are times when a little lipstick and eye makeup add to a feeling of being "dressed up" and special. You decide, but make your choices conscious. Is there a neutral color palette that looks good with everything? Can you buy products that are relatively free of chemicals? How were your products manufactured and tested? Would a little natural oil on the lips and a healthy glow from fresh air and sunlight be just as effective? And what's "beautiful" anyway? Whose idea was all this goo? If you follow the money I think you'll come up with your own answers.

A word about hair cuts: they don't have to cost a lot either. I've taught myself to cut my husband's hair and now he won't go anywhere else. I can do in-between trims on my own, but occasionally need a more expert cut. Walk-in haircutting establishments are popping up all over. They're economical, and if you find someone who does your hair the way you like, get his or her name and wait the extra time to get your favorite haircutter. Trade hair cuts for something else you do well, like mending or a neck and shoulder massage, or offer some homemade food or garden produce in exchange.

Simple Wisdom

"Those who make their dress a principal part of themselves, will, in general, become of no more value than their dress."

—William Hazlitt

How much time do you spend on appearance? What part of each day is spent putting on makeup and grooming, shopping and caring for clothes, even choosing clothes? If you ever decide to keep a time diary to see where your time is going (like the spending record we talked about earlier), you may be surprised at home much time you would reclaim by simplifying your routine in this area.

Find a style that suits you. Buy or make clothes that really work, that are of the best quality you can afford, and that are classically designed. Then wear them, repair them, and keep them until they wear out. Use them then for rags or recycle them into something else (quilting, anyone?). The clothes you wear shouldn't cost the shirt off your back. Make new decisions and free yourself from fashion tyranny!

The Least You Need to Know

➤ Becoming conscious of how the fashion industry works and what messages underlie clothing advertising can simplify how we decide to dress.

➤ Developing a classic style gives you a framework for building a wardrobe and a ready pool of used garments to work with.

➤ Learning how to care properly for your clothes will help them last longer and look better.

➤ By simplifying your grooming routines and making some of your own products, you can save money and time.

Chapter 13

Seeking Shelter and Keeping House

In This Chapter

➤ Living in the home you're already in and liking it more

➤ The ins and outs of remodeling

➤ Building or buying a new house the simple living way

➤ Alternative housing arrangements and how to know if they're for you

---

Whether you live in the country or the city, rent or own your own home, your living situation can either support you in your efforts to create the simple life, or it can get in your way. So how do you keep a roof over your head without getting complicated? Read on!

What Makes a Home?

First of all, a house or an apartment should be good, basic shelter, but I believe it should also be a home. A home is a place you want to come back to, a nest, a center. To me it's "home base" or the center of operations from which I launch my life and to which I retreat. How does it feel when you walk into your current place of residence? Does it reflect you? Is it in line with your values? Does it support the activities you do there? Is it uplifting? Is it healthy? What does "home" mean to you?

Some people have beautiful homes but they're "house poor." They have a lot of money tied up in their dwelling and spend most of their life energy working to make the payments and keep it up. In some cases, they're working 40 hours or more a week to do it and hardly ever spend time there! If that's what you're doing, then how much house do you really need if you're never home?

Simple Wisdom

"Try to make everything you do in your home, no matter how insignificant it may seem, part of your authentic path to wholeness and it shall become so."

—Sarah Ban Breathnach, *Simple Abundance: A Datebook of Comfort and Joy 2000*

Beyond Basics

A great book on sensible and problem-solving decorating for apartment dwellers (or anyone living in small spaces) is *The New Apartment Book*, by Michele Michael (with Wendy S. Israel). You'll find lots of easily adaptable ideas for storage, creating breathing space, and just generally sprucing things up.

A simple living approach to housing would match the living space to what you can afford and still allow you to spend your time doing what matters most to you. The simple living approach to housing considers alternatives that provide the most quality and value for the least amount of money spent. It's about living more with less and building in a way that's energy efficient and that has a low impact on the environment. A simple home is a happy, healthy home. It's also a place where we can find our spiritual center, nurture ourselves, and celebrate good times.

As more people are working at least part-time at home, our shelter also becomes part of our daily sustenance, much as it was in an earlier time.

Love the One You're In!

The best place to start is always where you are. You may notice this is a recurring theme for me. Often we don't fully appreciate our current situation or resources. And if we need to make a change, we usually make more informed choices if we have a clear picture of where we are now and how we got there.

Before thinking about where else you might want to live, start from where you are. If you evaluated your location already when you were reading Chapter 8, "Location, Location! The Simple Truth About Where You Live," and you determined you're in a good place, then your work is clear: Improve on what is already a good thing! If you haven't given serious thought to your current location, I suggest you do so now.

Assuming for a second that you've decided you're where you want to be, how do you feel about your current dwelling? If you're renting, you'll need to evaluate whether this is where you want to remain for now and whether it suits your financial goals. What do you like about your apartment? What don't you like? Are there any changes the landlord would let you make to correct the things you're not too happy about? Most will let you do things to improve the place, make it more energy efficient, and spruce it up. Ask. Perhaps you can even make improvements to your apartment in exchange for reduced rent or a partial refund of your security.

Apartment space can often be made more livable with more careful attention to use of space, storage, and decorating. Again, know what you can and can't do, then make a list of problems and look for solutions.

If you own your own home, challenge yourself to look at it through new eyes—how can you make better use of space, create a better atmosphere, make the place more reflective of who you are and your values, and develop it into a center of activity and a place of harmony? What rooms do you spend the most time in? What is wasted space? Can changes be made to double up on the usefulness of certain spaces?

Be aware of which spaces you feel most comfortable in. Spend a day looking at houses with a realtor or attending realtor open houses, even if you're not planning to buy right now. Sometimes looking at other people's houses gives you a new appreciation for your own, and you can garner lots of ideas to use now or in the future.

Sizing Things Up

The first step to evaluating where you are now is to look at actual space. How many square feet of living space do you have and how many people are using it? Remember, you're paying to heat and cool that space, to insure it, to maintain it, and to clean it!

Maybe the kids have moved out and you're still living in a large house with four bedrooms. Is the space filled with things you actually use or are you just living in a glorified storage facility? If you have a very large house that you enjoy living in but don't need all the space, could you share it or remodel it to create more than one private living space? Do you use all the rooms in your house? How often?

Is there any way you can bring your employment or business into the space? Can you turn your house into a business by renting out rooms or

Quick Starts

Go through each room with a pad and pencil and note what you'd like to make better plus any items in that room you don't use. (Later we'll be decluttering, and this will come in handy.) Some things that you don't like you may only be able to change with a remodel. Look first at the things you can do with the house as it is now, but note the more serious flaws as well.

Avoidance Techniques

One key thing to consider if you plan to downsize is capital gains tax. You'll need to look at your own situation based on your age and how much you might lose all at once as opposed to what you'd gain over a period of years. As part of your information-gathering process, talk to an accountant about what selling your house and moving into a less expensive one might mean financially.

creating a bed-and-breakfast, by offering space for workshops, by creating a studio for a writer or artist, by giving workshops or holding retreats? I'm not saying you're going to do these things. I'm just trying to get you to think more creatively about your existing space.

If the problem is that your home is not big enough, could you create more space instead of moving? Do you use all of the garage or basement? Could you add another story or use the attic as it is with some finishing?

While you're evaluating size, don't just look at living space. How about the size of things like windows, appliances, furniture, doors, stairways, cabinets, sinks, and tubs? Look for features and objects that are oversized as well as undersized. For instance, do you have a two-car garage and only one car?

Beyond Basics

If you're looking for ideas for increasing the efficiency of a small house or apartment, *Making the Most of Small Spaces,* by Anoop Parikh is a good read. For all kinds of ideas for making a house into a home the simpler way, subscribe to (or borrow copies of) *Natural Home* magazine, 201 E. Fourth Street, Loveland, CO 80537-5633; www. naturalhomemagazine.com.

Energy Efficient or Energy Suck?

Now let's look at energy consumption where you live. Even if you live in an apartment, this is a worthwhile effort, and there may be things you can do even if you don't own your dwelling. You can start by taking a look at your electric and fuel bills. How much do you actually spend each month? Which are your peak months? Remember, that's your life energy going out the window!

Next, find out what local energy resources might be available in your area. Does your state or utility company offer energy conservation tax credits? Free or low-cost energy audits? Contact your local cooperative extension service (check the phone book) and see what publications they might have available such as energy conservation checklists, instructions on how to do simple energy-saving projects, and tips for making appliances and heating and cooling plants more efficient. Check out your local library, too. Gather information on what can be done, then look at your own home and see what's feasible to do right away and what you might budget for in the future.

While you're doing your energy information search, here are some things to gather information about and then concentrate on in your own home:

➤ **Hot water heater.** This appliance uses a lot of electricity heating water even when you don't need it. Is it working properly? Is it the right size for your needs? Does it have an insulation blanket around it (cost: only about $10)? When you go on vacation do you shut it off (for electric heaters) or turn it down (for gas)?

➤ **Appliances.** There are more and more options available when purchasing appliances to select energy-efficient ones. How efficient are yours? Do you maintain your appliances to keep them efficient (vacuuming refrigerator coils regularly, for example)? Do you rinse clothes in cold water and run full loads in your clothes washer? Can you dry clothes outside on sunny days? Do you clean the lint filter on the dryer after every load? Have you checked the dryer vent hose lately? Do you only run the dishwasher when it's full and use the "air dry" or "energy saver" settings? Do you leave the TV or radio on when you're not there?

➤ **Lighting.** How much natural light is available in your home? Do you open blinds and curtains in the winter to take advantage of it and close them in the summer to keep things cool? Do you turn lights on when you could open a blind or curtain and take advantage of sunlight? Do you turn lights off when you're not using them? Are you using higher wattage bulbs than you really need? Can you substitute compact fluorescent lights for incandescent ones in some areas? How about using nonelectric lighting once in a while?

➤ **Windows and doors.** How well are these sealed? (If you're not sure, hold a lighted candle near them and look for drafts.) Have you caulked them recently? If you have double-pane windows, are the seals still good? If not, have them replaced.

➤ **Plumbing.** Do you have leaky faucets? Have you installed an energy-efficient showerhead (cost: $5 to $15)? Do you leave the water running when shaving or doing dishes? Do you have water-saving aerators on the faucets you use the most? Are the hot water pipes insulated where they run through unheated areas of the house? Are all your toilets in good working order?

➤ **Heating and cooling systems.** Do you have these serviced regularly? Are they properly sized for your living area? Do you clean or replace filters regularly? Do you turn up the thermostat when you're cold instead of putting on warmer clothes? Would a fan do the job rather than turning on the air conditioner? How well is your home weatherized? Do you know how much insulation is in your attic and walls? Can it be improved? Do you have a clock thermostat that

Quick Starts

If you have a computer and an Internet connection, you can get lots of helpful energy-conservation information quick and free! Try the Department of Energy "Consumer Energy Information Home Page" at www.eren.doe.gov/consumerinfo and the American Council for an Energy-Efficient Economy at aceee.org for starters. Challenge yourself and your family to find ways to save energy and check the next month's utility bills to see the results!

you can set to automatically lower the heat when you're sleeping or at work? Are there ways of landscaping to provide shade and reduce air conditioning costs?

These are just a few of the questions you'll be prompted to ask yourself as you do a simple energy audit. Keep looking for and implementing simple tips for saving energy and you'll be saving money, too. Home improvements that decrease energy consumption are one of the simplest ways to cut costs. Once they're completed, you don't even know you're saving money. If you're trying to get out of debt and become financially independent, this is good!

A Matter of Place

Are you making the most of where you are? Do you know your neighborhood, avail yourself of community resources, and participate in local activities? Is it the house or you?

This may be the most difficult question of all to answer honestly. You know the old saying, "Wherever you go, there you are." Perhaps you're in the perfect place and don't know it. Maybe all it needs is some loving care, some fixing and cleaning up, some attention. Only you can answer this question, but it's an important thing to consider in assessing whether you're living in the right place for you.

Get Organized!

We've talked before about decluttering and organizing, but it can't be emphasized too much. You may not need a new house, just a new way of living! An orderly home contributes to well-being as well as less consumption, conservation, and contentment. Getting rid of excess and organizing the rest brings comfort and joy into your home. Make your sleep places a haven, your bath a place for delighting the senses and self-healing. As you pare down and assign your possessions a permanent place, your life will become simpler with each step. Simplicity soothes.

If you pare down and get organized, you may see immediately that you don't need as much space. Get rid of the furniture you don't use, the books you don't read, the stuff you never look at; you might be amazed at what you find under all that clutter. Before you decide to move on, move stuff out!

If It's Not Model, Why Not Remodel?

If you like *where* you are but your current dwelling doesn't fit the bill in terms of how you live, the next thing to consider is remodeling. If you've lived in the same place for some time, your mortgage situation may make this even more attractive.

You made a list earlier of what's right about the house and what's wrong. If you've determined that the things that are wrong are significant enough that more drastic changes need to be made, what would it take to make them right?

There are other reasons to remodel, too. Maybe the house was fine at an earlier time, but changes in your living situation may have changed your housing needs. Maybe you've changed from working outside the house to working at home. Maybe your family has expanded. Perhaps you want to remodel to turn part of your house into income-producing property—by creating rental space, for instance, or turning it into a bed and breakfast.

Remodeling can be as simple as tearing down a wall or putting up a new one. You might go looking for space upwards or down. Maybe that garage could be reconfigured. Or you may want to consider an actual addition. You'll need to evaluate all the options, and unless the solution is obvious, you'll probably want to consult a licensed remodeling contractor.

If you know what part of your home you're going to use for needed space or which existing spaces need remodeling, look for information about those specific kinds of renovations. The editors of Better Homes and Gardens have some excellent books for getting ideas on specific projects. Try *Attics: Your Guide to Planning and Remodeling* and *Basements: Your Guide to Planning and Remodeling*. There's also the *Better Homes and Gardens Remodeling Your Home* book and CD-ROM for Macintosh and Windows; it gives you a 3D tool for visualizing and costing out what you have in mind.

Avoidance Techniques

Don't pay more than you have to! If you know the changes you want to make and have a pretty good idea of what needs to be done, consider being your own contractor and hiring the various subcontractors you'll need to complete the job. Need help? Consult *Be Your Own Home Renovation Contractor*, by Carl Heldman for ways to "save 30 percent without lifting a hammer."

Quick Starts

Whether you're building, buying, or renting, get some ideas for quality earth-friendly products for your home from the Real Goods catalog, 1-800-762-7325 or visit their Web site at www.realgoods.com.

Build or Buy?

Now, lets say after all this you decide neither reorganizing, fixing up, or even moving walls or ceilings can make your current home work for you. Or perhaps you're renting now and want to invest in your own home. Do you build or buy your new dwelling?

Avoidance Techniques

Be careful with salvaged materials. They may not be energy efficient, they may not fit (measure carefully), they may not be up to current building code, and they may even contain some health or safety hazards. Then again, salvaged materials can be beautiful, cost effective, and perfect for your application. Just choose carefully and ask an expert if you're not sure.

Beyond Basics

Whether you renovate or build, you'll want to learn something about permaculture. This philosophy takes into account natural systems as a model for land use. To find out more, read *Earth User's Guide to Permaculture*, by Rosemary Morrow and *Permaculture: A Designers' Manual*, by Bill Mollison.

Well, yes and yes! From a simple living perspective, there are advantages to both. First let's look at buying an existing structure:

➤ The structure is ready to move into right away.

➤ You know what you're getting.

➤ The land has already been cleared, so you're not using up any new land. Same with building materials.

➤ The cost is often lower than starting from scratch using traditional building techniques.

➤ If you purchase an older home, you're often getting better building materials and practices as part of the bargain.

The advantages of building are equally compelling:

➤ You can design the spaces specifically to suit your needs.

➤ You can choose the materials you want including those that are earth-friendly and energy-efficient or even salvage materials from structures that have been torn down.

➤ You can oversee the building process and check for quality materials and workmanship.

➤ You get to choose the exact location of your home.

With both buying and building, be willing to think beyond the usual. Existing spaces for homes don't necessarily have to be houses—people live on boats, in old schools or gas stations, former mines, and even abandoned ICBM missile silos! Sometimes an old house can be revitalized. If you're handy, look for fixer-uppers. Keep your ear to the ground for foreclosures and distress sales. Be open to the possibilities.

If you're considering building, don't overlook unconventional building materials like adobe, cob, or rammed earth. Consider solar alternatives, underground building, and log or even manufactured homes, which are made of much higher quality materials than years ago and have the advantage of being low maintenance, affordable, and space-efficient.

Housing Alternatives "Outside the Box"

If you really want to think "outside the box," consider other options besides traditional home ownership or renting altogether. Some of these options are

➤ **Cohousing:** This is a trend that's catching on. According to The Cohousing Network (www.cohousing.org), it's "a type of collaborative housing that attempts to overcome the alienation of modern subdivisions in which no one knows their neighbors, and there is no sense of community." It is characterized by private dwellings with their own kitchen, living-dining room, etc., but also extensive common facilities. The common building may include a large dining room, kitchen, lounges, meeting rooms, recreation facilities, library, workshops, childcare.

Avoidance Techniques

It's important to seriously consider *all* of the implications of cohousing or shared housing situations. Some people just aren't cut out for sharing living quarters with others, and it might make your life more complicated rather than simpler. Know thyself.

The definitive book on the subject is *Cohousing: A Contemporary Approach to Housing Ourselves,* by Kathryn McCamant and Charles Durrett.

➤ **Communal housing:** There are intentional communities, both rural and urban, that might be the perfect match for your lifestyle, your values, and your financial goals. Find out more by reading the following:

Communities magazine, "The Journal of Cooperative Living." Write to 138-W Twin Oaks Road, Louisa, VA 23093, or call 540-894-5798 or toll-free 1-800-462-8240. You can find more information online at fic.ic.org/cmag/subscribe.html.

Communities Directory: A Guide to Intentional Communities and Cooperative Living. For people interested in finding or creating a community, more information is available from the Fellowship for Intentional Community at directory.ic.org/order/index.html.

Builders of the Dawn: Community Lifestyles in a Changing World by Corinne McLaughlin and Gordon Davidson.

➤ **Shared housing:** Perhaps you have a house that's bigger than you need and can share it with one or more person. Or maybe you're looking for such a living situation. Before you do, you might want to read *House Mates: A Guide to Cooperative Shared Housing,* by Lori Stephens for the ins and outs of doing it successfully.

The options for living within your means, simply and sustainably, are growing. As we seek to uncomplicate our lives and live more harmoniously, we can make new choices or enhance the ones we've already made.

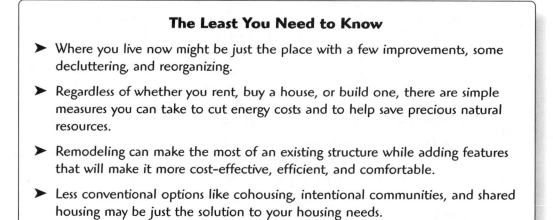

The Least You Need to Know

➤ Where you live now might be just the place with a few improvements, some decluttering, and reorganizing.

➤ Regardless of whether you rent, buy a house, or build one, there are simple measures you can take to cut energy costs and to help save precious natural resources.

➤ Remodeling can make the most of an existing structure while adding features that will make it more cost-effective, efficient, and comfortable.

➤ Less conventional options like cohousing, intentional communities, and shared housing may be just the solution to your housing needs.

Getting Off the Grid: Is It for You?

What does it mean to be living "off the grid?" Basically, the grid we're talking about is the electrical utility system that brings "juice" to the switches and outlets most of us use without thinking. When someone chooses to live off the grid, they take responsibility for making their own power whether that means using an alternative method for generating electricity or going completely nonelectric like the Amish communities we learned about in Chapter 4, "Culture Shock: Lessons from Alternative Living."

Some people who are energy independent still have all the modern conveniences. They are simply nondependent on public utilities and don't pay any utility bills. If the grid goes down in a snowstorm or a hurricane, it doesn't faze the energy-independent household.

Even if you're not interested in either of these scenarios, this chapter will give you lots of ideas to help you reduce your utility bills and to lower your dependence on the Anytown Electric and Gas Company.

What Pulling the Plug Can Mean

So is getting off the grid really simple living? At first blush, it didn't sound "simple" to me. But the more I read and the more I ponder the subject, the more I see it as a desirable trade-off—independence and lower costs for a bit more work in other areas (and often higher initial cost). It may be a matter of whether you want to spend your life energy working at a job and then paying the utility company or whether you want to spend your life energy doing things to provide for yourself directly like chopping wood or growing your own food. However, many of the measures I'm going to share with you take very little effort and can result in big savings.

Producing your own power completely is especially cost-efficient if you're planning to live in an area where there are no existing utilities at the dwelling and you would have to pay to have them brought in. The other scenario in which investing in independent energy production also makes sense is if you're going to live in the same place over a long period of time. It's important that you do the math and weigh cost versus other considerations.

If you choose to get off the grid instead of getting your "juice" from energy that's produced miles away from nuclear energy, coal, or water power, you'll be turning to water, the sun, wind, the earth, or an alternative fuel instead.

You'll need some sort of equipment to harness the energy sources you choose and to disperse it to where you need it. You'll most likely need equipment to store energy, such as batteries, which are an ongoing expense that needs to be factored in when you do your calculations.

Solar energy is the most independent energy source since it requires no fuel that needs to be replaced, it's free, and it's renewable. You may need a backup system like a propane generator or a wood stove for heat, but essentially, the energy from the sun is free and plentiful.

Quick Starts

Do a vulnerability check. Even if you have no intention of going off the grid, at least be aware of the extent of your dependence on "the almighty juice." Go through each room and the outside of your house and note how many things must have electricity to run. Don't forget hidden things like water pumps. While you're at it, for safety's sake, note where your utilities enter your house and where the shut-off valves or breakers are. Make a thorough and basic inventory of your current power usage. What absolute necessities do you need to find a battery or non-electric backup for?

Another consideration if you're thinking of going off the juice is whether you're building a new home or trying to retrofit an existing conventional house. There are ways to build to make the most of solar energy or the earth's natural insulating qualities so your system doesn't need to be that large or complicated. We talked about some of these in Chapter 13, "Seeking Shelter and Keeping House." It's much harder and more costly to retrofit a conventional house. But that doesn't mean it can't be done. People are coming up with economical and innovative solutions all the time! Hire someone who knows how to take a look at your place and see what can be done. You may be surprised.

Your physical location will make a difference as well. Know your area and the limits of your structure and equipment. Consider the orientation of your home on the land relative to the sun as well. If you live in New England, it's probably not wise to turn off the heat in winter; but if you live in the Southwest, it might be an easy way to save energy.

As in your overall plan for creating a simpler life, it's important to distinguish needs from wants. It's important to decide what you absolutely have to have to lead a full, satisfying life that is dependent on energy. If certain electric conveniences mean that much to you, you'll want to allow for them in your overall utility-independence plans.

Decide what your bottom line items are. If you had to go into deep conservation mode, what could you give up easily and what would be a hardship? These things are good to know, say, while you're working on your financial independence plans from Chapters 6 and 10 and working on cutting costs drastically to get out of debt. Knowing what you can do without is very empowering. If you practice doing without them when you don't really need to or as a preliminary step before pulling the plug for real, you'll be giving yourself even more personal power.

Beyond Basics

The best book I've found on the subject of living off the grid is Anita Evangelista's *How to Live Without Electricity and Like It*. She and her family have run the gamut from living with no stored power at all to trying out just about every kind of system imaginable for creating alternative power. It's a no-nonsense guide with something for everybody.

A Different Light

So if you had to light your own way, what would your options be? You can still have electric lights and be off the grid. Solar energy storage systems allow you to flip the switch much as before using energy stored from the sun during the day. But it may behoove you to cut down on your demands on the system. When it comes to reducing energy dependence, light is one of the easiest areas to make a difference.

It helps to think of lighting in a new way. Instead of flooding the room with light, you'll be lighting specific areas, specific tasks. Remember the last time the power went off? You lit a candle or an oil lamp and did what you needed to do where the light was or carried it with you.

The supplemental lighting we've chosen for ourselves is kerosene and oil lamps. They're efficient and they're beautiful. We have two lovely Aladdin kerosene lamps. They aren't the most expensive or decorative ones this company offers, but they're beautiful in an unadorned way and provide excellent light. We also have some smaller, handcrafted oil lamps we use regularly plus two rugged "hurricane"-style lamps for outdoors.

Avoidance Techniques

Be careful! You need to think differently when using alternative lighting, especially anything with a flame. Never leave a flame unattended, blow it out if you leave the room or think you might fall asleep, and remember that flames consume air, so make sure any room where one is burning isn't too airtight.

Beyond Basics

If you want a good overview of what options are out there from the people who know, get yourself a copy of the Lehman's Non-Electric catalog by calling 330-857-5757 or take a look at their online catalog at www.lehmans.com. This company has been serving the Amish for over 40 years, and they know what works. Just reading through the catalog is an education in itself. You can see some useful lighting products in the Real Goods catalog. Call 1-800-762-7325 or browse at www.realgoods.com. Another catalog you'll want to have on your shelf is the Cumberland General Store. Call 1-800-334-4630 to order yours. They've got still more tools for the nonelectric lifestyle.

Candles are a handy backup, but they give off far less light and aren't terribly cost effective for regular use. You'll have to increase the number of candles for the work you need to do; to sew, for instance, you might need four or five candles burning at a time to illuminate your work. But I still use candles a lot for dining. I like the look and the atmosphere they create. Look for bargain ones at thrift stores, factory outlets, and yard sales. Candles burn more efficiently if they're surrounded by a glass chimney. Save your candle wax for making your own now and then, which is easy and fun.

Of course, in the old days, people rose early and went to bed early, limiting the amount of lighting they actually needed. When we're without power, we naturally tend to do the same. If you chose to live off the grid, you could adjust your lifestyle somewhat to take greater advantage of the natural light of the sun and reduce your dependence on artificial light in general.

Whither Water?

We're so used to turning on the faucet and having clean, pure water instantly come out that we rarely think about what would happen if it didn't. Humans need about a gallon of water per person per day. This does not include the water needed for cooking and basic cleaning. Pets need water every day, too, so don't forget to count them in. Water basically comes from two sources: It comes out of the ground or falls from the sky in the form of rain. Once you get it, you need to store it so it's available and clean, free of disease-causing bacteria or parasites, and free of toxic chemicals.

In some parts of the country, there's enough rainfall each year to provide water for the average household. Where we live in Arizona that's not the case, but we can still provide some of our needs from the sky. We have above-ground rain barrels for collecting water off the roof, and we use this water for the garden and outdoor cleaning. If we needed this water for drinking, we'd have to treat it in some way to make it safe.

Simple Wisdom

"The future of civilization depends on water. I beg you to understand this."

—Jacques Yves Cousteau

I don't have adequate room to go into rainwater catchment systems in detail here, but Anita Evangelista's book gives you a good overview, and you can find specific detailed instructions in some of the other books I've recommended here. For some free, interesting, and practical information from Canada about what can be done with rainwater collection systems, check out www.cityfarmer.org/rainbarrel72.html. Also have a look at Xenia and Basil Arrick's Homesteading and Simple Living site at www.homestead.org/water.htm. Check back issues of magazines like *The Mother Earth News*, *Backwoods Home* and *Back Home* magazines, and *Countryside and Small Stock Journal*. Ask around your area, too. You may be surprised at what some of your neighbors are already doing!

Beyond Basics

Two excellent books on alternative water systems are *Cottage Water Systems: An Out-of-the City Guide to Pumps, Plumbing, Water Purification, and Privies* by Max Burns and *The Home Water Supply: How to Find, Filter, Store, and Conserve It* by Stu Campbell.

If you're getting your water from a well, you'll need to have a means of pumping it out. That's true of underground rainwater collection systems such as cisterns, too. You'll need to make sure your ground water isn't contaminated, and as with all water sources, you'll need a means of filtering it and keeping it free of disease-carrying organisms. To learn more about ground water systems and water purification, consult the sources I've already given you. If you're looking at alternative water sources for emergency backup, there are some high quality water filters available at a reasonable cost from companies like Katadyn, PUR and First Need. I've already mentioned the Real Goods catalog for other things, but check them out as well for water purifiers and filters. Also contact Jade Mountain at 1-800-442-1972 or www.jademountain.com, Emergency Essentials (also a good source for long-term food storage) at 1-800-999-1863 or www.beprepared. com, and even REI, the hiking equipment folks, at 1-800-426-4840.

Cooking a Whole New Way

If you didn't have access to your electric stove and oven, electric gadgets, and microwave, could you get a meal on the table? It's easier than you might think! After all, how did the pioneers and homesteaders do it? And farm or ranch wives before they had electricity? Many old farm and ranch houses had a wood cook stove, and they're still for sale today (just look at the Lehman's catalog!). A wood stove used for heating can often be used to cook a meal in a pinch if there's enough surface area to put a pot.

Other options include nonelectric-ignition gas stoves and ovens (yes, they still make them!) and, believe it or not, solar cookers. There are small solar cookers for as little as $20 or larger ones that'll cook a medium-size turkey for around $250. The catalogs I've already mentioned have solar cookers for sale, or you can build your own with the help of the book *Cooking With the Sun: How to Build and Use Solar Cookers* by Beth Halacy and Dan Halacy. For tons of free information and plans for building a variety of solar cookers, plus recipes and lots of other useful information, point your Internet browser to www.solarcooking.org.

An old-time cooking method that works just as well as ever is cooking in a pit using wood and a dutch oven. If you go on a western trail ride, chances are your hosts will use this method to make your evening meals. There are lots of good books to show you how, but the one I'd recommend is *Cooking the Dutch Oven Way* by Woody

Woodruff. Woody passed away in 1990, but this former Scoutmaster and dutch oven designer knew it all about pleasing tummies the "dutch oven way." It's the book we use.

You'll also need to think about refrigeration. Options include gas refrigerators (more expensive than electric to operate and the refrigerator itself is more expensive), solar-electric refrigerators like the SunFrost (cheaper to operate than both gas or electric), and as a supplement, the old-fashioned root cellar.

Another area to consider in the cooking department is preserving food by canning and drying so you don't need refrigeration. You can find excellent information on home canning and drying from your local cooperative extension office or by doing a search on the World Wide Web.

If you have a home garden and a passive solar greenhouse, you'll be able to grow some simple fresh foods like salad fixings and culinary and medicinal herbs year round. As I mentioned in Chapter 11, "Food Fancy: You *Are* What You Eat!," the more raw foods you eat, the less you have to cook!

Beyond Basics

You can read all about making root cellars in *Root Cellaring: Natural Cold Storage of Fruits and Vegetables* by Mike and Nancy Bubel. You can even create a mini root cellar in a garbage can! For complete instructions, log on to Taunton Press' *Kitchen Garden* magazine site at www.taunton. com/kg/features/techniques/ 6rootcellar.htm or call for back issue #11 at 203–426–8171. Also check out The Root Cellar Home page sponsored by Walton Feed at www.lis.ab.ca/walton/old/ cellar.html.

Keeping Your Cool and Staying Warm

Without electricity, you'll have to decide what kind of system you're going to use to keep warm in the winter and cool in the summer. The first step is to do a thorough energy audit of your home as outlined in Chapter 13: insulate, winterize, and take advantage of natural sunlight whenever possible. Dressing properly for the temperature, both inside the home and out, can also go a long way to cutting your demand for power to heat and cool.

Options for home heating include wood stoves (which can also be used for cooking) and wood furnaces, kerosene heaters, gas heaters, and solar heat. You'll need to factor in how you're going to heat water for washing dishes, bathing, and doing laundry as well.

Solar systems today have come a long way. They're easier to install and maintain (and they're cheaper), plus the technology, especially storage technology, has improved by leaps and bounds. It would be worth your while to make a study of the solar heating and cooling options available before making any final decisions.

Quick Starts

Don't forget to use your house's "greenhouse effect" to your advantage right now. During the day, uncover your windows and let the sun come in. At night, pull down your insulating shades so the heat doesn't escape. You'll be surprised how this simple conscious step will make a difference.

Beyond Basics

One of the best primers on residential solar power is Adi Pieper's *The Easy Guide to Solar Electric: For Home Power Systems*. Also check out *Home Power* magazine, which has a complete collection of back issues available on CD-ROM. They're located at www.homepower.com. To order a subscription, call 1-800-707-6585 or e-mail subscription@homepower.com

One of the simplest and cheapest ways to add some solar heat to your house is to construct a greenhouse. All you really need is something to hold the heat like straw bales or dark water drums, which are put up against the house, some PVC pipe, and some clear polyvinyl sheets. Your greenhouse will store heat during the day and disperse it to the house at night. An added advantage is you can grow food all winter long.

Look at both passive solar applications and active solar systems. Active solar systems are more expensive and require more maintenance, but they're more flexible and can provide more conventional solutions. In either case, you'll still want to work on ways to conserve energy so you can manage on a smaller system. The lower the load, the smaller and less expensive the system you'll need.

It's amazing how, when it takes more human effort to "turn up the heat," like chopping wood for the wood stove, you're more likely to so something simple like put on more clothes when you're chilly or caulk the windows to keep the draft out. Even if you don't intend to go off the grid completely, turning off the heat and experimenting with providing your own is an eye-opener. As I keep reiterating, simple living is *conscious* living.

Now, what about cooling? The most important single thing to remember is that hot air rises. If you provide hot air a place to go and escape, you'll keep your house cooler. Air circulation helps the process along.

One way to regulate the temperature is to regulate the sun and outside air that comes in the windows. At night, open the shades and windows to let the cooler night air in, and during the day, pull them shut. Ceiling fans can help with air circulation. Also take a look at awnings to shade the windows that receive the most intense sun. And keep in mind that good insulation works both to keep a house warm and to keep it cool. Use trees and shrubs to your advantage as well.

A Line to the Outside World

How would you communicate or gather information about what was happening beyond your immediate area if you had no electricity and no phone? What alternative communications systems do you have in place?

I would definitely suggest a solar-powered radio (again, the Real Goods catalog is a good source) or at least a battery-operated one (with plenty of fresh, spare batteries). Some solar models are even radio/flashlight combinations. A battery-operated scanner is another handy thing to have. You'll need someone to program it for your area (our friend in Search and Rescue did ours), and you'll be able to access a much broader spectrum of information. There are regulations governing these transmissions, however, so make sure you familiarize yourself with the law. CB radios are cheaper than dirt these days and still offer handy emergency communications. There's always amateur (or "ham") radio, but this requires a license and some specialized equipment. Better yet, find out if there's an amateur radio enthusiast in your neighborhood and make friends.

Taking Care of Business

I couldn't think of a polite way to say it, but what are you going to do with your, er, waste? You may not have water to flush the toilet if the power fails or if your solar system isn't working because the sun hasn't shined in days. There are more options to the modern flush than I ever realized and certainly more than I can cover here. But do consider waste treatment and disposal as part of your off-the-grid investigations or emergency backup plan.

One option to check out is composting toilets. Did you know you can build one yourself? The Clivus Multrum is probably the best-known commercial composting toilet. There's also something called the "dry toilet" and other short-term solutions for you to look into.

Beyond Basics

I know it sounds a little weird, but if you read *The Humanure Handbook: A Guide to Composting Human Manure* by Joseph A. Jenkins, you'll think it's perfectly practical and sane! The book describes the composting system he's used on his farm for 20 years. It's simple, it's clean, and it works!

You Don't Have to Go All the Way!

My husband and I looked into going off the grid a couple years ago and decided it just wouldn't be cost effective for us right now, however desirable it may be. Instead, we decided to reduce dependence in areas that made sense and were relatively low cost. We began by collecting rainwater, turning off the heat, and dressing more warmly. We've slowly been working on using fewer electrical appliances. We've put skylights in our dark center kitchen, so we no longer need electric lights there during the day and can use task-directed lighting at night. We've started using our oil lamps on more occasions. We're looking into a solar water heater as our next major purchase and will be doing some outside construction that will help shade the part of the house that gets the most of our summer Arizona sun, thereby helping to cool the house.

What measures could you take now to begin living less on the grid? How could you wean yourself off "the juice" and have fun doing it? What would you do to keep your family warm and fed in the event of a blizzard or another condition that knocked out the power for a prolonged period of time? You'd be way ahead in the event of an emergency (or even a financial hit) if you knew how you'd handle things like cooking, water, heat, and waste disposal. Try hitting the breaker one weekend and see how well you do!

The Least You Need to Know

➤ Whether you're planning on becoming totally utility independent or are just looking for ways to provide power in an emergency, reducing your consumption is an important first step.

➤ There are many inexpensive and attractive alternatives to electric lighting that can also add atmosphere and enjoyment.

➤ Options for cooking without electricity are many, and some are as easy as turning to the sun!

➤ Using and controlling the natural rays of the sun and attending to the insulation in your house can go a long way toward helping with heating and cooling.

➤ Being able to reach the outside world is important for safety, but it doesn't need to be dependent on the usual power sources.

Chapter 15

Rethinking Getting from Here to There

America's love affair with the automobile is deep and longstanding. The mobility of owning your own car is exhilarating. Yet it comes with a price. Put aside the impact on the environment we've heard so much about. Owning a car is complicated. We have to first earn enough money to buy one, which is no mean feat. The cost of a new car today is easily the same as a down payment on a house! It may well be the second largest (or in some cases, *the* largest) expenditure we'll make in our lifetime. Then there's the care and feeding of our prize possession. We have to give it the gas, oil, and other fluids to make it go and to keep it healthy. We have to insure it, pay taxes on it, register it, keep it clean, and avoid accidents. And then there's the traffic!

Automobile: The Movie

If you made a movie about transportation, the automobile would definitely be the star. He's made to look sexy, slick, alluring, and independent. He's full of adventure, and he knows how to please. Put yourself in his hands, and he'll take you anywhere. In the right automobile, you're a star, too. There's a vehicle to suit every ego. But there's a dark side to our hero, and we need to know the whole story.

Car Dependence

When does love become addictive? I don't know, but I'd say we're there! I don't advocate getting rid of the automobile altogether, although I know there are people who do. I'm just asking that you stop and think about it once in a while before you turn the key. What are your driving patterns? If that sounds complicated, let me put it another way—how often and how far do you take your car or truck each week? How many of those trips are really necessary?

Simple Wisdom?

"Baby you can drive my car. Yes, I'm gonna be a star. Baby you can drive my car. And baby I love you ... Beep-beep 'm beep-beep YEAH!"

—The Beatles, "Drive My Car"

Joe Dominguez and Vicki Robin, authors of the book *Your Money or Your Life*, recommend keeping an auto log to get an accurate handle on your driving habits. They suggest including "everything done to the car along with the date and odometer reading when it was done." This includes gas records and calculating your gas mileage, every time you add oil and how much, when you rotate or replace tires, plus any repairs, regular tune-ups, and replacement of parts you do yourself. If you're keeping track, you'll be able to anticipate when things need to be done and replace them before they cause a problem. Frequent oil changes are probably the most important single thing you can do to prolong the life of your car. You'll also begin to notice and pay attention to whether you make the most of your time on the road or whether you're driving in circles!

If your car were out of commission, how would you get around? Do you have an emergency backup-transportation alternative? You might find that, if you had to do without because of circumstances, you could learn to do without a car by choice. Can you reduce the amount you use your car or eliminate it altogether by paying someone else to drive, renting a car, or taking a cab when you really need to?

In the book *Living More with Less,* Doris Janzen Longacre recommends four major things to live more responsibly while owning an automobile: drive less; drive smaller, more fuel-efficient cars; drive tenderly (practice safe driving); and maintain your automobile properly. We'll look into all of these later in this chapter.

Fuel and You

What kind of mileage does your vehicle get? Do you know? Keep track of how many miles you go between fill ups (set your trip indicator to zero) and then note how many gallons you put in. From there, you can compute your car's fuel efficiency by dividing the number of gallons it took to fill the tank into the number of miles you went.

There are many ways to reduce fuel consumption once you start paying attention. Here's a list of tips to get you started:

1. Keep the tires properly inflated. Not only is this good for fuel consumption, it's also a lifesaver! Underinflated tires waste fuel and wear out the tire tread. You'll want to have the tires checked regularly for proper alignment and balance as well. Remove snow tires once winter is over.

2. Do regular tune-ups. A properly tuned engine burns gas more efficiently. Do all the regular maintenance on your car, too.

3. Don't carry unnecessary stuff! You lose fuel efficiency for each pound of extra weight you carry. Keep only important emergency items and not a lot of junk.

4. Keep an even speed and don't make fast starts or sudden stops. Smooth driving saves fuel!

5. Lower your speed. You'll save gas at 55 even though sometimes you might be able to go faster.

6. Don't warm up your car longer than a minute or so, even on cold mornings. It's unnecessary and wastes gas. Don't rev the engine, either.

7. Don't be a lead foot. Resting your left foot on the brake will drag and gobble up gas. It'll cause your brakes to wear out faster as well.

8. Plan your trips to combine errands and take the best route.

9. Make sure the gas cap is secure. Fuel will evaporate if it doesn't seal properly or is missing altogether.

10. Keep the windows closed. It's actually more efficient to run the air conditioner if you're doing highway driving than it is to keep the windows open due to resistance. In stop-and-go traffic, however, open the windows.

11. Telecommute, start your own home business, or find a job closer to home. Ask if you can shorten your workweek by working longer hours four days a week and having three days off.

12. Shop by phone or the Internet. Bank by mail or online. Buy in bulk; you'll make fewer trips.

13. Look for fuel efficiency when you buy a car. The EPA publishes a list each year of the top cars and trucks in the fuel-efficiency game. If you pick one, you'll save some real bucks over the life of your car.

How Many and How Long?

How many vehicles do you own and how long should you keep them? Only you can answer these questions, and no one's trying to point a finger. Maybe you really do need to be a three-car family. But maybe you don't. Just consider how much money you'd save if you could eliminate one vehicle.

If you really do need the vehicles you currently own, how long should you keep them? There are different schools of thought on the subject, but most sources that look at it from both cost-effectiveness and impact on the planet recommend keeping a car until you absolutely have to replace it.

Beyond Basics

Two worthwhile books to help you keep your car going for a long time are Bob Sikorsky's *Drive It Forever: Secrets to Long Automobile Life* and *Car Talk: With Click and Clack, The Tappet Brothers,* by Tom and Ray Mag–liozzi, National Public Radio's favorite mechanics.

Should you buy a new car or a used one? Well, there are advantages and disadvantages to both. With a new car, you know exactly how it's been taken care of since you're the original owner! And you can do all the right things along the way to make the car last. Overall, you'll get a long life out of the car if you buy it new. Plus some newer cars pollute less and are safer.

But there are distinct advantages to buying a used car, especially a "gently used" one that's a fairly late model year. Cars depreciate rapidly in the first couple of years, so you've already saved a bundle before you even begin. Registration, taxes, and insurance are usually lower for an older car. If you buy a much older car that's been well-maintained, it may be easier and cheaper to keep running since newer cars are more complex and cost more to repair.

Take care of the vehicle you have. Whenever possible, do it yourself. Buy quality. Buy a vehicle that serves several functions. Comparison shop. Never buy a car on credit.

Avoidance Techniques

Don't throw away those old belts. Keep them as spares in the trunk if they're not completely gone. They may save you time and aggravation on the road as a spare and can save you the cost of a tow.

Make a list of the things you can do on your car yourself and schedule them on your calendar so you don't forget. Almost anyone can do an oil change on almost any car. Take an auto-maintenance course at an adult-education program. Replace belts and filters regularly. They're cheap, and if they fail, it can lead to a bigger problem.

Make sure you buy parts with a lifetime warranty if they're available when you're doing your own maintenance. Keep your receipts and make the manufacturers honor their warranties if the parts wear out.

Find yourself a reliable, competent mechanic before you need one. Ask if your mechanic will install parts you've obtained yourself by comparison shopping. Some will. Some won't.

Avoidance Techniques

Don't buy a used car without checking first with the Auto Safety Hotline run by the National Highway Traffic Safety Administration. They have several databases that allow you to search for things like recalls and customer complaints by make and model year. You can reach them by calling 1–800–424–9393 or by typing www.nhtsa.dot.gov/cars/problems/index.html into your Internet browser. If you have a problem to report, the number is 1–888–327–4236. If you're buying a new car, *Consumer Reports* magazine is always a good place to start, and for older models, look for back issues at the library.

Compare insurance rates. Older cars cost less to insure (another incentive for keeping yours), but the cost to insure newer cars can vary widely from company to company as well.

If you must junk your car, take off whatever parts are still good and sell them separately or give them to someone who can use them.

Automobile: The Sequel

Now, what are the alternatives to the Hollywood script with the big guy automobile in the starring role? If the automobile is no longer the hero in the sequel, who's the new star? Well, dust off your walking shoes and pull out the bicycle pump. You're in for a whole new script!

Human Power

Bicycles aren't just for kids anymore! They've gone mainstream and are showing up in cities and towns in greater numbers every day. Using your own body to provide transportation may sound like work, but it can also be play. Try walking for a change. Check out ways to get there under your own power.

Quick Starts

Haven't ridden a bicycle since you were in grade school? Then start small and just ride around your neighborhood. Gradually lengthen your rides—pretty soon you'll be pedaling everywhere!

Beyond Basics

A good book to teach you the basics of bicycle maintenance is *The Haynes Bicycle Book: The Haynes Repair Manual for Maintaining and Repairing Your Bike* (Haynes Automotive Repair Manual Series), by Bob Henderson and J. Stevenson. And just for fun, try *Bike Cult: The Ultimate Guide to Human-Powered Vehicles,* an interesting read by biking enthusiast David B. Perry.

We're friends with a couple who lives in a charming cottage close to our downtown. They own one car, two bikes, and a motorized scooter. I hardly ever see them in the car! Jim and Charlene seem to do just fine with their nonauto choices, and yet they live in an area where they can have a great garden on a tree-lined street. Living in town doesn't mean giving up a lot of simple living choices. The technical editor of this book also lives close to downtown and is raising most of her family's food on the roof of their garage! You can make the choice to cut down on the need for transportation and still live close to nature if you choose the right place to live. You don't need lots of land to live sustainably!

If a bicycle becomes either your main mode of transportation or a regular supplement, you may want to add a cart to your bike to haul stuff or take the kids along. Check out the ones from Bykaboose at www.bykaboose.com or call 1-800-441-9163 for product information. There's also Cycletote (www.cycletote.com; 1-800-747-2407) and Equinox (www.efn.org/~equinox; 1-800-942-7895) for innovative quality products. You'll want to learn how to maintain your bike and be prepared for emergencies, plus you'll need to refresh your memory on bicycle safety.

Check to see if there are biking groups in your town. This is a good way to learn what you need to know without starting from scratch, and you may want to join together to lobby for bicycle paths and safety measures in your area. For information on bike safety and choosing the best helmet, contact the Bicycle Helmet Safety Institute at www.bhsi.org. There's also a group trying to make roads safer for biking, among other things, called the Bicycle Transportation Alliance. They're based in Portland, Oregon, and can be reached at www.bta4bikes.org.

If you're not all that far from the things you need to do, how about walking? Or maybe you could drive part of the way and walk the rest. Just as with biking, work up to walking longer distances if you're not used to it. What may now seem like too far to walk may be a breeze after you get in better shape.

I like to park downtown and walk to my errands. I'll sometimes take the entire afternoon, enjoying our beautiful town square and getting some fresh air and exercise to boot. It's the short hops that wreak havoc on your car, so making the 12-mile drive into town, leaving the truck, and walking the shorter distances makes good sense. Weigh saving time and convenience against conserving energy and saving money. I'd rather walk to do my errands than pay someone to let me use their exercise machines! Having a cart to carry items might be necessary. I just pack a couple of canvas bags and can usually hold most items I might need to carry. Plus I don't end up with all those awful plastic bags!

Everybody in the Pool

Everybody knows about car pools, but a lot of people don't take advantage of them. Even if you don't want to use a car pool to go to work every day, consider one at least a few days a week. And don't just think of the car pool for the daily grind. Any excursion involving several people with vehicles is a candidate for car pooling. It may not always work out, but it's worth a try to see if one can be coordinated.

Beyond the conventional car pool is the "pooled car." This is actually called car sharing. If you drive less than 10,000 miles a year, owning a car with a couple other people might make real sense. Portland, Oregon, has a model program that's gotten a lot of publicity. You might be able to get some ideas for your town by looking at what they've done at www.carsharing-pdx.com/index.html.

Perhaps you have a small, fuel-efficient car but occasionally need a van or a pickup truck. Some people go in together on these specialized vehicles and find it to be a good arrangement. Each person chips in an equal amount on a used vehicle. When someone wants to use it, everyone is contacted to reserve the time. The last person to use it fills it with gas, vacuums it out if necessary, and if someone tends to use it a lot, he or she might wash it or pay for some needed repairs or an oil change. As long as everyone does his or her share, this can be the perfect arrangement and can allow everyone in the "pool" to own only one energy-wise vehicle.

Quick Starts

Not sure exactly what car sharing is or if it's for you? Log on to www.carsharing.net for all the basics and then some.

If you don't want to actually go in together with other people on a vehicle, you may be able to make an arrangement with a friend that has a car or truck to share it periodically in exchange for an agreed upon amount and a full tank of gas. If you don't need the vehicle on a daily basis, this may be a perfectly adequate arrangement. You'll need to work around your friend's schedule, but if you pay your share and are considerate, it just might be the solution. Or if your friend or neighbor doesn't like the idea of you driving his or her car or truck, maybe you can pay to have the person drive you where you need to go.

Transportation Goes Public

Does your town have public transportation? How good is it and how often do you use it? Could you use it instead of taking a car? Or could you take a car to one location and then use public transportation for part of the trip? When choosing a location, you may want to consider what public transportation is available.

Oftentimes, other simple living choices place us in a location where there isn't any public transportation. That's the case where we live, although some bus service is available in a limited area. You'll have to weigh the other advantages against the need to own a car to get around.

Travel in a Simple Vein

What's the goal of leisure travel? For many people who aren't living the simple life, travel is for destressing and "getting away from it all." When you're living the simple life, travel takes on a whole new meaning. It can actually be an extension of the simple life, an opportunity to learn new things, share ideas with people, create new experiences for yourself, and maybe even give the gift of your time and energy to improve something. Through travel we can learn to live lightly, do with less, slow down, and break our normal patterns. By disrupting our usual patterns, we notice things we missed before. We become enriched.

Beyond Basics

My writer-friend Evelyn Kaye has written a whole rash of books perfectly geared to the simple traveler. Try *Travel and Learn: Where to Go for Everything You'd Love to Know, Family Travel: Terrific New Vacations for Today's Families, Active Woman Vacation Guide, Eco-Vacations: Enjoy Yourself and Save the Earth* (out of print, but worth tracking down), and *Free Vacations and Bargain Adventures in the USA.*

So what would the simple living approach be to travel? Well, first I can tell you what it would *not* be. It's not the simple living way to go into debt to take a trip. Better to curb your spending and save for your excursions than to take out a loan (remember, charging on a credit card is the same as a loan if you can't pay it back right away!) or dip into your savings.

If you don't have the cash, can you accomplish the same thing and stay close to home? If what you're looking for is a change of scene, you may be able to just go across town!

One advantage of living the simple life is the freedom to arrange your schedule to take advantage of cheaper modes or periods of travel. Can you work out a deal with a rental-car company to drive back one of their cars so your transportation is free (actually, you'll probably earn a few bucks)? Can you take advantage of standby flights or less convenient routing? If you allow yourself to be "bumped" on an earlier flight, you'll get a free ticket to use for travel another time.

Look for creative ways to lodge yourself while you're on the road. Stay away from big name hotels and motels and check out small B&Bs and inns first. Some of the smaller, independently-owned motels have better rates and are, frankly, often a lot more fun to stay in. There are lots of ways to travel and sleep on the cheap if you make it your business to look for them.

Another way to make travel more meaningful is what I call "theme travel." I've often found my most memorable trips were planned around a theme. When I was researching my book about Victorian weddings, everywhere I went I looked for Victorian homes to tour, costume museums, vintage clothing shops, antiques shops, and anything Victorian. I've gone on bead-finding and quilt-exploration trips, wildflower expeditions, and birding jaunts. Other people I know have spent many trips tracking down their family history or tracing the route of Lewis and Clark. Pick an interest or theme and plan your travel around that. You'll see a side of things no one else would see, and you may even make lifelong friends that share your interests.

Another type of travel I like to call a visionquest. This is a spiritual journey, and no one can design it but you. It may be a trip back to childhood or a metaphysical journey to sacred sites. Or perhaps you'll go off in the woods to learn primitive skills and get closer to the land as our continent's early inhabitants did.

While you're on the road, your meals don't have to cost a fortune either. Eat less and eat better. Try eating only one real meal a day and snacking a couple of times on fresh fruit and nuts or cheese. Picnic. Shop in the local grocery store or open-air market. Eat with the locals. You'll spend less money, will come home with the same waistline (or even a little smaller), and will be less likely to have an upset stomach on your journey. Stick to bottled water if you can or get one of those portable sports-bottle water filters. Drinking water you're not accustomed to can really turn your system upside down!

Staying Home: The New Frontier

Working and playing at home goes a long way toward lowering transportation costs. Look homeward for entertainment, education, stimulation, companionship, and even earning a living, and you'll see your expenses go down, down, down. Centering your activities around home and doing for yourself are surefire ways to simplify your life and make it more frugal besides.

The Least You Need to Know

➤ Keeping track of your mileage, gas purchases, and repairs can give you a whole new picture of your driving habits and ways to lower your car dependence.

➤ Bicycles, walking, car pools, car sharing, and public transportation are all ways to get around having to own a car or at least using yours less.

➤ Travel need not put you in debt or cost a lot. Planning carefully and looking for bargains can mean more frequent trips without complicating your finances or your life.

➤ Making your home the center of most activities is another way of reducing auto dependence and making life simpler.

Part 4
Family, Friends, and Community

One of the greatest rewards of simple living is more time to spend with the people you love. But how will the choice to simplify affect these relationships? Will people treat you differently? Will they understand?

The next five chapters will answer your questions about simple living and relationships, from those closest to you to the wider community. You'll learn how to create a "quality circle" of people you cherish, why simplicity is a better way to raise kids, how play fits into the simple life, and how to create a caring, supportive community around your goals and values.

Chapter 16

Simple Living and Relationships

> ### In This Chapter
>
> ➤ Creating a quality circle of love and support
>
> ➤ Learning the importance of taking care of yourself first
>
> ➤ Working with your partner to achieve your simple living goals and have a better relationship
>
> ➤ Creating a balance between family, friends, and community and setting down clear, workable boundaries

The whole purpose of adopting the simple living lifestyle, in my opinion, is to orient your life less around things and more around the people you love. If that's not what's happening, then you need to take another look! Even when we're trying to embrace simplicity, we can get caught up in the process or even spend as much time being a miser as we were a spendthrift before. Relationships can get complicated, too. How do the principles of simple living apply to the give and take of being with other people? Well, that's what we're going to find out in this chapter!

The Quality Circle

I came up with the idea of a quality circle when I was working on my book about organizing. It seemed to me that life can just as easily be filled with "junk" relationships as it can useless "things." If we don't pay attention, a kind of emotional clutter can push out the good stuff. By creating a circle of quality people and relationships around us, beginning with ourselves, we have something so strong, so energizing, that we can depend on it for our whole lives.

After all, we only have so much time, so much energy, so much to give. To have quality in our lives, we need to be discriminating, to make choices—wise choices. We might like to think of ourselves as an eternal fountain with unlimited love to give, but in my experience, that's what gets us in trouble. Women especially, who are often taught to be nurturers, can overextend themselves and become depleted. If you don't put anything in, eventually there's nothing left to give! We can greet the world with a loving attitude, yes, but we need to focus our love with intent to create a quality circle of people we love around us.

So let's take this idea and begin from the center of the circle and work our way out.

Simple Wisdom

"In the hard decisions of living, to choose that which nurtures people is another guiding standard."

—Doris Janzen Longacre, *Living More with Less*

Simple Wisdom

"One's-self I sing, a simple separate person, Yet utter the word Democratic, the word En-Masse."

—Walt Whitman, *Leaves of Grass*

Song of Myself

I say that you're at the center of the circle; you come first. Singing your "song of myself" is the way to make music with the rest of the world. Now, to many of us, putting ourselves first sounds self-centered or selfish. It's smacks of the "looking out for number one" attitude that always puts "me" ahead of "you" or "we." But that's not what I'm talking about.

In the poem "Song of Myself," Walt Whitman begins "I celebrate myself, and sing myself, And what I assume you shall assume, For every atom belonging to me as good belongs to you." Old Walt knew the importance of cherishing oneself and understood that, by loving himself, he was showing love for the universe and the divine. He says as much when he writes "Divine am I inside and out, and I make holy whatever I touch or am touch'd from."

Self-love and care isn't selfish; it's a sacred principle. By loving ourselves, we love all.

Part of the simple living journey is self-knowledge. How much is enough? What are our *needs*? What do we count as needs that are simply wants? We have to know ourselves to break old habits, to make new decisions, to create different patterns. We have to be kind to ourselves and nurture our spirit. Simplicity is the atmosphere in which we can find our wings and soar.

I've met people in the simple living movement who seem to be under a cloud. They are "in judgment" continually and are sometimes hardest on themselves. Simplicity for them is about self-denial, like a punishment for past sins. When I read about the early proponents of simplicity such as the Puritans and the Quakers and some Utopian experiments, there's a self-righteous thread that I find repellent. Yes, we need to take better care of the earth. And yes, a simpler life would probably correct many of the ills of our society. These are hopes and dreams that I have, too. But primarily, I hope you've been looking at this book as a way to a better life—your life.

If you're happy and content, if you learn to love yourself the real way instead of trying to fill the void with material things, if you improve your relationships with the people closest to you and your joy spills out into creative expression or volunteerism, then that's just great! But it all starts with the individual and how he or she feels in his or her own skin.

Here are some things you can do for the person in the center of your quality circle (remember, that's you!):

Beyond Basics

A book that has had a significant impact on my own journey to know and love myself has been Shakti Gawain's *Living in the Light*. Along with her book *Creative Visualization*, Gawain teaches the concept of self-creation and the ability of the individual to overcome past hurts and destructive patterns. I highly recommend them both.

➤ Take care of yourself first. This means getting a good night's sleep, eating healthy food, and getting fresh air and exercise for starters. This is bottom-line self-care. Do this first and everything else will begin to fall into place more easily.

➤ Take a moment to read something uplifting, pray, meditate, worship—whatever you do to connect with your inner self and the universe within or beyond.

Self-care is an essential part of simple living. Things can get very complicated when you don't take care of yourself, in fact, they completely unravel. Find out your pleasures and preferences and be true to them. They don't have to cost lots of money or force you to consume. Usually the most satisfying ones are free.

Simple Wisdom

"Friendship with oneself is all-important because without it one cannot be friends with anyone else in the world."

—Eleanor Roosevelt

➤ Slow down—it gives you time to appreciate yourself and others. Set aside a day to nurture yourself when things are especially hectic. Stay in bed late and read, make yourself a special meal, soak in the tub and listen to music, or go for a ride to no place in particular.

➤ Indulge yourself regularly with pleasures like listening to music, making up a clean and crisp bed with sheets that have been dried in the breeze, picking yourself some fresh flowers, setting a nice table even if you're alone. Engage your senses. Express your feelings—skip, giggle out loud, whistle, give yourself a hug.

Quick Starts

Organizing for self-care makes you more likely to do it. Sarah Ban Breathnach recommends having a "comfort drawer" or a box filled with little things that make you feel pampered and cared for like bath salts, some massage oil, a favorite throw, some lozenges, and a book of quotes or poems you like reading over and over again. Some of these things are even more self-nurturing if you make them yourself. Find directions for making an herbal sleep pillow or make yourself a lap quilt. By having the tools for taking care of yourself ready and waiting, you'll get in the habit more often.

➤ Allow yourself time to be creative. Dance, sing, paint, sculpt, garden, write, sew, arrange some flowers, build a bookshelf or a birdhouse, read a poem aloud with the most feeling you possibly can muster.

I think you'll find that, by taking care of yourself first and paying attention to your needs, you'll gain greater self-knowledge, and knowing one's true self is the foundation of living a simpler life.

Significant Others: Not So Simple?

In my own life, my husband is the first recipient of my loving intent outside myself. He is my chosen partner, my best friend, my helpmate, my confidante, and he gets the very best of my time and attention. The rest of my family is terribly important to me, don't get me wrong. My children are the lights of my life. But they have their own lives to live and have chosen their respective mates.

If you're in a primary relationship, take a simple inventory of how you hold that person in your life. Take a pad and pencil and see if you can re-create how you spent your time this past week. How much did your "significant other" get? Of that time, what kind of quality would you estimate that time had? Was it detached chatter and daily business? Or was it focused conversation where you looked into the other person's eyes and listened and then spoke with authenticity and intensity? How "significantly" did you treat this "other?" How did you hold him or her in your esteem this week?

Then ask your partner how important he or she feels in your life. Just ask and be open to the answer without being defensive. Don't wait. Assess often. Pay attention to this most sacred of relationships. Give it the position in your life that it deserves.

Sometimes we come to things at different times, at different speeds, in different ways. I tend to be a little more enthusiastic about making changes than my husband is. I do the research, start talking about what I want to do, and he's not always very excited about it in the beginning. In time, however, if I respect his needs and his particular pace, he often warms to the idea (perhaps with some adjustments or changes to my original one) and we move forward. When I want to make a change and he doesn't, I simply make it for me and respect his choice.

Don't underestimate the importance of listening. Make it a rule that you let the other person finish without interruption. Sometimes that's very hard to do, but force yourself and ask that your partner do the same. You'll be amazed how much this improves the quality of your communication. It also sometimes short circuits thoughtless comments, and that can't be bad!

When was the last time you and your partner were out on a "date?" These can be as simple as an evening walk, a canoe ride, stargazing away from the city lights, or swinging in a hammock on the front porch. What makes it a date is that you've planned for it. Romance is a state of mind, but if we don't tend to it, we lose it. Memorize a love poem. Write one. Massage. Tickle. Take care of each other. Read to each other. Create a memorable evening by putting up your cots and sleeping out on the front porch.

Avoidance Techniques

Don't expect your partner to be a mind reader! If you're making a lot of changes toward a simpler way of life, have you engaged your partner in the process? What is his or her "take" on the whole thing? You honor each other and the simple life when you create the time to communicate carefully and consciously.

Simple Wisdom

"All who joy would win Must share it, Happiness was born a twin."

—Lord Byron

Beyond Basics

If you're not familiar with Alexandra Stoddard's books, I suggest you become acquainted. If you concentrate on her meaning especially, I think they have a lot to offer. Try reading *Living Beautifully Together* for some truly useful suggestions for making your life with your partner better and more gracious. And for learning how to nurture yourself in a myriad of small ways, be sure to read *Living A Beautiful Life.*

Avoidance Techniques

The two areas that cause contention in most primary relationships are money and domestic chores. However long you've been together, if you haven't worked these things out by now, do it! If you need help, get it! Don't let irritations or feelings of unfairness grow and fester.

Do chores together. Make a nest together. Create order for each other. Give each other space. Pay attention to the needs of the other person and try to accommodate him or her whenever possible. If you need something, ask for it.

Work on your communication. Watch your language. Give some thought to the major areas of your life and how you both feel about them. Work out your parenting styles as early on as you can. Decide how you're going to treat family occasions and demands from outside the relationship. Don't let these things just happen. Be conscious of them and build the relationship you've always wanted. Sculpt the home life you truly desire.

Create regular opportunities for both serious talk and frivolous play. Be careful not to take each other for granted. Have a partner appreciation day every so often to show and tell the love of your life how much he or she means to you. You can do this for another family member or a close friend, too. Just decide that you're going to devote some concentrated time to showing people how much you appreciate them. Tell them, show them, do for them.

Make sure you get both time together and time apart each day, each week. Always respect each other's need for solitude. Show that respect by asking and including. Share decisions. Respect privacy. Consult your partner's schedule before making arrangements.

Be quiet. Watch your tone of voice. Apologize when you know you should. Say "please" and "thank you." Do what you say you'll do. Keep your promises. Work on being understanding. Ask her how she really is. Put your partner in the spotlight. Be his champion.

Do simple, spontaneous things like writing notes and tucking them in unexpected places. Bring your partner breakfast in bed on no special occasion. Don't forget to touch. Don't forget to tell the other person "I love you."

Avoidance Techniques

Don't forget to apply simple living principles when dating or just beginning a relationship. I loved Janet Luhrs' description of her first date after her divorce in her book *The Simple Living Guide.* She had worked on creating a life that was authentic and honest in so many ways, and yet when she found herself in a dating situation again, she immediately resorted to a façade, "dressing up" and filling the evening with detached activity and conversation.

By going on a hike or some other simple activity, Janet found her "date" revealed much more of whom he was right from the start. The artificial setting of "dinner and a movie" was a barrier to really getting to know each other. Why spend time pursuing a relationship that's not going anywhere when you can find that out more quickly by being natural?

No significant other? Maybe you're looking for there to be. When I was a single mom for almost 15 years, I went through long periods during which I was content just being alone. It was during these periods that I learned the most about myself and grew the most. Learn to like your own company. I often found I was my own best date!

Family First

The next ring of the quality circle for me is my family, specifically my children and stepchildren (and now their children!). Although we're quite far flung, my psychic and emotional energy is still focused on them. Now, this may not be true for you. Perhaps you don't have children. Perhaps you're estranged from your family. Your quality circle might look totally different than mine! But I'm just asking you to consider these relationships and how they might fit into your particular quality circle picture.

Quick Starts

Need to add some romance to your relationship? For tons of creative and inexpensive ideas (you can skip the extravagant ones!), I often refer to Gregory Godek's *1001 Ways to Be Romantic* and *1001 More Ways to Be Romantic.* They're playful and creative. You're sure to find something you'd never thought of. Greg even offers a course in romance!

Communication with this part of the circle is paramount, too. Now that my children are grown and are living all over the country, it takes a real effort to stay in touch. E-mail is one technological advance I find very helpful! But not just any e-mail. We send scanned pictures back and forth, type in quotes, and follow up on important events. E-mail isn't a substitute for voice and face-to-face communication, but if used properly, it can help you "cut to the chase" when you finally do connect on a more personal level.

If you have younger children, your focus will be closer to home. We'll go into much more detail about raising kids the simple living way in the next chapter, but what I want you to notice here is how you hold your children in your life.

Important events don't have to be an extravaganza. Concentrate on the meaning, create an atmosphere, pay attention to words and actions, get everyone involved.

Family rituals, even if carried out from afar, add to the closeness. Start early and keep them going, even going to great lengths to make sure they happen regardless of where you all are.

Just as with your partner, as you make choices toward simple living, you need to explain to your family what you're doing and why. You also need to respect their right not to make the same choices. Try not to be judgmental or preachy. There's no one more insufferable than a zealot.

Simple Wisdom

"Your children are not your children. They are the sons and daughters of Life's longing for itself. They come through you but not from you. And though they are with you they belong not to you."

—Kahlil Gibran

Treat your family with respect, engage them in the discussion, explain what you're doing, and give them the space to do things their own way as much as possible. They may actually have ideas that are better than yours or ways of achieving your goals that you never thought of.

Reach out to your extended family and be there when you can. At the same time, protect your privacy and the integrity of your immediate family. Don't allow other family members to disrupt or interfere but honor them. Include them when you can. If you are estranged from your family, create one!

A Few Choice Friends

There are lots of people we know, but how many are truly friends? How do you define the word "friend?" What are your expectations in friendship and what are you willing to give?

After myself, my husband, and my family, I only have room in my life for a few more people to which I can give well. I choose to have a group of four or five close friends that I consider part of my quality circle, and whatever's left after they get my best goes to the rest. That may sound harsh, but it really simplifies things and makes my choices a lot clearer. I find that other people "get" where my priorities are and know that there are others who come before them. It's clear and I'm clear. If it's a choice between doing this or that or spending time with someone in my quality circle, the choice is a no-brainer. I simply say to myself, "This person comes first, period."

If you did the time and relationship inventory that I asked you to do earlier in the chapter, and you found you were spending very little time with the people who matter most and lots of time with those who matter little, then you'll need to take steps to change that. You may actually have done damage to those most important relationships and have wounds to heal and bridges to repair. Well, get to it! Do the right thing! It's never to late to start again.

The disposability attitude (that newer is better) in our society filters over into relationships. We don't commit. We exchange a relationship that's become difficult or boring with a new one rather than looking to our inner resources to revitalize or improve an existing relationship. Be genuine in your evaluation of the people in your life and the rewards and challenges, but cultivate loyalty and be in the relationship for the long haul.

In looking at your time and how (and with whom) you spend it, be aware that there are lots of messages to forego the activities you used to do with other people, like making music or gardening, and purchase them instead. What things do you do now that you could make into a meaningful experience with one of your quality circle?

Being more exclusive in your relationships doesn't mean there's no place for lots of other people in your life, but you need to decide what priorities come first in the use of the limited personal resources we all have. Not that there aren't special times when someone not that close to you needs some real help and attention. If you're "taking care of business" in other areas of your life, chances are you'll be able to give to that person in need freely and happily, without shortchanging the people to which you're most committed.

Of Boundaries and Breaches

Part of managing your relationships and keeping them safe and healthy is setting boundaries. When other people try to co-opt your time, you need to let them know you're not going to allow it. Among the most powerful words in the English language are "yes" and "no." Who do you say "yes" to and why? By saying "yes," are you by default saying "no" to the people you really care about?

There's nothing wrong with asking someone to defer to a better time. There's nothing wrong with saying "I'd love to, but I have other things to attend to." If you don't set limits, other people may define them for you.

Don't be afraid to let people know when they've violated your time and space. If you allow it to continue, you're doing a disservice to yourself, to the people to whom you're most committed, and to the offender. They can't know what the limits are if you don't make them clear. Boundaries that aren't enforced aren't boundaries at all.

Know when to call it off. Sometimes we take on too much, say "yes" too often, overestimate our capabilities. You may feel bad about having to renege, but it's better than landing in bed from exhaustion or giving the short shrift to everything else.

Don't overschedule. This hurts both you and your relationships. Get your time priorities straight. Ask, "What will happen if I don't do this? What will happen if I say 'No?'"

What Happened to the Neighborhood?

Another priority of ours has become getting to know our neighbors. Beyond our quality circle, we make an effort to at least get to know our neighbors' names and, within our agreed-upon boundaries, offer assistance whenever possible. We feel this creates an important local support network that can never be underestimated.

What's your neighborhood like or is there even a "neighborhood?" Do you know your neighbors' names and where they're from? When someone new moves in, have you ever thought of stopping by with a little something and introducing yourselves? It doesn't take a lot of time, but it's one more step in creating a connectedness and a sense of community where none existed before.

The Least You Need to Know

➤ Quality relationships are one of the main goals of simple living.

➤ Creating a quality circle with yourself at the center makes making choices and keeping priorities straight much easier.

➤ Paying attention and being conscious of the time you spend with your quality circle, how you hold them, and what you say will go a long way to enriching your life.

➤ Setting limits and saying "no" is another way of honoring yourself and the others in your life you hold most dear.

Chapter 17

Raising Kids the Simple Living Way

Being a parent today is no easy job. But then again, maybe it never has been. Some folks in the simple living movement choose not to have children because they feel the planet's future is too uncertain. I respect that choice, but I also honor the decision to bring a child into the world and nurture him or her to become a steward of our planet for the future. The challenges of parenting are great but so are the opportunities.

In this chapter, we'll explore how to share your values with your kids, how to enlist them in helping you make the simple changes to which you've committed, and how to make the most of the lessons they can teach us about simplicity.

Finding Your Own Little Kid

Perhaps the best advice to give new parents is to tell them to become a kid again. How in touch are you with your own inner child? I'll bet you're rediscovering your "little kid" already. Simple living naturally puts us closer to who we were when we were at our most authentic.

So what were you like when you were a kid? What are your best memories? What are your worst? What issues from childhood do you still have? Remembering all the feelings of our child state (yes, your child is still with you) will better prepare us for what's ahead. It's important to know when to be a parent and when to be a kid, but certainly we don't want to lose our own inner child just because we're raising kids of our own.

Have you forgotten? Here are some ideas to help you remember:

➤ Look at pictures of yourself as a child. My hus band and I have a framed picture of each of us that greets us each morning in our bedroom to remind us to nourish and protect each others' child and our own.

➤ Do something physically challenging, that makes you feel awkward and requires you to practice. I remember trying to learn how to crochet as an adult. Just holding the needles and the yarn was a challenge, much less doing the stitches. A humbling experience. Imagine standing upright when you've never done it before!

➤ Try writing or drawing with the hand that's the opposite of the one you normally do. Throw and catch with the opposite hand. That's how it felt to learn the first time!

➤ Get dirty! You know, put on some old clothes and get really filthy. Dig in the dirt. Roll around in the grass. Run, jump, slide, and do somersaults.

➤ Get naked! Not in front of the kids, of course, but close the door, take off all your clothes and run around your room. Do some of your regular activities that way. Remember? If you can do it without getting caught, go skinny dipping!

➤ See the movie "Big" with a big bucket of popcorn and your favorite movie theater candy.

➤ Re-read your favorite kids books, then share them with your own. Who used to read them to you? What made you love them so much?

➤ Sing the songs you learned when you were little. How about "Twinkle, Twinkle Little Star" or "Over the Rainbow"? How many nursery rhymes can you remember? Make some music any way you can.

Simple Wisdom

"What its children become, that will the community become."

—Suzanne LaFollette

Simple Wisdom

"Some of my best friends are children. In fact, all of my best friends are children."

—J. D. Salinger

➤ Play some simple kids' games like jacks or cat's cradle. Make a hopscotch board on the sidewalk and see if you can remember how it's played. Can't? Then find out!

The Essence of Parenting

I always wondered how I was supposed to know what to do when I became a parent. No one told me which course to take, what manual to buy, or where I could sign on for an apprenticeship. Yet, all those things sure would have helped a heap.

In later years, I actually did take a couple of workshops that were very enlightening. I read some super books that taught me how to nurture my own inner child and thereby become better able to honor the child-spirit in my own kids. And the rest I guess I just learned by making mistakes and observing what other people did and didn't do.

My children are all grown now and are beginning to create families of their own. We've had our ups and downs as all families do, but overall, they turned out to be people I really like and respect. I'm proud of them, and they fill my life with wonder and enjoyment.

Some of the things I am embracing in my life more fully now, I was struggling to accomplish then. Sometimes I was effective in enlisting their cooperation, and sometimes I wasn't. But I've discovered there are some basic parenting principles that go hand-in-hand with the simple living ones we've been discussing in this book. They're cut of the same cloth.

Creating Order

Getting rid of clutter, putting your finances on the right track, determining your priorities, and saying "no" to forces that sap your energy are all steps you've been taking that will bring harmony and order into your life. This is the essence of simplicity and the essence of a good family life.

Quick Starts

To refresh your memory of the games you played as a kid, I recommend *Hopscotch, Hangman, Hot Potato, & Ha Ha Ha: A Rulebook of Children's Games* by Jack Maquire. For hand-clapping games, try *Hand Clap! "Miss Mary Mack" and 42 Other Hand-Clapping Games for Kids* by Sara Bernstein. If you were ever a Girl Scout, pull out your old copy of *Games for Girl Scouts* for more ideas.

Beyond Basics

One book that had a profound influence on my appreciation of my own inner child and therefore my own children was *Born to Win*, by Muriel James and Dorothy Jongeward. My second recommendation as required reading for every parent is *Homecoming : Reclaiming and Championing Your Inner Child*, by John Bradshaw.

By creating order for yourself (and taking care of yourself!), you teach the same thing to your children. Chaos and conflict make kids insecure and confused. Bring in order and you have the foundation for simpler parenting. Routines and rituals are the keys. Here are some areas to consider:

➤ **Mealtimes.** Try having meals on a fairly regular schedule and making them a time for appreciation of each other and gratitude for abundance. If your mealtimes are hectic, consider revamping your cooking style (see Chapter 11, "Food Fancy: You *Are* What You Eat!") and using slow cooking or bulk cooking techniques to help things go more smoothly. At the very least, plan menus for the week.

➤ **Mornings.** How does your family begin the day? Are you setting things up to be positive or getting off on the wrong foot? Organizing things like clothes, papers, and breakfast the night before, getting up early enough so you don't have to rush (kids, too!), and making sure everybody begins with a good breakfast will make a huge difference in your whole day.

➤ **Homecomings.** Does your family have a homecoming ritual? Asking "How was your day?" is just a little thing, but it tells a child you've been thinking of him or her, and it provides a regular time for communication. Maybe there's a snack waiting or a few moments on the front porch. It's just as important to create an atmosphere of love and support at the end of the day as at the beginning. Just a few words, some undivided attention—how powerful that is!

➤ **Chores.** Having a routine when it comes to household tasks, in which everyone knows what's expected and is praised for following through, is the beginning of learning how to set goals and meet them. You're not only getting work done, you're teaching life skills. No fair for parents to shirk their duties either!

Simple Wisdom

"A child is fed with milk and praise."

—Mary Lamb

Setting Limits

Just as we need to have boundaries in our relationships with our partner, our extended families, and others outside the household, so, too, must we set limits with our children. Policies about how much television watching is allowed, when and how homework gets done, family time, and free time all need to be made clear and enforced. The earlier you start, the easier it is!

Respect from our children comes from respecting ourselves and our own needs. Set limits on the demands they can make on your time and time spent with your partner. If you follow the principle of the quality circle discussed in Chapter 16, "Simple Living and Relationships," you'll know what comes first!

No Shame, No Blame!

In *Your Money or Your Life,* Joe Dominguez and Vicki Robin discuss the destructiveness of being judgmental, even with ourselves. They stress the concept of "no shame, no blame" when we begin to confront our relationship with money. Well, this goes for any area in which we are attempting growth and understanding.

Cultivate unconditional love. Learn to listen and find out where your kids are coming from. Give them a safe place to share their innermost feelings without fear of being criticized.

Be careful when correcting not to humiliate. What values do you transmit when you strip a child of his dignity?

Honor Personal Space

Just as you've learned the importance of self-care and solitude for yourself, make sure you respect the same for your partner and your kids. Learn how to let go and trust them to find their own process and experience their own joy. Support but don't smother.

Give your child a space where he or she can decide everything about it—his or her own personal haven. Help if asked but don't dictate.

Encourage Diversity

Appreciate your children's individual personalities and give them room to express themselves. Allow support for divergent opinions. Encourage intelligent debate and challenge them to support their point of view.

How can a child learn the value of his or her ability to think if you don't provide a forum to express his or her own opinions and ask questions?

Simple Wisdom

"In solitude we give passionate attention to our lives, to our memories, to the details around us."

—Virginia Woolf

Building a Better Family

Simple living gives you so many more opportunities to be a teacher and to learn from your children. You're teaching them self-reliance and respect for the earth by taking control of your life and your own choices. You're freeing up time from the endless pursuit of material things to concentrate on what matters. There are no better lessons to give.

Quick Starts

Not sure what kinds of crafts you and your kids might like? My book, *The Complete Idiot's Guide to Crafts with Kids,* offers an overview of scores of crafts, simple projects, resources to go further, and lots of tips for helping your kids and you get the most out of the experience.

Here are some more simple living ways to bring you closer together:

➤ Pass on a self-reliance skill like carpentry, cooking, money management, or gardening.

➤ Make something by hand. Crafts teach physical dexterity, patience, creativity, organization, independence, and self-expression. Children learn practical applications of the things they learn in school like measuring, mixing, the effects of heating and cooling, spatial relationships, and even history.

➤ Engage in some sort of spiritual practice together. Share your spiritual beliefs and rituals with your children, then let them design their own. Acquaint your kids with other faiths and systems of spiritual thought so you all learn respect for the many paths to the divine.

➤ Find a hobby the whole family can enjoy.

➤ Limit television watching. I know, I keep harping on this. Try it. You'll like it! Some parents find removing the TV altogether is the best solution. Others set limits, like no TV on weekdays. By limiting television, you're also interrupting the constant bombardment of consumerist messages aimed at kids and adults alike.

Avoidance Techniques

Somehow having a baby has become just another excuse for consuming. Not that some of the new baby equipment and gadgets aren't useful, but how many are truly necessary? If we're looking at spending money in terms of life energy, how much better to convert that item into time and attention? Try making your own baby food and clothes, use cloth diapers instead of disposable ones, and make your child's toys instead of buying them. You'll save money, ensure the quality of the products with which you surround your child (because you made them!), and avoid creating more rubbish for those overflowing landfills that are taking over our earth.

➤ Encourage kids to read at an early age. By putting emphasis on kids entertaining themselves, rather than being entertained, you're teaching your children to be self-reliant and responsible for their own enjoyment. Give them the love of learning, curiosity, and reading.

➤ Teach your children to honor their bodies. Again, your own self-nurturing example will say far more than words. Do active things together. Relax together.

➤ Teach them a love of nature. Take note of the seasons. Feed the birds and learn their names. Plant a seed.

Avoidance Techniques

Don't snoop! Sure you want to know what's going on in your child's life, but ask. Unless he or she's given you good reason not to trust, respect your child's right to privacy.

➤ Have rules. Set standards. If you don't explain what you expect, your child will never be able to please you.

➤ Teach kids about money at an early age. We tend to overlook teaching kids about money, debt, and consumerism as parents. Yet this is part of our responsibility. Think what it could mean if your children never got into debt, started putting money away as soon as they get their first coin from the tooth fairy, and could choose to live as they want before they're 30? It could happen! What an incredible gift.

➤ Tell your children the truth. You may think you're protecting your child by keeping things from him, but they know when you're being dishonest. Teach the value of honesty by being truthful yourself.

➤ Create family traditions. By observing family traditions, we teach continuity and a reverence for the past. Carry on those traditions that you find meaningful from childhood or create new ones with your children.

➤ Don't forget the simple things, the little things, like making Valentines, baking cookies from scratch (don't forget to lick the bowl), and playing checkers.

➤ Learn from your kids.

➤ Introduce your children to your heroes and let them pick their own. Be a hero for them.

➤ Champion your child! Promote his or her positive qualities whenever you get the chance.

➤ Teach the value of connecting with the generations.

➤ Teach the importance of caring for those less fortunate.

➤ Give the gift of your time—the time you've freed up by living more simply.

Never forget that a child is a living, breathing, thinking, feeling little human being and the most precious gift imaginable. But to help that child develop into a charitable, responsible, and successful adult takes effort and creativity. Parenting is a contact sport!

All's Clear: Values and Boundaries

Values are part of communication but are broader and deeper. I guess you could say that communication reveals our values. Raising children, more than any other experience, can test our boundaries and help clarify our values.

Simple Wisdom

"Children need models rather than critics."

—Joseph Joubert

Beyond Basics

Advertisers have your kids in their sights from the time they're born. How do you combat the influences of the consumerist society on your kids? A good start is Mary Hunt's (of *The Cheapskate Monthly* fame) *Debt-Proof Your Kids.*

What you do is what they learn, not what you say. If you're not clear on your values, they'll be fuzzy, too. They may not adopt yours, but it helps for them to have a standard to measure against.

What do you do when other people criticize your simple living efforts (and your child's)? Have you discussed how to handle the situation in advance with your family? Considering the possibilities and planning a response makes it much easier to handle. The pressure to conform to peer pressure is great. It's important for kids to know they must make their own judgments and follow their hearts. If they're not taken by surprise and have a chance to work out ahead of time what's most important to them, you'll be giving them the ultimate support.

You need to pay attention to how your kids are being targeted by the media and the marketers. One way is to turn it off as much as possible. The other is to arm them with information.

Part of simple living is defining what success is to you. Let your children know your definition of success and discuss how the world sees and presents success. Does your child also know there's room to fail?

Learn the difference between healthy competition and pushing oneself to the limit (competition with yourself) and destructive "win at all costs" competition.

Communicate the value of delayed rewards, the value of putting off immediate gratification and saving for something really important. Resist overindulging your children and substituting material things for time and energy, no matter how strong the pressures.

I Heard You!

As with ourselves, our partners, and everybody else we come in contact with, communication is the key to good relationships. Why is it we think communication with kids is somehow different or more difficult?

One truth about communication with our children is that, for it to be effective, we need to start early and keep it up. Think about how you hung on your new baby's every word. What happened? How did what he or she says suddenly become so much less important? Communicate with your children using the same focus, preciseness, and tone of voice that you'd like other people to take with you.

The Simple Baby

I couldn't do this chapter without saying something about the baby boom. I'm not talking about the one I'm supposed to be a part of, but the one that's going on right now in the world of advertising and marketing. How are babies so different today that they need all this stuff?

I remember being in the hospital with my first child, and my husband and I weren't sure the crib we'd ordered was going to be there on time. The nurse said, "well, you can always use a dresser drawer for the first few months." Somehow, that seemed like a perfectly practical solution. Today that would probably be seen as akin to child abuse!

Somehow having a baby has become just another excuse for consuming. Not that some of the new baby equipment and gadgets aren't useful, but how many are truly necessary? If we're looking in terms of spending money as spending life energy, how much better to convert that item into time and attention?

Every baby item imaginable is readily available secondhand. All you really need are a few basics. I honestly believe the fewer pieces of "baby equipment" in a baby's environment, the more he'll be inspired to explore the real world around him. Babies learn and grow pretty much the way they

Beyond Basics

There actually is a course to help you be a better parent and a textbook for the course. I took this program back in the 1970s, and it's just as relevant today as it was then. The foundation of the course is communication. Get yourself a copy of *P E T: Parent Effectiveness Training*, by Thomas Gordon and find someone who's giving the workshops in your area. You'll never regret it.

Avoidance Techniques

Beware the baby shower! Instead of having family, friends or colleagues throw a consumer orgy to anticipate the coming blessed event, ask that they simply throw a party and contribute toward the baby's college fund.

Beyond Basics

For the things you do need to buy for your baby, why not make your choices the most simple and wholesome possible? Here are some great resources for cloth diapers, diaper covers, wraps and organic cotton bedding:

Mother-ease: www.motherease.com; 1–800–416–1475

Bummis: www.bummis.com; 1–888–828–6647

EcoBaby: www.ecobaby.com; 1–800–ECOBABY

Beyond Basics

For more ideas on how to enjoy your kids the simple living way, read Elaine St. James' book *Simplify Your Life with Kids: 100 Ways to Make Family Life Easier and More Fun.*

always did. And in many instances, the old-fashioned way is still a good way.

Dirty diapers don't need to be another excuse to add to the landfill, either. Sure, disposable diapers are convenient, but just think of the price, both real and symbolic. Cloth diapers are a little more work, but neither of my daughters ever had diaper rash. And a clean washcloth is still just as effective as a disposable baby wipe. Cornstarch makes a great baby powder, too—no additives, no scent, no rash!

Who ever heard of "baby food" a hundred years ago? I made my own just as my grandmother did. If I knew it was going to be a busy week, I made several foods ahead and froze them in ice cube trays. I chuckled recently when I saw the same idea had been "reinvented" by Martha Stewart. By going back to the older, simpler ways, we often avoid additives, preservatives and other chemicals, which we have to accept as a trade-off for convenience. If you make your family's meals simple and wholesome and wait until the food reaches the table to season it, baby can eat what you eat. All you need is a blender, food processor, or manual food mill.

Don't worry about giving your baby all the right stuff! The right stuff is the simple stuff—keeping him warm and dry, well fed, and cuddled till the cows come home. Tell your baby "I love you" every day and never stop. Don't forget for one single day.

Where Are You Running To?

You've heard of "soccer moms." They spend their time in SUVs running from gymnastics lessons to soccer games to band practice to the PTA. You can collect activities much as you do things. If you're always running, when do you ever get to be "with" your children in any real sense? Some people are enrolling babies in classes and activities before they can walk! Your child is a human being, not a do-it-yourself project.

The "families on the fly" phenomenon is an epidemic, it seems. Everyone I know with children seems to be caught up in it. The only cure I can see is the same one we've been talking about all along. Slow down. Look at what's important. Simplify. Be selective.

Children need structure, but cramming every hour with patented activities is stifling and just plain silly. When every moment is spoken for, there's no room for just dreaming or acting on a whim. There's no creative space. And again, activities are just another way to *consume*—consume money, consume time, consume energy!

Simple Wisdom

"Remember, money is not love. Love is."

—Alexandra Stoddard

With overpacked schedules, everyone is stressed out and going in different directions. If you plan your family life around important times together, there will be a balance. Eat most meals together. Insist on it. Bring back the Sunday dinner! Limit the number of activities your kids can sign up for. Limit your own. How can you be a family if you never see each other?

The Least You Need to Know

➤ By getting in touch with the child we were and still are, we can be better parents.

➤ Simple parenting is much the same as simple living—it takes slowing down, knowing what's important, and paying attention to what matters.

➤ As with all relationships, communication is one of the great keys to effective parenting.

➤ Constant activity only consumes time, it doesn't build healthy families.

Chapter 18

When You Know How to Play, Who Needs Recreation?

In This Chapter

➤ Examining the entertainment industry and its relationship to the consumer society

➤ Focusing on inexpensive or free activities for the entire family

➤ Finding substitutes for games and sports that require expensive equipment or clothing

➤ Turning work into play

We have more choices than we could possibly view or do when it comes to entertainment and leisure activities. At any given time, we can watch 200 plus channels on satellite TV, play an endless array of video or computer games, go to our local multitheater complex for 10 or more first-run films, or select from thousands of titles at the local video store. There are "sports parks" and "entertainment malls" open into the wee hours.

But why do some people seem to be as stressed by their "recreation" as they are by their jobs? Doris Janzen Longacre suggests we look at the word "re-creation" and wonders if what we do for amusement actually gives us enough time to renew, to rest. Despite all the entertainment experiences offered us, she suggests, "The best recreation may still turn out to be staying home and fine-tuning our senses."

Entertainment: Giving You the Business

Entertainment isn't often homemade anymore. It's a multimillion dollar industry seeking to capture both your initial media-buying cash and continuing "after market" purchases like clothing, toys, and even products that make increasingly frequent cameo appearances.

With communications and entertainment in the hands of a smaller number of very large corporations, there can be an almost seamless product promotion machine. It's no accident that the hero of the latest action flick is hoisting a particular brand of beverage or the monster from the gooey depths just stepped on a well-known fast-food restaurant. It's all calculated to sell, sell, sell.

We need to be asking the hard questions about what we're taking into our minds and hearts. I find myself asking, "Who is making movies and television shows and why are they making them?" The more I see of the entertainment community, the less I think it has to say to me.

How well do you know the people who are controlling and manipulating this incredibly powerful force? What are some of the values being offered by the creative output of this industry and is it in line with your own?

Quick Starts

How can you make your kids more aware of how they're being targeted to consume? Make it a game to observe "hidden persuaders." Analyze regular ads and look for the more subtle forms of advertising. Start a "logo watch" and see how many you can spot.

What your kids see on TV, in the movies, and in magazines geared for their tastes and interests is echoed now in their schools, where corporations are advertising in exchange for supporting and helping to fund education. Called "in-school branding" by Naomi Klein in her recent book *No Logo: Taking Aim at the Brand Bullies,* the trade-off is educational equipment and materials for access to young, impressionable minds with unprecedented amounts of their own "disposable income" with more to come in the future.

So what are we seeing? Pull out the paper and go down the list of movies currently playing at your local theater. What are their themes? Let your remote control do some walking and get a quick picture of what's on the tube at any given moment. Make it a game and try to capsulize what you see in just a few words, then move on to the next. I see people who barely seem to work living in attractive apartments in big cities sporting designer wardrobes. The message: Upscale spending is for everyone! Research has shown that the more TV a person watches, the more they spend. I also see lots of conflict and the inevitable use of violence to resolve it (if it gets resolved at all). I see disaffection, boredom, anger, and restlessness. Love, peace, tranquility, and contentment don't make good TV!

Most of our modern amusements involve sitting and observing. Our pleasures are passive. We even have a word for people who engage in little else—the "couch potato."

Then there are the more subtle influences of the media. The entertainment industry, by its very nature, promotes certain conditions in the human mind and body. Jerry Mander, in his book *Four Arguments for the Elimination of Television,* goes into these. Mander talks about what he calls "the mediation of experience," or entering totally fabricated environments where we're disconnected from the natural world. We begin to substitute, for example, a television show that shows people studying lions in Africa for the experience of knowing how lions live in Africa. Our image of Africa and lions is from a television program, not from direct experience, but it is difficult for our minds to distinguish between the two.

Mander also explores the implications of media dominated by a few commercial giants and what the potential is of this centralized control, the physical effects of TV on the human body, the "ingestion of artificial light," and how we become the images we see.

I'm presenting some of the more extreme arguments here to get you thinking. That's not to say there aren't good movies, worthwhile television shows, and other quality forms of entertainment. But as with all the other areas we've discussed in this book, the goal is to be more *conscious* and to be critical of what we may be doing automatically, without any thought at all about its value or effect on us.

Beyond Basics

If Mander's arguments aren't enough to make you at least question the effects of our current forms of entertainment on your mind, heart, and soul, two more thought-provoking books on the subject are Thomas S. Hibbs' *Shows About Nothing: Nihilism in Popular Culture from "The Exorcist" to "Seinfeld"* and *Amusing Ourselves to Death: Public Discourse in the Age of Show Business* by Neil Postman.

And perhaps, in the process, we might choose to get our entertainment in a different way. Perhaps, like Thoreau, we might "… wish ever to live as to derive my satisfactions and inspirations from the commonest events, everyday phenomena, so that what my senses hourly perceive—my daily walk, the conversation of my neighbors—may inspire me."

If enjoying yourself usually means having to "get away from it all," you might want to look at what's going on at home, on the job, in your life. When you no longer find the ever-changing landscape right under your nose to be a source of wonder or curling up with a good book a thrilling night's entertainment, something is amiss!

Cheap (Even Free!) Thrills

Let's just say for argument's sake that your entertainment budget for this month is zero. You heard me—zip! And let's throw in that you've decided to unplug your TV for 30 days, just to see if you can stand it. If you take away the typical fare, what's left? Try making a list and see what you can come up with. Open closets and drawers, dig a little, and I'll bet you'll easily come up with 30 things to do just with what you already have in your house!

Make your own list of "homemade" entertainment. Consider picnics or camping, making music or crafts, exercising or gardening, and reading or writing. Keep adding to your list as you think of things. When you're looking for something to do, just consult your list!

Beyond Basics

Why not join or start an adult or junior Great Books discussion group? For more information on what to do point your browser to greatbooks.org/ for the Great Books Foundation Web site.

Simple Wisdom

"Like the bee, we should make our industry our amusement."

—Oliver Goldsmith

When Work Is Play

When you pursue the simple life, you may find your need for recreation just isn't there. A lot of people I know have found work that's so close to what they do for play that they can hardly tell the difference.

My friends Diane and Doug Iverson have turned their play into work (or vice versa). Diane is an illustrator and writer who creates books about nature for children. Husband Doug is a retired English teacher who loves photography. Together they travel to beautiful areas, hike, camp, and canoe while they gather material for Diane's next books.

Another friend who knows everything there is to know about the Grand Canyon and loves to spend as much time there as possible works as a guide for various organizations and as the owner of his own business. Yet another outdoors-loving friend has founded a primitive-skills school, sharing with others all he's learned about surviving in the wild.

My own work is so integrated into my pleasures it's hard to separate what I do for a living from my hobbies and interests. One feeds the other. I don't need to find time to play. I do it every day!

Beware of Games Requiring New Clothes

A lot of what passes for sport or recreation today requires all sorts of special clothes or accessories. Thoreau warned us to beware of enterprises requiring new clothes, and our leisure time activities are no exception.

Not that an investment in some tools or equipment isn't worthwhile, just make sure what you're buying isn't going to end up in the closet for years after the first month's enthusiasm fades away.

Fitness experts tell us to find a "lifetime sport" rather than going from one activity to another. Find something that you enjoy doing and make it a regular part of your life. If that involves an initial investment in some equipment, then so be it. Borrow or rent what you need first, and if it looks like you've found something you'll stick with, buy good-quality equipment that will last a long time.

Think of the values I've been asking you to clarify throughout this book and see if your leisure activities are in line with them. I know a lot of people enjoy playing golf, but here in Arizona, where water, or rather the lack of it, is increasingly becoming an issue, I have a hard time justifying acres of green lawns in an arid landscape.

How about croquette or horseshoes in the backyard instead of golf? Lots of sports that cost a lot of money if done the commercial way can be played on your own for less or for free. Skating on the sidewalk or in an empty garage rather than at a rink, sledding instead of skiing or snowmobiling, playing baseball at a park rather than joining a league.

Avoidance Techniques

Even if you love your work a whole lot, make sure you balance it with other activities and time with your quality circle.

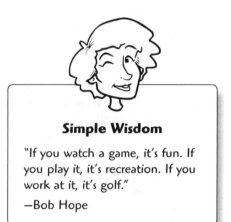

Simple Wisdom

"If you watch a game, it's fun. If you play it, it's recreation. If you work at it, it's golf."

—Bob Hope

You don't need a lot of special equipment for hiking either. A good pair of shoes and comfortable clothes, something to carry water and a light lunch, maybe a day pack and a cap—that's all that's needed. Walking doesn't cost anything and gives so much. And a walk can be anything from discovering animal tracks to studying birds or trees, from a challenge of the body to a trip for gathering berries or responsibly wildcrafting medicinal herbs.

Rent or borrow equipment first. Make sure an activity is something you're going to do long-term. Then, whenever possible, buy used. Watch the papers for great values on sports equipment or check out consignment shops like Play It Again, Sports; thrift stores; or even sports stores that sell off older equipment customers have traded in for new.

Avoidance Techniques

I know so many people (myself included) who were sure they wanted to take up a new activity, but first they had to have all the right stuff to do it right. Then they never started. Improvise, make do, substitute, borrow, rent, use something used. Delay the purchase until it really seems to make sense. Put it on a wish list and wait a month. Examine whether you're buying something because it will really make the sport more enjoyable or because you've been suckered into keeping up with the sports Joneses or have fallen for a clever ad.

For any new activity, ask what its positives and negatives are. Doris Longacre says to ask the positive question: "Does this strengthen my own spirit and my relationships with others?" And a negative one: "Is it expensive in terms of money, energy supplies, or the natural environment?" Come up with your own criteria for play times.

For children, ask the same things when buying toys and games. Find ways to involve kids in adult work and play whenever possible. What could you make as a toy instead of buying one? Learn about the toys of times past and other cultures. A lot can be made from a tin can or some old tires.

Old-time activities like making ice cream (we bought a nonelectric ice cream maker for $3 at a yard sale), making lariats, simple weaving, or whittling cost little or nothing and can occupy many satisfying hours. Make history recreation. Learn geography. Play word games. Write a play or story together. Start a scrapbook. Tell stories by the fireside and play cards, Ping-Pong, or pool (find used tables and equipment). Introduce yourself and your kids to stamp collecting. Find out more about your community. Study what's in your own backyard. Try your hand at drawing. Start pressing flowers. Discover the world under a magnifying glass. Play with some basic science equipment. Take apart an appliance or a piece of electronic equipment and study how it's made. Put together a box of tricks for rainy days or times when kids are sick. Learn to do some magic tricks. The possibilities are endless once you start to think simple!

The Least You Need to Know

➤ Entertainment and recreation is big business, and it often prompts us to consume when simple pleasures are just as fun if not more so.

➤ We need to help kids see how they're being targeted by marketers, especially to spend their money on entertainment.

➤ Old-fashioned hobbies, games, and activities are inexpensive, easy to pursue, and fun for the whole family.

➤ Substitutes can usually be found for expensive sports and sports equipment.

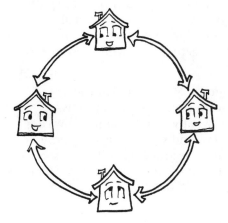

Chapter 19

Circle of Community: You Can't Do It Alone

In This Chapter

➤ Discovering the barriers to community and how to overcome them

➤ How to create communities that are supportive of your values

➤ Starting a simplicity circle

➤ Finding balance between individuality and community, privacy and sharing

---

Although we've talked about joining with others in different contexts in previous chapters, we haven't specifically discussed the challenges and opportunities of joining with others to work toward simplicity.

In this chapter, we'll explore both existing communities you may be a part of and new ones you can create and their roles in helping you achieve your goals.

What Makes a Community?

What does the word "community" mean to you? If you look at it in its broadest sense, it can encompass a family or the entire human race. In fact, some people extend their definition of community to include all living things.

What community or communities are you a part of? What commitment do you feel to your community? What do expect from it? What communities could you create or strengthen? Can you be part of a community and yet not experience "community"? How are decisions made in your community? What is your role? Are there things you would change? What are they and what would changing them mean?

Certainly, a family can be a community. So can a neighborhood, a church or spiritual group, a political or social-change group, a group organized around a particular hobby or activity, a group organized to create something, or a group devoted to learning something together. Sometimes communities come together for a while and then fade away or break apart.

Much has changed in our society concerning community, even just in the last 50 years. Our whole economy seems to be geared toward single-serving options—individual goods and services. This trend is part of what generates so much waste. You're more often than not "on your own." You may find yourself driving alone to work, wanting to be alone, partially as a reaction to overcrowding and because you like the independence of "having your own wheels" and just spending time alone with your own thoughts.

Beyond Basics

For some thought-provoking ideas on communities today and how to make them more livable, try reading *Building Communities from the Inside Out: A Path Toward Finding and Mobilizing a Community Assets,* by John P. Kretzmann and John L. McKnight; *Once There Were Greenfields: How Urban Sprawl Is Undermining America's Environment, Economy, and Social Fabric,* by F. Kaid Benfield, Donald D. T. Chen, and Matthew D. Raimi; and *Changing Places: Rebuilding Community in the Age of Sprawl,* by Richard Moe and Carter Wilkie.

We also tend to do things individually because of fear or lack of trust. We don't get to know each other that easily, and our institutions don't facilitate our getting to know each other. Sometimes our lack of trust extends to the greater environment. We find ourselves drinking bottled water, for instance, because we don't trust the public water supply. Or we fear public transportation because we don't trust its safety. These private, individualistic choices made out of fear or distrust are not always the best ones, but they create new markets that many are eager to take advantage of, and they are understandable on some levels.

So what are the other barriers to community? What keeps us from joining together and sharing time, skills, and resources?

Well, for one thing, we're spreading out. Urban sprawl is a real phenomenon, and it's having a huge impact on how we relate to one another. We're also a mobile society, moving many times in a lifetime rather than staying in one place as we did only 50 or 60 years ago.

Television and other media entertain us and are the sources for so much of our "information." We don't rely on other people the way we once did to learn skills and enjoy each other's talents.

We're running all the time. Busy, busy, busy! The so-called "time famine" makes it difficult to keep up with our immediate families, much less make time for other people.

The automobile has certainly had an impact. It used to be "the family car," now most families have more than one vehicle, with each family member driving off in a different direction. We commute farther and farther to work—because we can.

Our consumer culture fosters competition ("He who dies with the most toys wins") that again isolates us and tends to work against forming lasting communities. We adopt many of the stereotypes that come with class, occupation, location, education level, and other distinguishing characteristics rather than seeing similarities and common ground.

We seem to have lost the basic rules of civility and common courtesy. Without them, relationships have a hard go of it. Larger goals and shared priorities give way to squabbling and in-fighting.

Violence and crime keep people behind closed, locked doors and security systems. It's safer to "keep to oneself."

Simple Wisdom

"Cars remold communities and the character of daily life as cities sprawl, public transit atrophies, and suburban shopping centers multiply. Even workplaces have begun to scatter; just half the residents of the San Francisco Bay area, for example, now work in the town where they live. The greater mobility of the private car has the paradoxical effect of lengthening how far people go rather than saving them time."

—Alan Durning, *How Much Is Enough?*

Technology has both opened up new doors and served to isolate us from our neighbors, sometimes even our housemates. How often do you hear the complaint "Oh, he's always in front of the computer these days!" We don't even have to leave home to spend money. A click of the mouse brings everything right to our door.

For there to be community, some people argue, there needs to be a center, a gathering place. Cohousing communities are based on this, with a community square or center at the heart and residences surrounding it. In some newer suburbs, the only "community center" is the mall!

Avoidance Techniques

Don't allow technology to rob you of the experience of community. Make conscious choices to shop locally, and you'll be creating links to the community through your buying choices. Not that online shopping isn't convenient and doesn't have its place. But it also has its price.

Simple Wisdom

"Because we face a crisis in the interconnected global system, changes at every level are needed. At the personal level, we need a magnified global awareness and simpler ways of living. At the neighborhood level, we need new types of communities for sustainable living. At the national level, we need to adopt new policies with regard to energy, environment, education, media, and many more."

—Duane Elgin, *Voluntary Simplicity*

And there's a paradox within the simple living movement itself. Simple living folks tend to be mavericks and quite individualistic. It's this very quality that allows them to go against the norm and forge a new way.

Juliet B. Schor, in *The Overspent American,* talks about discovering this with her interview subjects: "While most of the people I interviewed had a strong community orientation, there are aspects of this lifestyle that emphasize separateness, independence, and self-reliance."

Helen and Scott Nearing hoped to be part of the towns in Vermont and Maine where they farmed, but they found it to be one of the more difficult challenges. Their collective ideas were not greeted well by the existing community, and the couple was seen as peculiar, subversive, and against the grain.

Some simple living folks are upper-middle-class high-achievers who opted out. Although that gives them a financial advantage and a strong skill set to work with, one of the hardest things for some of them has been leaving an entire social structure behind and starting over.

Do-It-Yourself Communities

Many people who have adopted the simple living lifestyle report that they are not necessarily accepted by the community at large, but they have found support from smaller subcommunities. These, they say, can be created when none exists.

Communities, whether "natural" or created, need a center to gather. In planning our communities, we need to think about creating gathering places. One of the things my husband and I liked about our current house is the existence of a pleasant room to hold neighborhood and community meetings. We've kept the furniture to a minimum there, so it's easy to convert it into meeting space. Where are your community centers? Are there spaces that aren't being used that could be converted to meeting and gathering places?

The old "neighborhoods" are virtually gone. The way I grew up in New York City, everyone spent evenings sitting on the front stoops watching their kids play in the streets. It takes more of an effort to create a feeling of "neighborhood," but we can if we do it consciously. Approach your neighbors. Invite them over. Get to know them.

Concentrate on one neighbor at a time if that's your style. Welcome new people to the neighborhood with some cookies or even a little package of helpful information you've collected; include some local maps and free booklets from the Chamber of Commerce.

Shopping in local stores helps foster community, too. Our food co-op has become a kind of community center, as has our health food store, with people of like interests sharing resources of information. Sometimes a local bookstore or coffee shop can serve a similar function.

Here are some other ideas for creating community:

➤ Community celebrations are one way to get to know your neighbors. Go to the parade, the Christmas tree lighting, and the local house tour.

➤ Form a cooking co-op. You cook less and have the fellowship of sharing daily meals with others.

➤ Reach out to share childcare. Back in the '70s when there were few daycare options and I was a single mom going back to school, I shared childcare with other student moms. Sometimes it was a little difficult coordinating schedules, but we planned together and occasionally shifted children in the college parking lot!

➤ Organize a neighborhood yard sale.

Beyond Basics

The Sustainable Communities Network is concerned with helping people build more earth-friendly and people-centered places to live and work. Their Web site at www.sustainable.org is filled with resources and links to still more ideas and tools. Especially helpful is their huge resource list at www.sustainable.org/creating/vision.html.

Simple Wisdom

"Simple living is not mainly about spending less, but about living differently."

—Juliet B. Schor, *The Overspent American*

Avoidance Techniques

Yard sales are a great way to get rid of clutter and get to know your neighbors at the same time. Just stick to your commitment not to come home with more junk. On the other hand, you may find you have items among you that could be shared.

Simple Wisdom

"Residents of Colorado's Grey-rock Commons put colored flags by their doors when they plan a trip to the store, so neighbors can drop off shopping lists; simple assistance—fixing leaky faucets or installing software, for instance, is often handled 'in-house'; and care once provided by extended families is sometimes supplied by the community."

—Gary Gardner in *World Watch* magazine (July/Aug 1999)

➤ Talk to your neighbors or community members (your church group, supper group, book discussion group, any "community") about sharing tools, yard equipment, luggage, freezer space, storage space, recreational equipment, and household appliances.

➤ See if there's a car-sharing program in your area. If there isn't, find out about getting one started (see Chapter 15, "Rethinking Getting from Here to There," for more information).

➤ Investigate shared housing options (see Chapter 13, "Seeking Shelter and Keeping House," for ideas).

➤ Join or start a community garden.

➤ Pool skills and services like home repairs, computer expertise, childcare, car repairs, sewing and tailoring, and hair cutting.

➤ Investigate the service credit programs operating in 150 U.S. communities.

➤ Look into the viability of "community currency" or "local currency" in your area. Start by contacting E. F. Schumacher Society, 140 Jug End Road, Great Barrington, MA 01230 (413-528-1737; www.schumachersociety.org).

The benefits of joining with others in a community include lower environmental impact, less time spent shopping and maintaining things, less need for storage, lowering costs, and gaining emotional and spiritual support from others.

And what about online communities? Are they really communities or substitutes for communities? I think they are and can be both. Last year, I contracted Lyme disease during a visit to New England. It was diagnosed early, and I've since nearly completely recovered, but because I live in Arizona and Lyme disease is a rarity here, I turned to the online community for advice, information, and support. It was there, ready and waiting. People online can be so very generous!

Quick Starts

Want to find out what a service credit program is? Start by reading *Time Dollars: How to Build Community Through Social Capital* by Edgar S. Cahn, the originator of the idea, and get started in your community. You can also get the basics from the TimeDollar Institute at www.timedollar.org.

Then check out Womanshare, a "skills bank" founded in New York City by Diana McCourt and Jane Wilson. In this system, debts are paid with skills instead of cash and getting into debt is encouraged! Ask for information by writing Womanshare, 680 West End Avenue, New York, NY 10025, calling 212-662-9746, or e-mailing Wshare@aol.com.

Sometimes online communities become more personal when the people meet face to face. When I first moved to Arizona from Connecticut, I had trouble connecting with other writers in my area. I posted a message on a professional writer's forum asking if anyone wanted to get together to share "war stories," resources, and ideas. A group of around 10 writers formed out of that initial inquiry, and we met monthly for over two years. The group no longer meets, but some of us have remained close friends.

I think it's important to create face-to-face communities as well as the more anonymous online ones; however, I think both are useful. If you find yourself spending all your time online and rarely socializing "in person," you might want to examine why this is so and how you might benefit from breaking out of that mold.

Beyond Basics

For a quirky look at one of the pioneering virtual communities, ECHO, read *Cyberville: Clicks, Culture, and the Creation of an Online Town,* by Stacy Horn.

An important way that communities can support their members in living the simple life is to commit to common goals and encourage each other to stick to them. Communities or subcommunities can agree to set limits on spending or TV watching or anything they want. If the larger community won't do it, having a smaller community that will helps enormously. Let's say you're in a church group, and everyone in that group decides to limit TV watching to weekends only. That helps the kids with the outside pressure in the larger community to be able to say "Well, my church group isn't watching TV during the week. We're all doing it!"

Simplicity Circles and How to Start One

If you create a community that has simplicity as its main goal, your strides in that area can be made more quickly. Something called "simplicity circles," the brainchild of Cecile Andrews, seems to be catching on. You can locate one in your area or start your own.

Your simplicity circle can make it easier to stick to your goals. It also can make it easier for your kids to resist peer pressure in other groups. If you know you're not alone in making new choices, you can feel stronger. You have a built-in, resource-sharing network and a place to help answer some of the questions and clear up some of the confusion about the American dream together.

My daughter Rachel, a naturalist and wildlife rehabilitation specialist, joined a simplicity circle at the New England Aquarium where she was a graduate school intern. This was set up as an 8-week-long workshop using materials from the Northwest Earth Institute (www.nwei.com). There was a facilitator from the institute for the first "lesson" and then individuals in the group took turns facilitating. As a result, Rachel made some simple changes. She decided to stop buying coffee in disposable cups and now brings her coffee mug to work. She started composting regularly and examining why she purchases things. She and her husband contacted people in their neighborhood and began sharing resources like lawnmowers and snow blowers.

Quick Starts

For more information on simplicity circles, go to Seeds of Simplicity, the Simplicity Circles Project at www.seedsofsimplicity.org/cecile.htm.

To see if there are any simplicity-circle study groups in your area, point your Web browser to www.simplicitycircles.com for a study group database with listings by state.

Some friends and I just started our own circle, and we're fairly loose in structure. Basically, we've decided to go through the book *Your Money or Your Life* on a weekly basis using their program outline and then decide what we'd like to do from there. We've been doing potlucks, although that may not be every week. I'd like to see us work on sharing resources, and I'm making my simple living library (which is extensive from researching this book) available for the group and other groups that might like to start circles of their own. I'd like to see us become the initial facilitators for new groups that would like to start as well.

When Things Don't Work

What happens when community breaks down? Neighbors clash, groups fall apart, organizations end up rife with fighting from within. Before you give up, first evaluate what's happening and see if there are ways to do things differently. There are lots of good books on facilitating and helping groups work more effectively together. Perhaps it's just a matter of focusing on each person's objectives or working through some hurt feelings. Step back and agree to take some time to clear things up.

Sometimes an outsider can give a new perspective. If everyone agrees, bring in someone with more experience or background in group facilitation or mediation and see if that can help. You began with good intentions. Getting back to the mission of the group, the original vision, may also refocus attention on what's important.

And then again, sometimes communities form for a time, are viable, and then cease to meet the needs of their members. This seems to be part of the very nature of human endeavor. Allow things to evolve. Groups sometimes can dissolve and re-emerge in a slightly different incarnation or might break into several parts that are more satisfying for individual participants. Be open to change.

If you find that most of the communities you become a part of don't work out, perhaps, frankly,

Avoidance Techniques

If things just don't seem salvageable, even after making sincere efforts, let it go. Sometimes groups just don't mesh. The timing could be wrong or the personality mix not compatible. Learn from your mistakes and move on.

it's you! Look in the mirror. How are you an obstacle to community building? Could your own competitiveness or fear of getting close be involved?

Seek also a balance between community and time alone. Ultimately, we each have our own levels of need for privacy and solitude coupled with our needs for companionship and community. Seek to know and understand yourself and strive for the right balance in your own life.

The Least You Need to Know

➤ There are many barriers to a sense of community in our modern society.

➤ We can take positive steps to strengthen the communities of which we are a part to support us in our goals.

➤ Simplicity circles are one way of creating small communities to learn about simplicity and more sustainable living.

➤ Sometimes groups hit rough spots or even fall apart. There are steps we can take to salvage them, but sometimes we just need to let it go and move on.

Part 5

What If Everybody Did It?

Living more simply and lightly on the earth is a personal choice that has many bene-fits and rewards. But what if it really caught on and lots of people decided to make fundamental changes in their lifestyle? These final chapters speculate on the political, economic, and social changes that simple living implies and how we as individuals might cope with those changes.

We'll consider alternative ways of educating our children and ourselves, how to live in greater harmony with the environment, and ways in which we might redefine wealth as a tool for social change.

Chapter 20

The Politics of Paring Down

In This Chapter

➤ Understanding the political diversity of the simple living movement and considering a politics of simplicity

➤ The myths of the American economy and some possible alternatives to "conspicuous consumption"

➤ How self-reliance and simplicity might threaten some of our existing institutions

➤ Taking simple living beyond our own households

People who choose simple living are generally mavericks who tend to be self-reliant and act as individuals. Many feel disaffected from the political and economic scene. They might be seen as almost apolitical. In some ways, living the simple life is a protest in itself. But instead of being only a reaction against what appears to be unworkable, it is a positive commitment to a set of principles. It's living the American dream we choose to create rather than the one created by Madison Avenue and Hollywood.

Which Wing Are You? Choosing Bridges, not Poles

You may be tempted to stereotype people who are interested in simple living. One assumption is that people who are interested in simplifying are holdovers from the 1960s, aging hippies, politically "liberal," probably vegetarian, maybe even "left-wing."

A second stereotype is of the conservative Christian, often labeled as being on the "extreme right," leaving crowded cities to live in the country and reconnect with old-fashioned values, with Mom staying home and home-schooling the kids and Dad acting as traditional breadwinner.

Perhaps a third stereotype is that of the yuppie high-achievers that have "made it" in the city or upscale suburbs, accumulated their loot, and decided they want out of the rat race. With their substantial bundle carefully invested, they've scaled back, built a custom log home in a rural community, and are living off their stock dividends.

And finally, there are the so-called "survivalists" who expect some sort of natural or political disaster and are dedicated to becoming self-reliant so they can be ready for whatever happens. They mistrust the government, keep to themselves, and know how to shoot straight.

I would submit that all of these are true and none of these is true! The people I've interviewed for this book are all over the lot and are none of the above. If you knew me well, you'd find it difficult to find a label and fit me into any one of these stereotypical groups, yet I probably share some characteristics with them all.

Yes, simple living is a political issue, and it cuts across all philosophical doctrines and all political parties. It's about quality of life for us as individuals, but in a broader sense, it's about the future of us all.

By making certain individual choices, we are making a political statement whether we intend to or not. Opting to "go off the grid," for instance, has an economic and, therefore, political impact, even if only on a small scale. Choosing to buy goods locally has an economic and political impact. Shifting our emphasis from mindless acquisition of cheap consumer goods to sharing, reusing, and only buying the essentials—and then demanding the highest quality—is bound to have both economic and political implications in the long run. Whether there are enough people making these choices to have an effect remains to be seen.

Some people are making an effort to identify the political issues of plain and simple living. Jerome Segal, for example, a former House Budget Committee staffer and author of the book *Graceful Simplicity: Toward a Philosophy and Politics of Simple Living,* has grappled with the subject.

"What we need in America today," says Segal, "is not primarily a new set of programs, but a rethinking of the fundamentals of economic life." Although making the personal choice to spend less, work less, earn less, and spend more time doing the things that matter to us is important, for it to be embraced by more people, the cost of "core needs" would have to go down. Segal identifies these needs as safe neighborhoods, good education, transportation, economic security, and health care. Segal feels we need shifts in public policy so a family isn't pressed to have two cars so that both parents can work to supply health care, buy a house in the "safer" suburbs, send the kids to private schools to get a good education, and have an IRA or 401(k) to be economically secure.

The basic idea is to reform the current system so that a modest income produced by a shorter workweek would take care of core needs. We then could use our leisure time to pursue what mattered to us. Segal recommends that we be open-minded about seeking alternatives and policies to achieve them.

But we know that economics drives politics. "It's the economy, stupid!" is what it's all about, right?

Simple Economics: What They Don't Want You to Know

The foundation of our current economy, not just in America but worldwide, is "growth is good." We are obsessed with economic performance, growth, and expansion. If we don't consume, we aren't being good citizens and contributing to "the growth of the economy." We worry about "consumer confidence" and "disposable income," unemployment, and inflation. What's wrong with this picture?

If everyone scaled down and stopped consuming beyond what they really needed, wouldn't the economy collapse and throw us all into a depression?

Simple Wisdom

"Any intelligent fool can make things bigger, more complex, and more violent. It takes a touch of genius—and a lot of courage—to move in the opposite direction."

—E. F. Schumacher

A pioneer in rethinking these economic assumptions was E. F. Schumacher. In his more than 25-year-old entreaty for a new economics, *Small is Beautiful: Economics As If People Mattered*, Schumacher contends that our current thinking is an obstacle to peace, a threat to the environment, and a prescription for unhappiness and alienation. Schumacher has become the catalyst for a variety of concrete solutions and the search to "find another way." His basic concerns are summed up in the mission statement of the Schumacher Society: "human scale, respect for the land, mutual aid, community renewal."

Beyond Basics

For more information on E. F. Schumacher and his ideas and what's grown out of them, contact the E. F. Schumacher Society, 140 Jug End Road, Great Barrington, MA 01230. You can also call 413-528-1737, go to the Web site at www.schumachersociety.org, or e-mail efssociety@aol.com.

As Cecile Andrews puts it, "We need to have a new way of measuring what is going on in the economy and society." The gross domestic product is no longer an accurate measure, and Andrews advocates adopting something like the genuine progress indicator. She notes that, although the Exxon Valdez oil spill had a terrible environmental cost, it helped raise the GDP. If factors like pollution, crime, resource depletion, and damage to the environment were included as negatives along with community service and the work of homemakers as positives, this would be a more "real" indicator of economic health.

It's beyond the scope of book to discuss all the ideas and programs currently being experimented with to create a more human and earth-centered global economy, but I'd like to touch on a few to get you thinking. These are actual programs being tried in real towns and cities. I don't know about you, but I'll be eagerly watching the results.

Local Currencies

One of the fundamental ideas of *Small is Beautiful* is to take care of local needs from local resources. One area where this is taking place is in banking. Communities are establishing what are called "regional" or "local" currencies. This practice harks back to the days when bankers knew the people in the community well and loans were made based on character and integrity, not strictly on collateral. Banks could issue a local scrip, which meant that the money could circulate only within a limited area. This kept money from traveling to the big industrial centers, and the economy was decentralized. During the Great Depression, forms of exchange emerged that competed with the national currency.

In the 1970s, economist Ralph Borsodi and Robert Swann issued a local currency called the Constant. The experiment lasted for a year and received a great deal of publicity. When asked by a reporter if the currency was legal, Borsodi told him to check with the Treasury Department. The reporter was advised that all that mattered was whether the currency could be exchanged for dollars so that transactions could be recorded for tax purposes. It proved that, as long as the community has confidence in the currency issued and it was accepted as cash, it was legal.

In 1982 in Great Barrington, Massachusetts, home of the Schumacher Society, a nonprofit organization called the Self-Help Association for a Regional Economy (SHARE) was created to establish a local currency, which is still in existence. In Ithaca, New York, the Ithaca HOURS local currency system is perhaps one of the most well known and well established. More than 65 American communities are experimenting with community currency including Kansas City, Eugene, Boulder, Philmont (a small town in New York), and my own town, Prescott, Arizona. Each program is tailored to and reflects the people of the area and their needs, culture, and the products they produce.

Quick Starts

If you think you might want to start a local currency in your neighborhood, you'll get all the information you need from the folks at Ithaca Hours, the local currency exchange for Ithaca, New York. Contact them at P.O. Box 6731, Ithaca, NY 14851. Or you can call 607-272-3738, e-mail ithacahours@lightlink.com, or go to the Web site www. ithacahours.org. At Paul Glover's (Ithaca Hours founder) site, www.lightlink.com/hours/ ithacahours/, you can order your local-currency starter kit and the book *Hometown Money: How to Enrich Your Community with Local Currency.*

Also check out the books *Local Currencies in Community Development or too much mng-wotngwotiki is bad for you,* by Tony Savdie and Tim Cohen-Mitchell and *Rethinking Our Centralized Monetary System: The Case for a System of Local Currencies,* by Lewis Solomon.

Local currencies are completely legal as long as the bills themselves do not resemble Federal Reserve Notes and as long as they are treated as cash for tax purposes. The local dollars can only be spent locally and with the merchants who participate in the program, which keeps residents investing in the community.

GANE—General Agreement on a New Economy

In an effort to come up with a new economic model, the Economics Working Group in Washington, D.C. has drafted a proposal for "full employment, equity, and environmental sustainability." They call the new, innovative model "community federalism." Here's an excerpt from that draft:

> "The GNP-growth/consumption-driven basis of the present economy generates increasing levels of global production that are environmentally unsustainable. This means we are not replenishing the natural resources we use so future generations will also be able to meet their needs.

Beyond Basics

To find out more about GANE and the Economics Working Group, contact 3407 34th Places N.W., Washington, DC 20016. You also can call 202-244-0561 or go to the Web site at www.greenecon.org/gane.

"Nor has this growth approach been able to ensure employment for all who want and need it. Job creation and maintenance of a decent standard of living in the United States is being hindered by the cumulative effects of corporate downsizing and large-scale layoffs, the increased reliance on temporary and contract workers to replace permanent workers, the transfer of production overseas in both the manufacturing and service sectors, and the increasing use of technology to replace human labor."

GANE's goals are full employment, protecting and restoring the environment for future generations, ensuring healthy communities, and changing the measurements of economic health to include factors other than "total monetary value of economic activity."

Whether you accept this particular model or not, the idea of questioning our existing system and replacing it with one that contributes more to the overall well-being of the people and the planet seems to make sense.

Shorter Work Hours

In *The Overworked American: The Unexpected Decline of Leisure,* Juliet B. Schor makes the point that most Americans are working an average of 163 extra hours of paid employment each year compared to 20 years ago. Those who are employed are working longer hours, while others are unemployed or "underemployed."

A movement to shorten the workweek, interrupt the work-and-spend cycle, and revalue leisure time is afoot. To learn more, contact the Shorter Work-Time Group, c/o Barbara Brandt, 69 Dover Street #1, Somerville, MA 02144 (617-628-5558; www.swt.org/) or the Society for the Reduction of Human Labor, c/o Benjamin Hunnicutt, 1610 East College Street, Iowa City, IA 52245 (hunnicut@blue.weeg. uiowa.edu).

A site that also has lots of background and makes the case persuasively is www.vcn. bc.ca/timework/, the TimeWork Web from Canada.

Self-Reliance and the Government

Self-reliance and a commitment to simple living may put you at odds with your government at times. Using alternative building methods or energy sources may create conflicts with local zoning ordinances or building codes, for instance. There's even some question as to whether long-term storage of food and supplies for emergencies may be contrary to recent antiterrorist laws.

Make it your business to know your state and local officials and to familiarize yourself with the laws governing what you may want to do. Chances are, sooner or later you'll find yourself getting involved. I did.

Here are a few pointers from my and others' experiences:

➤ **Read your local paper.** And if you're thinking of relocating, make sure you subscribe to the local newspaper before you go. Find out who the various players are, both in government and out. Read, especially, the op-ed page. Write letters to the editor to express your opinion.

➤ **Attend meetings periodically.** There's nothing more enlightening than a meeting of the city council, county board of supervisors, or planning and zoning commission.

➤ **Question authority.** This is not to say you should be impertinent or impolite. Just ask questions and don't accept things on face value.

➤ **Respect the individual, not the office.** Learn who the people are that are sympathetic to your objectives and values.

➤ **Avoid political stereotypes and polarization.** Make it your business to understand all sides. Your own views will be better informed and clearer. Read magazines now and then that have different perspectives. Some of my favorites are *The National Review, Reason, The Utne Reader,* and *Harper's.* Visit Web sites from different organizations and consider different points of view.

Avoidance Techniques

Don't reinvent the wheel. Get yourself a copy of *How to Save Your Neighborhood, City, or Town: The Sierra Club Guide to Community Organizing,* by Maritza Pick and read it. You'll find lots of ideas for making your community a better place to live.

Simple Wisdom

"A politics of graceful simplicity focuses on time, money, and work. It seeks a society in which ordinary people have: a high level of leisure time; the ability to satisfy core economic needs at low levels of personal income; economic security and dignified work."

—Jerome Segal

Making Time for Changes

As we live more consciously, I believe we will begin to demand a greater consciousness from our institutions from the local level on up. As it becomes more essential to us that they be shaped by the realization that it's not just "profitability" that counts but the "total cost" of our way of life, we will naturally get more involved. We will begin to see a connection between personal economy and self-government and the larger picture. The debt and irrational consumption that leads to spiritual bankruptcy and impoverishment on the personal level becomes more apparent on a global level.

But how can we make a difference? I personally think it's important to make time for influencing our political destiny as part of my daily life. I'm not sure what I can do on the national level or beyond, but my husband and I have become active in preserving and improving our small area of the world. I've run into many people who seem to share the pervasive attitude that "you can't stop growth and development" or "you're fighting a losing battle." Maybe so, but if I believed that, I wouldn't be wasting my time.

Simple Wisdom

"Trust thyself: every heart vibrates to that iron string. Accept the place the divine providence has found for you, the society of your contemporaries, the connection of events."

—Ralph Waldo Emerson

Simple Wisdom

"I predict future happiness for Americans if they can prevent the government from wasting the labors of the people under the pretense of taking care of them."

—Thomas Jefferson

Critical thinking is essential. Asking questions constantly of ourselves, our leaders, and our institutions and questioning the "common wisdom" is a fundamental skill of those leading simple lives. Why shouldn't we ask these questions of our government, politics, and economics?

By making the choice to live more simply, we've made a stand for a new way of thinking. Even shifting something as simple as diet can have a profound effect on world hunger. Acting locally affects the whole.

Self-reliance and being able to live with less gives us a kind of power, both personal and political. We need to recognize that power and use it wisely. I believe simple living tends to give us the time and space to do that, and it presents the challenges to complacency that we tend to miss when we're caught up in the rat race.

Ultimately, self-reliance and simple living are good for government. It means a more involved, informed, and active citizenry. It means less of a burden on social programs, less money spent on cleaning up the environment, a smaller burden on the health care system, and more resources freed up for making improvements that will benefit us all.

So think through what's important to you and what actions you can take to have your voice heard. Consider ways in which a simple living approach might help change things in your neighborhood. Reserve some time for getting involved and giving back. Volunteer, write letters, attend meetings, and begin to shape the future.

The Least You Need to Know

➤ Stereotypes are barriers to understanding and creating change.

➤ Old models for the economy don't necessarily reflect reality and the total costs of our way of life. We can create new models for the future.

➤ Experiments at the local level like community currencies and shorter work-weeks have promise and are worth watching.

➤ Taking charge of our lives on a personal level can make us more demanding of our institutions. The next step is getting involved in making them better.

Chapter 21

New Directions in Education

Educating our kids today is not a simple matter. There are so many issues facing parents of school-age children that it's nearly overwhelming. First, there's the issue of safety and simply protecting our children from random violence, predators, and drug peddlers. Then there's whether enough time is even spent learning after all the other bureaucratic and behavioral tasks are taken care of. The basic quality of education is in question, and more kids are graduating from high school as functional illiterates and with no knowledge of geography, history, or the basic foundations of democracy and a free society.

Some may disagree with me, but I believe there's a fundamental paucity of the debate and discussion of values. What makes an "educated" person? What life skills are our children taking with them when they leave "the system?" What have we taught them about personal responsibility and making their own way through the moral challenges they are about to face? How have we contributed to their ability to think critically, to question, and to dig out information for themselves?

As with many other aspects of simple living, the things we can do at the outset may not seem simple at all. They may actually take more effort, more time, and require us to pay closer attention to how we do things. But I submit that, in the long run, we will greatly simplify our lives, our relationships with our kids, and their future success and happiness.

Education or Learning: Which Is Which?

Think back to which aspects of your education you are using now. I don't mean specifically in your career or way of making a living but in your everyday life. The skills I believe you'll most likely mention are

➤ **Problem solving.** When faced with a challenge or a puzzle, you rely on your ability to look at a variety of solutions and choose the best one.

➤ **Critical thinking.** This skill allows you to hear a series of persuasive arguments, challenge the assumptions on which they're based, and come up with your own conclusions.

➤ **Curiosity and a love of learning.** Instilling the "fire" of inquisitiveness is what fuels the best of what we can become.

➤ **Communicating.** Verbal skills as well as the confidence that you can make yourself heard clearly and understand the response are keys to successful living.

➤ **Finding information.** When you don't know something, you know how to research, interview, or otherwise ferret out the information you need.

➤ **Reading.** Simple reading skills not only allow you to keep up with your world and gather important information, they also provide you with a world of free or nearly free entertainment and education for the rest of your life.

➤ **Working compatibly with other people.** The ability to work in groups or teams, making the most of individual strengths and minimizing weaknesses, will multiply both your effectiveness and your enjoyment.

➤ **Self-esteem.** This is something of a "can of worms" as to how we go about building self-confidence and a sense of self-worth, but the ultimate positive sense of identity forms the foundation for the rest of life.

➤ **Connectedness with the natural world.** It seems the lack of connectedness, as a result of the technological age and the information age, is a major cause of our desperate search for simplicity.

These are life skills, and we want our kids to come out of the educational environment with them. The schools can't do this alone, but they certainly shouldn't *undo* them! There's a body of knowledge as well that, as a society, we need to pass on to future generations if our civilization is to survive. Our political and historical foundations as a nation, the principles of our government and our system of laws, and a basic set of moral values that help create a civil society all need to be transmitted in some way by public educators and by our children's first teachers, ourselves.

We need to clarify for ourselves what we believe constitutes a good education and then evaluate how well the schools we have to choose from are doing. And there's something more.

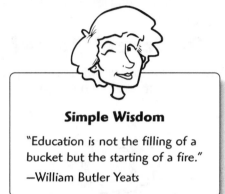

Simple Wisdom

"Education is not the filling of a bucket but the starting of a fire."

—William Butler Yeats

What things that you do *not* want to be instilled in your children are the schools teaching, either directly or implicitly? Do you know? How, for instance, is public education teaching our kids to be "good little consumers?" Some people feel that the schools are heavily involved in social engineering, which is basically the science of controlling attitudes and behavior at the societal level. What are the "hidden agendas" in your schools and are they compatible with your beliefs and what you want for your children?

Beyond Basics

Never thought about what your kids might be getting in school that you don't want them to? Read John Taylor Gatto's *Dumbing Us Down: The Hidden Curriculum of Compulsory Schooling* for more thought-provoking ideas on the subject of programming our kids through the public school curriculum. According to Gatto, an award-winning New York public school teacher, the hidden curricula can be broken down into seven basic categories: confusion, class position, indifference, emotional dependency, intellectual dependency, provisional self-esteem, and one can't hide. It's a must-read for anyone trying to evaluate our current educational system!

I believe getting these things straight with yourself as a parent will make the whole process of choosing how you want to educate your children and then being involved in the process that much easier.

Do Schools Work?

Our first responsibility as parents of school-age children is to become familiar with their learning options and evaluate them. How do you do that? Simple: Go there! Ask to meet the principal, your child's teachers, and other school staff members. Sit in on classrooms. Volunteer some time if you can and get to know more about the inner workings of the place where your child is learning. You'll pick up the pluses and minuses pretty quickly if you pay attention.

Simple Wisdom

"I have never let my schooling interfere with my education."

—Mark Twain

If you don't have children yet or your children aren't yet ready for school, all the better. Now's the time to do your homework!

Come prepared with a checklist based on what you'd like to see in the educational environment and what you *don't* want to see. Aim high, be critical, but also look for the things they're doing right.

➤ How are they handling safety?

➤ What procedures are in place in the event of an emergency? What is the student-to-teacher ratio?

➤ How much time is actually spent learning and how much seems to be spent in procedural activities, play, and handling behavioral problems?

➤ What provisions are there for students who are not keeping up or who have special needs?

➤ What provisions are there for students who are ahead and may be bored or unchallenged?

➤ What is the curriculum for the year and what materials are being used to teach it?

➤ Are there any supplemental materials available to kids who want to know more?

➤ What seem to be the underlying values of your child's teacher? The school? How are these being transmitted? Do they agree with your own? Are there ways for different value systems to be expressed and honored? How are conflicts and disagreements handled?

➤ Get a copy of the "school policy." Read it and ask questions.

➤ Read about what good schools should look like, how kids learn best, and what you can do as a parent to both make your child's school better and help him or her gain the most benefit. Come up with a clear idea of what you expect from your child's school.

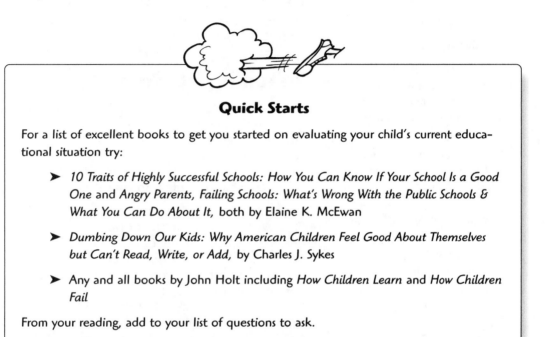

Quick Starts

For a list of excellent books to get you started on evaluating your child's current educational situation try:

➤ *10 Traits of Highly Successful Schools: How You Can Know If Your School Is a Good One* and *Angry Parents, Failing Schools: What's Wrong With the Public Schools & What You Can Do About It,* both by Elaine K. McEwan

➤ *Dumbing Down Our Kids: Why American Children Feel Good About Themselves but Can't Read, Write, or Add,* by Charles J. Sykes

➤ Any and all books by John Holt including *How Children Learn* and *How Children Fail*

From your reading, add to your list of questions to ask.

The next step is to research the alternatives. Look at all of them, even if at first glance you might not think they'd fit your criteria. If part of being an educated person is having an open mind and possessing critical-thinking skills, then use yours! Look at religious schools, "alternative" schools, charter schools, private schools, Montessori schools, Waldorf schools, and anything else that might be available to you. Don't even think of the price tag to start off. You're gathering information, educating yourself, and assessing the educational "marketplace."

If you're not sure what's available in your community, check in the phone book under "Schools." Then make some phone calls requesting information. If you don't know anything about some of these different educational options, find out. Waldorf, charter, and Montessori schools have very definite philosophies behind them, and the specific methods used to teach are quite different from the public schools and each other. I no longer have children in school, but just for my own information, I checked our local phone book to see what was available for elementary school options. We have several religious schools associated with individual denominations, a Montessori school, a Waldorf school, and several different "learning centers." Lots of stuff to investigate!

Beyond Basics

If you'd like to know more about educational options with which you might not be familiar, here are some books to give you additional background:

➤ *Rudolf Steiner Education: The Waldorf Schools,* by Francis Edmonds

➤ *Charter Schools in Action: Renewing Public Education,* by Chester E Finn Jr., Gregg Vanourek, and Bruno V. Manno

➤ *The Montessori Method,* by Maria Montessori

Avoidance Techniques

I said "help" with homework, don't *do* it! Taking an interest is one thing; taking over is another. Children learn by doing things themselves and by making their own mistakes. Make sure you keep your distance but keep in touch.

After you've gotten some grounding in the various options available, also try to find some criticisms of each method and talk to adults who were educated in these systems. Do they feel they got the tools they needed? What do they feel was lacking? What are the general criticisms of the method and what are your specific criticisms based on your idea of a good education?

Teaching at Home

Whether we realize it or not, we're all teaching our kids at home. Our kids learn most from what we do and say. Much of what we may find lacking in our child's school may actually come home to us. We need to decide where the school's responsibility begins and ends and what our role is in educating our child.

My daughters attended public school in the 1970s and '80s. We lived in an affluent Connecticut suburb, but our income was actually only slightly above the poverty level. I was a single parent. One of the reasons I chose this particular community was the schools. Both of my girls were identified as "gifted," and I knew the school system in this town had a highly respected gifted program.

It didn't take long, however, to see that the school could not provide the kind of enrichment I wanted my daughters to have. That was my responsibility, and I took it seriously. Today, one daughter is a naturalist and wildlife biologist, and the other is a copywriter. Both are happily working in their chosen professions. I attribute this to a good fundamental education supplemented by additional experiences and skills taught at home. From my own experience, here are some things you can do to enrich your child's educational experiences at home:

➤ **Do homework together.** My kids often did theirs at the kitchen table while I was preparing dinner. You'll know how much time they're spending, can keep up with what they're learning, and will be able to help when they need it.

➤ **Set up rules about TV and stick to them.** In some houses, it's no TV at all during the week. In others, it's chores and homework before TV. In still other households, there *is* no TV! Whatever you decide, do it early and stick to it.

➤ **Learn along with your kids.** If your kids are studying bugs, find out more about bugs yourself. Use your child's education to improve yours, and you'll enjoy the learning process together.

➤ **Provide tools.** Much of learning comes by accident. It's what I call "following your nose." It helps to have the tools to explore and learn on your own: some good reference books, perhaps a computer and the Internet, and some simple scientific tools like a good magnifying glass, possibly a simple microscope, some binoculars, and maybe even a telescope. (I found mine at a yard sale!) Consider how having tools available at home will enhance what your child is learning in school.

➤ **Provide enriching experiences.** If they're studying the solar system in school, visit a planetarium. Find out what astronomical events might be coming up and plan to observe them together. Look for videos that might add to the information provided in the textbook. Make a model of the solar system together. Not only are you enriching the educational experience, you're spending quality time with your child.

➤ **Challenge your children.** Challenge them to make dull subjects more interesting. Encourage them to do more interesting presentations. Ask them to think outside the ordinary. Ask thought-provoking questions. Present the "other side" in an argument.

➤ **Create a place.** Make sure your child has both the space and the quiet time to explore things on his or her own. Create an area for crafts, reading, outdoor exploration, experiments, and otherwise making a mess.

➤ **Encourage creativity.** Try storytelling, making up songs, writing a play, or building something from scratch.

➤ **Include kids in family decisions.** One way children learn problem solving is by (duh!) solving real problems. Bring kids in on issues you're dealing with and include them when coming up with solutions and ideas. I can't stress enough the importance of the family meeting, and now we see yet another benefit—it's an educational experience!

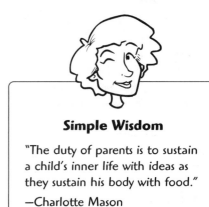

Simple Wisdom

"The duty of parents is to sustain a child's inner life with ideas as they sustain his body with food."

—Charlotte Mason

Quick Starts

To get a good overview of what home-schooling is like and whether it's for you, read *Home-schooling Handbook: From Pre-school to High School: A Parent's Guide* and *The Unschooling Handbook: How to Use the Whole World As Your Child's Classroom*, both by Mary Griffith. In fact, I'd recommend these two books to parents even if you'd just like to learn more about supplementing your child's education at home!

Beyond Basics

The resources on the Internet for both evaluating the home-schooling option and actually teaching your kids at home are enormous. Just type "home-schooling" into your favorite search engine, and you'll see what I mean. About.com is a good starting point for evaluating various methods and finding out about state laws and resources and a host of other things. Point your browser to homeschooling.about.com/education/homeschooling/.

➤ **Learn about the resources your community has to offer and exploit them!** It doesn't have to cost a lot. In fact, there are probably more free things available than you could ever take advantage of. Be aware of people in your neighborhood as resources as well. Help your child find mentors and encourage other kids by being a mentor yourself.

➤ **Make learning a priority.** If learning new things is a priority in your life, your kids will always be learning, too. The most important messages about the value of learning will come from your example.

Teaching kids at home for some goes beyond supplementing a public or private school education. There's a national trend toward home-schooling, and it's no wonder. For the parents who are willing to make the commitment and can arrange their circumstances, home-schooling is an important educational option.

One of the reasons some parents are choosing the simple life is to give this option to their children. By scaling down, spending less, and freeing up more time for what matters, you put more time into educating your children. When my children were in school, home-schooling was unusual and was not too accepted by the mainstream. Today, there are legions of home-schooling parents, some of whom are banding together for support, information, and shared teaching.

Home-schooling is a huge commitment, but then so is parenting. I think if you asked those parents who have made it, many of them would tell you that the rewards make it well worth the sacrifices. Their child's safety, the individual attention they're able to give, the quality of the educational experience, and the opportunity to impart the values a parent feels are important are all benefits to home-schooling. If this is an option you'd like to consider, weigh the pros and cons, research the literature thoroughly, and talk extensively with other home-schooling parents before making your decision.

Teaching Yourself

A discussion of simple living and education wouldn't be complete without at least mentioning self-education and lifelong learning.

One of the main reasons I've chosen my particular lifestyle is so I can continue to learn for the rest of my life. To me, the very essence of simple living is learning. By slowing down, we have time to really look, to think, to read, and to observe the seasons changing and nature's intricacy and splendor. By simplifying our lives, we can concentrate on the inner journey, experiment, grow, question, and find our own answers.

There are many options available to us for continuing the learning process long after we've left the formal education setting. In fact, there's a case to be made for availing ourselves of these options instead of pursuing the usual college degree or vocational training.

Some of these options are new; some of them are simply a rediscovery or new twist on age-old concepts.

One such option, "distance learning," makes use of new technology to study with a professor and other students but from the privacy of your own home and according to a schedule that's convenient to you. College credit courses are available, and even college degrees can be learned through distance learning.

Independent study is usually seen as a way of supplementing or enhancing the curriculum in a formal education setting. I contend that all study is "independent!" Pick a topic that you've always wanted to know more about and design an independent study program around it. When I was in college, I did an independent study project on William Butler Yeats. It led me into all sorts of nooks and crannies I would never have investigated if I'd stuck only to what was being taught in the classroom. The Rosicrucians, the Order of the Golden Dawn, Irish folklore and song, and Celtic history were only a few of the paths I embarked on while working on my project.

If you have a university or college in your area, see if it has a lifelong learning or continuing education program. Again, I see my own life as "continuing education" or "lifelong learning," but if you'd like a more structured setting to work within, check into these programs. Investigate, as well, the Elderhostel program.

Simple Wisdom

"What is a course of history or philosophy, or poetry, no matter how well selected, or the best society, or the most admirable routine of life, compared with the discipline of looking always at what is to be seen? Will you be a reader, a student merely, or a seer? Read your fate, see what is before you, and walk on into futurity."

—Henry David Thoreau

Beyond Basics

A helpful book for you to design your own lifelong education program is *Peak Learning: How to Create Your Own Lifelong Education Program for Personal Enlightenment and Professional Success* by Ronald Gross. For more information on distance learning programs, try *Peterson's Guide to Distance Learning Programs, 2000* (*Peterson's Guide to Distance Learning Programs,* fourth edition).

Elderhostel, Inc. is a not-for-profit organization with 25 years of experience providing high-quality, affordable, and educational adventures for people age 55 and over. They provide short-term educational programs on a wide range of subjects and even international travel experiences. To find out more about the Elderhostel program, visit their Web site at www. elderhostel.org or contact them at 75 Federal Street, Boston, MA 02110-1941 (877-426-8056).

If you enjoy learning with others, consider using a study circle to pursue any interest or subject. If you can find other people who care to learn about the same topic, organize a study circle and you're off. A useful guide on the subject is Leonard Oliver's book *Study Circles: Coming Together for Personal Growth and Social Change.* You can also contact the Study Circles Resource Center at P.O. Box 203, 697 Pomfret St., Pomfret, CT 06258 (860-928-2616; scrc@neca.com).

Another option for group study is starting a book club. Whether it's classic literature or the latest political tome, you can read along together and have a stimulating discussion.

An often-overlooked way to get an education for free is to volunteer! I learned more about Victorian architecture and nineteenth-century American culture as a docent for a house museum than I ever could have learned just in books. I got to see our costume collection firsthand, which was an education in itself, and through the questions and comments of visitors, I learned even more. When we moved to Arizona, I volunteered for a year at a wild animal park. To observe these magnificent animals over long periods of time, particularly the "big cats" that were the park's specialty, was the chance of a lifetime, and I even got to touch and play with three lion cubs for seven months as they were growing up. Priceless. Volunteer and learn!

Simple Living Is Simple Learning

Simpler living demands that we do many things for ourselves. It's a constant learning process that we can share with our kids and our communities.

The Least You Need to Know

➤ Deciding for yourself what makes a "good education" will make options for your child's schooling easier and clearer.

➤ Researching what's wrong with our schools and how to make them better will enable you to enhance your child's educational experience.

➤ Children learn at home regardless of whether you're home-schooling or not.

➤ Learning throughout your life is a fundamental goal and a principle of simple living, and there are lots of resources to help you.

Chapter 22

Future Planet: Living With the Natural Order

In This Chapter

➤ How simple living can help save the environment

➤ Making an environmental audit of your lifestyle

➤ Tips for taking immediate action

➤ Helping you to connect with your own environmental region

➤ Why we should make changing our consciousness the next step

Many of us begin to simplify because we want to improve our own lives. We want out of the rat race, we sense there must be a better way, we long to slow down and "smell the roses." When we start, we may have some sort of vague idea that we're "helping the environment," but perhaps we haven't given it a lot of thought.

As you've no doubt seen throughout the course of this book, simplifying our lives has everything to do with the environment. In each chapter, we've seen how a simpler life means a "lighter" life, and that has a potential impact on our natural resources and our future as a species.

Choosing the simple life enhances our own existence and, in my opinion, is nothing less than one of the great keys to happiness and contentment. But it is a greater choice than we may realize.

Losing Our Ways: The Cost of Estrangement

Many of us have become estranged from our sustainer, our caregiver, the source of all life, our Mother Earth. Without revitalizing that relationship, most environmental scientists say, our future is bleak.

If we separate ourselves from nature, we don't care about it or take care of it. The more we remove ourselves from the planet and insulate ourselves with stuff, the more endangered our home becomes. When we are actually at odds with our own life-sustaining environment—insulated from heat and cold, afraid of bugs and snakes—unknowing becomes uncaring. As the saying goes, "What we fear, we destroy."

Advertisers and marketers try to make us think we can buy nature. Get a sport utility vehicle, buy some camping equipment and the right clothes, sign up for a prepack-aged "outdoor adventure," and you'll experience the wild. Or we watch a television show or a movie or look at a beautifully photographed picture book and think we're experiencing an animal, a river, a mountain.

Avoidance Techniques

Watch out for the "consuming the environment" trap. Buying all sorts of gear to get closer to na-ture defeats the purpose. At the same time, be sensible and have with you the protective clothing, water, and other things you need to take care of yourself.

The truth is, these are all substitutes for experience, and they can easily waste our precious time, consume our cash, and keep us from experiencing the real thing. Actually, all you have to do is walk out your door on a regular basis, watch the sun rise, notice the stars, grow things, watch the seasons change. It's a smaller, more delicate, everyday "noticing" that teaches us what nature actually is.

We begin to notice how the machines we use to save us from work drown out the sounds of the people in our lives or the birds singing outside our window—perhaps even the "sounds" of our own inner voices.

When I was a little girl, I remember how my grandfa-ther, who lived on the water, kept a small record book in his pocket as well as a pencil he kept sharpened with his pocket knife. He noted every day when the sun rose and set, when the tide was low, and when it was high. He recorded the dates when his raspberries became ripe. He took note of where each of his crab traps was located and the catch in each. And along with these seemingly mundane observations were a record of the births and deaths of friends and family, phrases about storms and sunny days, and a mention of what he considered to be important occasions. He noticed. Slowing down and getting rid of clutter, freeing ourselves of the bondage of debt, and spending time doing what's important to us helps us notice.

There can be a cause for optimism amidst the darkness. Duane Elgin believes that voluntary simplicity can be an important part of coping with the current crisis and embracing "reconciliation and transition." In his book *Awakening Earth: Exploring the Evolution of Human Culture and Consciousness,* Elgin looks for an important synergy between the Western materialist view of the universe and the Eastern transcendental view, both of which promote a disconnection from nature. He calls this synergy "coevolution," which he believes is a middle path with the potential for global change.

Elgin acknowledges that simple living isn't the cure-all for all of the ills of the planet. "The problems generated by the past two centuries of industrialization cannot be suddenly erased," he says. "Our challenge is to rise to the occasion and begin, in earnest, the process of revitalizing our faltering industrial civilizations."

In some ways, the simple life makes it easier and clearer to see what needs to be done—what *can* be done. While we're making more conscious choices on a personal level, then working locally on a more human scale, we become aware of trends, shifts, and opportunities for change in the larger arena. We can't go back to a simpler time. We must go forward and build one.

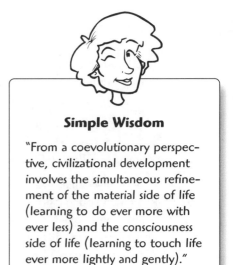

Simple Wisdom

"From a coevolutionary perspective, civilizational development involves the simultaneous refinement of the material side of life (learning to do ever more with ever less) and the consciousness side of life (learning to touch life ever more lightly and gently)."

—Duane Elgin

How Much Can We Do?

In the face of what we see around us as we connect more with our environment, we can feel overwhelmed, depressed, even paralyzed. But by slowing down, we will begin to see a path. By reducing the clutter in our lives, both physical and mental, we can start to see what's important. By living consciously, we can notice everything we do and begin to think about what the impact will be on the planet and on other people. Simple living creates the context for greater social change.

As you must know by now, my approach to almost any problem is first to take stock. By starting where you are, facing what exists, and then evaluating what needs to be done, you're less likely to go off in the wrong direction or waste your efforts. We have control over the choices we make every day. We decide how much energy we use and in what form. We decide how much or how little we consume and make choices about those products. Choices involving housing, work, diet, health, recreation, family, and community involvement are all ours to make. In the end, these individual choices multiplied many times over may decide whether our species survives the twenty-first century.

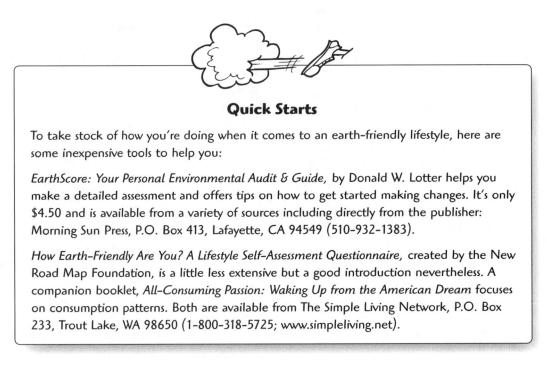

Quick Starts

To take stock of how you're doing when it comes to an earth-friendly lifestyle, here are some inexpensive tools to help you:

EarthScore: Your Personal Environmental Audit & Guide, by Donald W. Lotter helps you make a detailed assessment and offers tips on how to get started making changes. It's only $4.50 and is available from a variety of sources including directly from the publisher: Morning Sun Press, P.O. Box 413, Lafayette, CA 94549 (510-932-1383).

How Earth-Friendly Are You? A Lifestyle Self-Assessment Questionnaire, created by the New Road Map Foundation, is a little less extensive but a good introduction nevertheless. A companion booklet, *All-Consuming Passion: Waking Up from the American Dream* focuses on consumption patterns. Both are available from The Simple Living Network, P.O. Box 233, Trout Lake, WA 98650 (1-800-318-5725; www.simpleliving.net).

So, what can you do starting right now? Here are a few reminders:

➤ **No more plastic bags!** Get or make yourself some canvas tote bags and keep them in your car. Get in the habit of carrying at least one with you wherever you go. You'll be amazed how quickly this simple act on a consistent basis cuts down on waste and a constant eyesore on our countryside.

➤ **No more disposable cups!** This might be a little tougher to do consistently, but if you regularly buy coffee before work, bring your own mug. I even bring a mug when I travel, and when I go down to the motel lobby for free morning coffee, I bring it with me. It's a small thing, but over the course of one stay, I save several cups. Many stays, many cups.

➤ **Opt out of fast food and join the "slow food" movement!** Cook at home or eat at restaurants that don't use disposables. You'll be healthier and will create less waste.

➤ **Examine your driving habits.** Keep track of how much you drive and honestly ask each time "Is this trip really necessary?" Decide on changes you can make immediately and over time to cut down on driving time. You'll save time and money, too.

➤ **Take steps to lower your family's energy consumption.** Turn off lights, lower the thermostat in the winter, insulate and seal leaks, turn down the water heater, dry clothes on the line outdoors—make a list of the things you will commit to do personally to conserve. You'll be economizing while, at the same time, adding to the funds you'll have to apply to getting out of debt!

➤ **Keep tabs on consumption.** Follow the suggestions in this book and those I've recommended and buy only what you really need. When you need to make a purchase, make it one of sufficient quality to last a long time and, whenever possible, buy used.

➤ **Act locally.** By spending money in your own community, you lower energy costs and keep resources at home. Find local efforts to protect the environment and make a commitment to help.

➤ **Commit to finding more ways to live a more earth-friendly lifestyle.** Don't try to make too many changes all at once; you'll become frustrated and give up. Try committing to one thing a week. Define it, schedule it, do it, and make sure to give yourself a pat on the back.

➤ **Work with others to stay on track.** Recruit your simplicity circle, church group, study group, neighbors, friends, or family to join with you to live a more earth-friendly lifestyle. You'll make even more of a difference and will help each other stay on track.

Simple Wisdom

"Never doubt that a small group of thoughtful, committed citizens can change the world. Indeed, it is the only thing that ever has."

—Margaret Mead

➤ **Make it bigger.** Look for ways to change practices on a larger scale in organizations in which you participate. If you own a business, belong to a church or community group, or work in a corporation or school, lobby to make changes that will be multiplied many times over. Something as simple as using washable cups at a business or community meeting makes a big difference over time and interrupts the usual unconscious patterns.

I Thought You Said This Was Simple!

Making strides to turn the tide and reclaim the planet for a positive future is no simple matter. I wish it were. I'm optimistic, and I think there's hope that a widespread shift in perception and behavior is slowly taking place While we're working on the things we can do something about, such as consumption and waste, we can also be working on our own awareness of and connection to the earth and that of our neighbors. From that new awareness, the daily decisions become easier, the path clearer, and the possibilities for real change greater.

But how can you care about something you don't know very much about? If the closest you get to nature is through the window of your car on a Sunday drive, how can you experience the urgency to protect it? Yet, if someone was digging up your yard, throwing sewage in your driveway, and pouring smoke into your house, you know you'd be up in arms. That's because you're intimately connected with where you live. If we can learn to broaden that connection to the earth as our home, the motivation and the will to work to save it will grow as well.

What can you do to strengthen your connection to nature and to learn more about your earthly home? Start by taking "The Bioregional Quiz." Don't worry, I didn't know the answers either, but I'm working on it! I've paraphrased some of the questions and have added some from other sources:

Beyond Basics

Parts of this quiz originally appeared in the *Coevolution Quarterly* and were then reprinted in the book *Home! A Bioregional Reader,* by Van Andruss, Christopher Plant, Judith Plant, and Eleanor Wright. The book is out of print, but you may be able to find it in a used-book store or your local library. Learn more about bioregions and become familiar with the one you live in. You can take better care of something you understand!

➤ When you turn on your faucet, where does the water come from? Can you trace it from precipitation to the tap?

➤ What was the total precipitation in your area last year?

➤ When you flush the toilet, to what body of water does that effluent go?

➤ What happens to your garbage? At what point will the current landfill be full? Then what?

➤ From where you are sitting, point north.

➤ How many days until the moon is full? When is the new moon?

➤ What plant or animal is the barometer of environmental health for your bioregion? How is it doing?

➤ What kind of soil is predominant in your area? What kind of soil is on your own property? What grows best in it?

➤ What gardening zone are you in and how long is the outdoor growing season?

➤ Name five edible native plants in your region and when they're available for harvest. Name five medicinal plants in your region and when they're available. What are they used for? You might also want to include native grasses and wildflowers.

➤ Name five birds found in your area during the summer months. Which ones are migratory?

➤ What was your area like 50 years ago? 100 years ago? 200 years ago?

➤ Is there any designated wilderness in your bioregion? What pressures are there on this area? Have you ever visited it?

➤ What are the main geological events or forces that helps shape the land? Was there water covering it at one time? Ice? Volcanic ash?

I'll bet you could come up with another 10 questions or more to add to this questionnaire. This is a project to work on over time and is a fantastic one to do with kids. You may find yourself wanting to share the information-gathering process with a local school or community group or just a group of interested friends.

Get to know what's just outside your door. Walk and keep walking until you know your own home. If you begin to know the trees by name, if you notice which birds appear year round and which ones migrate to other climates, if you observe the health of your rivers and streams from day to day, you'll soon see your actions in a new light. You'll see how these relate to the turn of a faucet, the flush of a toilet, or the flick of a switch. If you change your definition of "home" to include what's outside your four walls, you'll begin to understand, and with understanding there can be change.

Starting Here, Starting Now

I don't know what the answers are, but I know I want to work daily on being less a part of the problem. It's hard to get my mind and heart around the enormity of it sometimes. At times, I'm not sure what to do or if what I am doing is really making a difference. By reading, looking for good teachers, making my own observations, and practicing my spiritual path, I believe I can have an impact. Simplifying my life allows me to find time to strike this balance between concrete action and a search for meaning.

Your reasons for simplifying your life may not be the same as mine. What matters is that you're clear about what you want to do and why. The benefits in your own life will lead you to the next steps for you. As you work your plan, all I ask is that you check in with your "Mother" now and then.

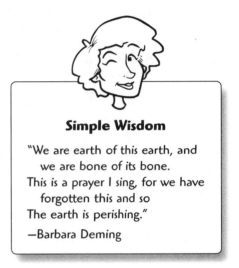

Simple Wisdom

"We are earth of this earth, and we are bone of its bone.
This is a prayer I sing, for we have forgotten this and so
The earth is perishing."

—Barbara Deming

Beyond Basics

The book *Let the Mountains Talk, Let the Rivers Run: A Call to Those Who Would Save the Earth* is no less than an outline of how to save the planet by David Brower, one of the elder statesmen in the ecology movement. Brower, controversial founder of Friends of the Earth and Earth Island Institute, reviews the successes and defeats of the past and poses a sensible plan for the future.

The Least You Need to Know

➤ The simple life puts us in a better position to reconnect with nature.

➤ There are some simple steps we can take to live more "earth-friendly."

➤ Besides taking concrete actions to live more in harmony with the environment, there needs to be a shift in consciousness as well.

➤ Learning more about our own bioregion and acting locally is the place to start.

Chapter 23

What's Rich? Defining Wealth for the Simple Life

In This Chapter

➤ The relationship between simple living and prosperity

➤ Redefining wealth so that it becomes an attainable goal

➤ Rediscovering generosity, stewardship, and philanthropy as the uses of our new-found wealth

Throughout this book, we've been taking a second look at how we define wealth for ourselves. We've taken steps to demystify money and divest it of the attributes we can only find in ourselves. We've talked about the concept of "enough" and how the fewer material goods we determine we need, the freer and more abundant life becomes.

Creating Prosperity

A funny thing often happens while living a simpler life—we experience abundance. It's not unusual for this abundance to include material success. Historically, groups that practiced simplicity, such as the Puritans and the Quakers, created wealth in spite of themselves. When we live within our means, find work we love and give it our passion, seek harmony and balance in our daily lives, and give back to our community, we create the conditions for success and prosperity.

Competition and greed are actually born out of a basic belief that there is never "enough," a sense of scarcity and insecurity that says, if we don't grab our share, someone else will have more and we'll be without. The shift in consciousness to the perception of an abundant universe that provides for the basic needs of all life often manifests itself in an accumulation of wealth.

In the philosophy of simplicity, wealth is not an end in itself, but when you work hard you often succeed and become prosperous, and there is a responsibility that comes with prosperity. I submit that it's our responsibility is to share our prosperity and do good. Simplicity also gives us the assets of time and energy to share.

Definitions for a New Age

If we redefine wealth as "having enough," then we are free to use any excess to care for our fellow man and to help heal the planet. Three ways we can do this are through generosity, stewardship, and philanthropy.

Generosity

> **gen er ous:** noble-minded, magnanimous; willing to give or share; unselfish; large; ample

When we have enough, we can afford to be generous. The pleasure of helping someone do something they really want to do, of giving a much-deserved gift, of lending a helping hand during a crisis adds richness to life. This is a direct act of sharing our abundance with others. It is often spontaneous and intimate.

Stewardship

> **stew ard ship:** (environmental science) the care of natural areas with an eye toward preservation

When we live in abundance, we take care of what surrounds us. We replenish, restore, and preserve. We're interested in managing our assets for future generations. Stewardship is often associated with churches and fundraising, but it has a deeper meaning—responsible management and use of our divine gifts, taking care of what we have, and sharing it with others. We are not owners of our wealth but stewards.

Philanthropy

phi lan thro py: a desire to help mankind

Once we've taken care of our basic needs and have provided for the future, we can invest our wealth in the greater good. To some extent, I believe the substitution of government programs for charitable works has left us impoverished. Caring for those less fortunate has become centralized in big government rather than being left as a function of local communities making direct contact with those in need among us.

Money isn't the "root of all evil," the *love* of money is! By knowing what constitutes "enough" and accepting the responsibility of being our brother's keeper, money becomes a tool for a positive future instead of creating an ever-widening gap between the "haves" and the "have nots."

For this to happen, we not only have to redefine wealth, we need to re-establish community and both individual responsibility and a duty to provide for those who cannot provide for themselves.

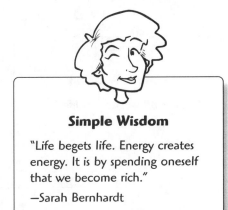

Simple Wisdom

"Life begets life. Energy creates energy. It is by spending oneself that we become rich."

—Sarah Bernhardt

Beyond Basics

If you doubt the power of individuals and organizations to work toward a more caring, compassionate society, find yourself a copy of the book *A Call for Connection: Solutions for Creating a Whole New Culture,* by Gail Bernice Holland. Holland offers concrete examples of individuals and organizations that make up what she says is a cultural movement emphasizing integrity, compassion, and spirituality. The book includes a 60-page resource guide that lists nonprofit organizations actively working to improve all areas of society.

When we redefine wealth to be "enough" rather than "more than enough," we can begin to see abundance as something accessible to everyone. A further revision in our definition of wealth expands it to take in the whole person. Just as health must encompass the whole person—physical, mental, and spiritual—so must our definition of wealth expand to be truly useful. How can we be wealthy if we have plenty in one area but are impoverished in another?

Simple Wisdom

"There is no wealth but life."

—John Ruskin

Beyond Simple Living

As you work though this book and make fundamental changes to simplify your life, I hope you'll look for ways to share with others the abundance that's sure to follow. As I've said before, simple living is a spiritual path, and whatever shape that takes for you, I believe it will be full of rewards.

There will be obstacles, without a doubt, but anything worth achieving requires diligence and hard work. May your efforts be blessed with the joys of sharing simple pleasures with those you love.

The Least You Need to Know

➤ Since simple living means living in abundance, it often creates material prosperity that can then be used to do good.

➤ We can redefine wealth to mean "having enough" and to include the whole person.

➤ Generosity, stewardship, and philanthropy are appropriate uses of wealth that benefit society as a whole.

Resource Guide

Here in one place are all the resources I've found to help you develop your own simple living plan. I've organized them by chapter to make it easier to refer to them as you're reading, and I've repeated some items mentioned in the chapters so you'd have the information all in one handy reference.

Chapter 1: Consuming Passions: How the World Got Un-Simple

Books

The Complete Idiot's Guide to Organizing Your Life, Second Edition, by Georgene Lockwood, Alpha Books, 1999; ISBN 0028633822.

Four Arguments for the Elimination of Television, by Jerry Mander, William Morrow & Co., 1978; ISBN 0688082742.

The Overspent American, by Juliet B. Schor, HarperPerennial, 1998; ISBN 0060977582.

Booklets

EarthScore: You Personal Environmental Audit & Guide, by Donald W. Lotter is available from a variety of sources including direct from the publisher: Morning Sun Press, P.O. Box 413, Lafayette, CA 94549; 510-932-1383.

How Earth-Friendly Are You? A Lifestyle Self-Assessment Questionnaire and *All-Consuming Passion: Waking Up from the American Dream* are available from The Simple Living Network, P.O. Box 233, Trout Lake, WA 98650; 1-800-318-5725; www.simpleliving. net.

Videos

Affluenza and *Escape from Affluenza* can be ordered from Bullfrog films at www. bullfrogfilms.com/catalog/affl.html.

Web Sites

PBS's Affluenza: www.pbs.org/kcts/affluenza/home.html

Chapter 2: Simplicity and the Spirit

Books

Migrations to Solitude: The Quest for Privacy in a Crowded World, by Sue Halpern, Vintage, 1993; ISBN 0679742417.

Pilgrim at Tinker Creek, by Annie Dillard, HarperPerennial Library, 1998; ISBN 0060953020.

Simple Abundance: A Daybook of Comfort and Joy, by Sarah Ban Breathnach, Warner Books, 1995.

The Complete Idiot's Guide to Meditation, by Joan and Eve Adamson Budiloysky, Alpha Books, 1998.

The Artist's Way: A Spiritual Path to Higher Creativity, by Julia Cameron, Jeremy P. Tarcher/Putnam, 1992; ISBN 0874776945.

The Best Guide to Meditation, by Victor N. Davich, Audio Renaissance, 1998; ISBN 1580630103.

Journey to the Center: A Meditation Workbook, by Matthew Flickstein, Wisdom Publications, 1998.

A Trail Through Leaves: The Journal As a Path to Place, by Hannah Hinchman, W.W. Norton & Company, 1999.

Breathe Deep, Laugh Loudly: The Joy of Transformational Breathing, by Peter Murray, 1999; ISBN 1929271018.

Nature Journaling: Learning to Observe and Connect with the World Around You, by Walker Leslie and Charles E. Roth, Storey Books, 1998; ISBN 1580170889.

Choices: Making Right Decisions in a Complex World, by Lewis B. Smedes, Harper San Francisco, 1991; ISBN 0060674113.

Chapter 3: What's Old Is New Again

Books

The Good Life, by Helen and Scott Nearing, Schocken Books, Inc., 1989; ISBN 0805209700 (contains *Living the Good Life* and *Continuing the Good Life* in one volume).

Loving and Leaving the Good Life, by Helen Nearing, Chelsea Green Publishing, 1992; ISBN 0930031636.

Simple Food for the Good Life: Random Acts of Cooking and Pithy Quotations, by Helen Nearing, Chelsea Green Publishing Company, 1980; ISBN 1890132292.

The Simple Life: Plain Living and High Thinking in American Culture, by David E. Shi, Oxford University Press, 1985; ISBN 0195040130.

Walden and Other Writings of Henry David Thoreau, by Henry David Thoreau, Modern Library, 1992; ISBN 0679600043.

Web Sites

A Thoreau site with lots of links: //miso.wwa.com/~jej/1thorea.html.

Chapter 4: Culture Shock: Lessons from Alternative Living

Books

Amish Home, by Raymond Bial, Houghton Mifflin Company, 1993; ISBN 0395720214.

The Amish in Their Own Words, compiled by Brad Igou, Herald Press, 1999; ISBN 0836191234.

Is It Utopia Yet?: An Insider's View of Twin Oaks Community in Its Twenty-Sixth Year, by Kat Kincade, Twin Oaks Publishing, 1994; ISBN 0964044501.

The Plain Reader: Essays on Making a Simple Life, edited by Scott Savage, The Ballentine Publishing Group, 1998; ISBN 0345414349.

Simple Gifts: Lessons in Living from a Shaker Village, by June Sprigg, Vintage Books, 1998; ISBN0375704329.

Walden Two, by B. F. Skinner, Allyn & Bacon, 1976; ISBN 002411510X.

Magazines

Communities: A Journal of Cooperative Liivng,
138-W Twin Oaks Road
Louisa, VA 23093
fic.ic.org/cmag/subscribe.html

Organizations

Twin Oaks Community
138 Twin Oaks Road
Louisa, VA 23093
Phone: 520-894-5126
Fax: 540-894-4112
E-mail: twinoaks@ic.org
www.twinoaks.org

Web Sites

Pennsylvania Dutch: www.800padutch.com/mem-cat.shtml

Ohio Amish: www.amish-heartland.com

Discovery's visit with an Amish family:
www.discovery.com/area/exploration/amish/amish1.html

Chapter 5: Finding Your Own Simple Living Way

Books

Voluntary Simplicity: Toward a Way of Life That Is Outwardly Simple, Inwardly Rich, by Duane Elgin, Quill, 1993; ISBN 0688121195.

The 7 Habits of Highly Effective People: Powerful Lessons in Personal Change, by Steven Covey, Fireside, 1990; ISBN 0671708635.

The Path: Creating Your Mission Statement for Work and for Life, by Laurie Beth Jones, Hyperion, 1998; ISBN 0786882417.

Wishcraft: How to Get What You Really Want, by Barbara Sher with Annie Gottlieb, Ballantine Books, 1986; ISBN 034530892.

How to Get Control of Your Time and Your Life, by Alan Lakein, New American Library, 1996; ISBN 0451167724.

Chapter 6: Going Debtless: How to Gain Your Freedom

Books

Your Money or Your Life, by Joe Dominguez and Vicki Robin, Penguin USA, 1999; ISBN 0140286780.

The 9 Steps to Financial Freedom: Practical and Spiritual Steps So You Can Stop Worrying, by Suze Orman, Crown Publishing, 1997; ISBN 0517707918.

Debt-Proof Living, by Mary Hunt, Broadman & Holman Publishers, 1999; ISBN 0805420789.

Newsletters

Cheapskate Monthly Online
P.O. Box 2076
Paramount, CA 90723
www.cheapskatemonthly.com

Organizations

Consumer Credit Counseling Service
1-888-GO2-CCCS (1-800-462-2227)
www.credit.org

Chapter 7: Earning a Life, not Just a Living

Books

Working Alone: Making the Most of Self-Employment, by Murray Felsher, Berkley
   Publishing Group, 1996; ISBN 0425152642.

*Working from Home: Everything You Need to Know About Living and Working Under the
   Same Roof,* by Paul and Sarah Edwards, J. P. Tarcher, 1999; ISBN 0874779766.

Chapter 8: Location, Location! The Simple Truth About Where You Live

Books

*How to Start and Operate Your Own Bed-And-Breakfast/Down-To-Earth Advice from an
   Award-Winning B&B Owner,* by Martha Watson Murphy, Owlet, 1994; ISBN
   0805029036.

Cities Back from the Edge: New Life for Downtown, by Roberta Brandes Gratz with
   Norman Mintz, John Wiley & Sons, 2000; ISBN 0471361240.

Country Bound! Trade Your Business Suit for Blue Jean Dreams, by Marilyn and Tom Ross,
   Upstart Publishing Co, 1997; ISBN 1574100696.

The Encyclopedia of Country Living, by Carla Emery, Sasquatch Books, 1994; ISBN
   0912365951.

Green Urbanism: Learning from European Cities, by Timothy Beatley, Island Press, 2000;
   ISBN 1559636823.

*The Urban/Suburban Composter: The Complete Guide to Backyard, Balcony, and Apartment
   Composting,* by Mark Cullen and Lorraine Johnson, St. Martin's Press, 1992, ISBN
   0312105304.

Web Sites

University of Florida's Online Composting Center: www.compostinfo.com

Economic Research Institute: www.erieri.com

Green City Project of San Francisco: www.green-city.org

Chapter 9: How Living With Less Can Mean More

Books

How Much Is Enough?: The Consumer Society and the Future of the Earth, by Alan Durning, W.W. Norton & Co, 1992; ISBN 039330891X.

How to Want What You Have: Discovering the Magic and Grandeur of Ordinary Existence, by Timothy Miller, Avon Books, 1996 ; ISBN 0380726823.

Organizations

Stop Junk Mail Association
c/o 3020 Bridgeway, Suite 150
Sausalito, CA 94965
1-800-827-5549

Chapter 10: In the Independent Republic of Finances

Books

Healthmate Medical Planner: A Practical Guide for Taking Control of Your Health and Having Your Medical Records Always Available—Even When Your Doctor Isn't, by Kathleen Deremer, Six Ponies Press, 1997; ISBN 0965635058.

The Simple Living Guide: A Sourcebook for Less Stressful, More Joyful Living, by Janet Luhrs, Broadway Books, 1997; ISBN 0553067966.

Booklets

For IRS publication number 552, "Recordkeeping for Individuals," call 1-800-829-3676.

Organizations

Equifax
P.O. Box 105496
Atlanta, GA 30348-54961
1-800-997-2493
www.econsumer.equifax.com/equifax.app/Welcome

Experian
National Consumer Assistance Center
P.O. Box 2104
Allen, TX 75013-2104
1-888-397-3742
www.experian.com/customer/mail.html

Trans Union Corporation
P.O. Box 2000
Chester, PA 19022
1-800-888-4213
www.tuc.com

National Association of Investors Corporation (NAIC)
P.O. Box 220
Royal Oak, MI 48068
1-877-ASK-NAIC (1-877-275-6242)
www.better-investing.org.

Software

Health-Minder: www.health-minder.com

Web Sites

CNET shareware.com

U.S. Disaster Preparedness Council: www.usdpc.net/finplan.htm.

Chapter 11: Food Fancy: You *Are* What You Eat!

Books

Cooking Like a Goddess: Bringing Seasonal Magic into the Kitchen, by Cait Johnson, Inner Traditions Int'l. Ltd., 1998; ISBN 0892817399.

Diet for a Small Planet, by Francis Moore Lappé, Ballantine Books, 1992; ISBN 0345321200.

Dining in the Raw, by Rita Romano, Kensington Publishing Corp, 1997; ISBN 1575661926.

Edible and Medicinal Plants of the West, by Gregory Tilford, Mountain Press Publishing Company, 1997; ISBN 0878423591.

The New Enchanted Broccoli Forest, by Molly Katzen, Ten Speed Press, 2000; ISBN 1580081266.

A Field Guide to Edible Wild Plants of Eastern and Central North America, by Lee Peterson, Houghton Mifflin Co, 1999; ISBN 039592622X.

The Green Kitchen Handbook: Practical Advice, References, and Sources for Transforming the Center of Your Home into a Healthful, Livable Place, by Annie Berthold-Bond, HarperCollins, 1997; ISBN 0060951869.

Home Made: Recipes from the Nineteenth Century, by Sandra Oddo, Antheneum, 1972; ISBN 0883652501.

Making the Best of Basics: Family Preparedness Handbook, by James Talmage Stevens, Gold Leaf Press, 1997; ISBN 1882723252.

The New Laurel's Kitchen, by Laurel Robertson, Carol Flinders and Brian Ruppenthal, Ten Speed Press, 1986; ISBN 089815166X.

The New Moosewood Cookbook, by Molly Katzen, Ten Speed Press, 2000; ISBN 1580081304.

Once-a-Month Cooking, by Mimi Wilson and Mary Beth Lagerborg, Thomas Nelson, 1994; ISBN 1561792462.

Recipes for a Small Planet, by Ellen Buchman Ewald, Ballantine Books, 1983; ISBN 0345324927.

Simple Food for the Good Life, by Helen Nearing, Chelsea Green Publishing Co., 1999; ISBN: 1890132292.

The Tassajara Bread Book, by Edward Espe Brown, Shambhala Publications, 1995; ISBN 157062089X.

Tassajara Cooking, by Edward Espe Brown, Shambhala Publications, 1973; ISBN 0394741935.

Wheat-Free Recipes and Menus: Delicious Dining Without Wheat or Gluten, by Carol Fenster, Savory Palate, 1997; ISBN 1889374059.

The Wild Food Gourmet: Fresh and Savory Food from Nature, by Anne Gardon, Firefly Books, 1998; ISBN 1552092429.

Booklets

Are You Ready? Your Family Disaster Supplies Kit and *Emergency Food and Water Supplies* is provided by the Federal Emergency Management Agency (FEMA), P.O. Box 70274, Washington, DC 20024; www.fema.gov/fema/.

Web Sites

Colorado State Cooperative Extension food publications: www.colostate.edu/Depts/CoopExt/PUBS/FOODNUT/pubfood.html

Sprouting information: www.sproutpeople.com/

Once-a-Month Cooking: members.aol.com/OAMCLoop/index.html

Chapter 12: Fashion: Trends or Tyranny?

Books

Natural Body Basics: Making Your Own Cosmetics, by Dorie Byers, Gooseberry Hill Publications, 1996; ISBN 0965235300.

Natural Beauty at Home: More Than 200 Easy-To-Use Recipes for Body, Bath, and Hair, by Janice Cox, Henry Holt, 1995; ISBN 0805033130.

Always in Style, by Doris Pooser, Crisp Publications, 1997; ISBN 1560524138.

Flatter Your Figure, by Jan Larkey, Simon & Schuster, 1992; ISBN 0671762966.

Gladrags: Redesigning, Remaking, Refitting All Your Old Clothes, by Delia Brock and Lorraine Bodger, Simon & Schuster, 1974; ISBN 0671217968.

How to Recycle Old Clothes into New Fashions, by Fenya Crown, Prentice-Hall, 1977; ISBN0134308190.

Jeanne Rose's Herbal Body Book, by Jeanne Rose, Frog Ltd., 2000; ISBN 1583940049.

Jeanne Rose's Kitchen Cosmetics: Using Herbs, Fruit, & Flowers for Natural Bodycare, by Jeanne Rose, North Atlantic Books, 1991; ISBN 1556431015.

Looking Good: A Comprehensive Guide to Wardrobe Planning, Color & Personal Style Development by Nancy Nix-Rice and Pati Palmer, Palmer Pletsch Publishing, 1996; ISBN 0935278427.

Simple Isn't Easy: How to Find Your Personal Style and Look Fantastic Every Day, by Olivia Goldsmith and Amy Fine Collins, Harper Mass Market Paperbacks, 1997; ISBN 0061093947.

The Yestermorrow Clothes Book: How to Remodel Secondhand Clothes, by Diana Funaro, Chilton Book Co., 1976; ISBN 0801964083.

Web Sites

About Face: about-face.org

ABE Books (used book search): www.abebooks.com/

Chapter 13: Seeking Shelter and Keeping House

Books

Better Homes and Gardens Attics: Your Guide to Planning and Remodeling, Better Homes & Gardens Books, 1999; ISBN 0696209144.

Better Homes and Gardens Basements: Your Guide to Planning and Remodeling, Better Homes & Gardens Books, 1999; ISBN 0696208970.

Better Homes and Gardens Remodeling Your Home, Multicom Publishing, 1996; ISBN 1888313005.

Be Your Own Home Renovation Contractor, by Carl Heldman, Storey Books, 1998; ISBN 1580170242.

Builders of the Dawn: Community Lifestyles in a Changing World, by Corinne McLaughlin and Gordon Davidson, Book Publishing Co, 1990; ISBN 091399068X.

Cohousing: A Contemporary Approach to Housing Ourselves, by Kathryn McCamant and Charles Durrett, Ten Speed Press, 1993; ISBN 0898155398.

Communities Directory: A Guide to Intentional Communities and Cooperative Living, Fellowship for Intentional Community, 2000; ISBN 0960271481.

House Mates: A Guide to Cooperative Shared Housing, by Lori Stephens, Verbatim Publishing, 1997; ISBN 0965883507.

Making the Most of Small Spaces, by Anoop Parikh, Rizzoli Bookstore, 1994; ISBN 0847818012.

The New Apartment Book, by Michele Michael (with Wendy S. Israel), Clarkson Potter, 1996; ISBN 0517887592.

Catalogs

Real Goods
1-800-762-7325
www.realgoods.com.

Magazines

Natural Home
201 E. Fourth Street
Loveland, CO 80537-5633
www.naturalhomemagazine.com.

Communities
"The Journal of Cooperative Living,"
138-W Twin Oaks Road
Louisa, VA 23093
540-894-5798 or 1-800-462-8240
fic.ic.org/cmag/subscribe.html

Web Sites

Department of Energy "Consumer Energy Information Home Page":
www.eren.doe.gov/consumerinfo

American Council for an Energy-Efficient Economy: aceee.org

The Cohousing Network: www.cohousing.org

Chapter 14: Getting Off the Grid: Is It for You?

Books

Cooking with the Sun: How to Build and Use Solar Cookers, by Beth Halacy and Dan Halacy, Morning Sun Press, 1992; ISBN 0962906921.

Cooking the Dutch Oven Way, by Woody Woodruff, Ellen Anderson, and Jane Woodruff, Globe Pequot Press, 2000; ISBN 0762706694.

Cottage Water Systems: An Out-of-the City Guide to Pumps, Plumbing, Water Purification, and Privies, by Max Burns, Cottage Life Books, 1993; ISBN: 096969220X.

The Easy Guide to Solar Electric: For Home Power Systems, by Adi Pieper, A D I Solar Electric, 1999; ISBN 0967189101.

The Home Water Supply: How to Find, Filter, Store, and Conserve It, by Stu Campbell, Storey Books, 1983; ISBN 0882663240.

How to Live Without Electricity and Like It, by Anita Evangelista, Breakout Productions, 1998; ISBN 0966693213.

The Humanure Handbook: A Guide to Composting Human Manure, by Joseph A. Jenkins, Jenkins Publishing, 1999; ISBN 0964425890.

Root Cellaring: Natural Cold Storage of Fruits and Vegetables, by Mike and Nancy Bubel, Storey Books, 1991; ISBN 0882667033.

Catalogs

Cumberland General Store
1-800-334-4630

Emergency Essentials
1-800-999-1863
www.beprepared.com

Jade Mountain
1-800-442-1972
www.jademountain.com

Lehman's Non-Electric catalog
330-857-5757
www.lehmans.com

REI
1-800-426-4840
www.rei.com

Magazines

Back Home Magazine
Wordsworth Communications
110 Third Ave. West
Hendersonville, NC 28792

Backwoods Home Magazine
P.O. Box 712
Gold Beach, OR 97444
541-247-8900

Countryside & Small Stock Journal
W11564 Hwy 64
Withee WI 54498
715-785-7979 or 1-800-551-5691
E-mail: csymag@midway.tds.net
www.countrysidemag.com

Home Power Magazine
1-800-707-6585
E-mail: subscription@homepower.com
www.homepower.com

Kitchen Gardener
The Taunton Press, Inc.
63 South Main Street
P.O. Box 5506
Newtown, CT 06470
1-800-888-8286
www.taunton.com/kg

The Mother Earth News
P.O. Box 56302
Boulder, CO 80322-6302
1-800-234-3368
www.motherearthnews.com

Web Sites

Rainwater collection systems: www.cityfarmer.org/rainbarrel72.html

Xenia and Basil Arrick's Homesteading and Simple Living site: www.homestead.org/water.htm.

Solar cooking site: www.solarcooking.org

The Root Cellar Home page sponsored by Walton Feed: www.lis.ab.ca/walton/old/cellar.html

American Solar Energy Society: www.ases.org

Chapter 15: Rethinking Getting from Here to There

Books

Active Woman Vacation Guide, by Evelyn Kaye, Blue Panda Publications, 1997; ISBN 0962623180.

Bike Cult: The Ultimate Guide to Human-Powered Vehicles, by David B. Perry, Four Walls Eight Windows, 1995; ISBN 1568580274.

Car Talk: With Click and Clack, The Tappet Brothers, by Tom and Ray Magliozzi, Dell Books, 1991; ISBN 0440503647.

Drive It Forever: Secrets to Long Automobile Life, by Bob Sikorsy, Atg Media, 1997; ISBN 0965757706.

Eco-Vacations: Enjoy Yourself and Save the Earth, by Evelyn Kaye, Blue Panda Publications, 1995; ISBN 0962623113.

Family Travel: Terrific New Vacations for Today's Families, by Evelyn Kaye, Blue Panda Publications, 1993; ISBN 096262313X.

Free Vacations and Bargain Adventures in the USA, by Evelyn Kaye, Blue Panda Publications, 1998; ISBN 0962623199.

The Haynes Bicycle Book: The Haynes Repair Manual for Maintaining and Repairing Your Bike (Haynes Automotive Repair Manual Series), by Bob Henderson and J. Stevenson, Haynes Publications, 1995; ISBN 1563921375.

Living More with Less, by Doris Janzen Longacre, Herald Press, 1980; ISBN 0836119304.

Travel and Learn: Where to Go for Everything You'd Love to Know, by Evelyn Kaye, Blue Panda Publications, 1994; ISBN 0962623156.

Magazines

Consumer Reports
1-800-208-9696
www.consumerreports.org

Organizations

Auto Safety Hotline
1-800-424-9393
www.nhtsa.dot.gov/cars/problems/index.html
To report a problem: 1-888-327-4236

Web Sites

Bykaboose: www.bykaboose.com; 1-800-441-9163

Cycletote: www.cycletote.com; 1-800-747-2407

Equinox: www.efn.org/~equinox; 1-800-942-7895

Bicycle Helmet Safety Institute: www.bhsi.org

Bicycle Transportation Alliance: www.bta4bikes.org.

Car Sharing: www.carsharing.net

Chapter 16: Simple Living and Relationships

Books

1001 Ways to Be Romantic, by Greogry Godek, Sourcebooks Trade, 1999; ISBN 1570714819.

1001 More Ways to Be Romantic, by Gregory Godek, Casablanca Press, 1992; ISBN 0962980323.

Creative Visualization: Use the Power of Your Imagination to Create What You Want in Your Life, by Shakti Gawain, New World Library, 1995; ISBN 1880032627.

Living A Beautiful Life: 500 Ways to Add Elegance, Order, Beauty, and Joy to Every Day of Your Life, by Alexandra Stoddard, Avon Books, 1988; ISBN 0380705117.

Alexandra Stoddard's Living Beautifully Together, by Alexandra Stoddard, Avon Books, 1991; ISBN 0380709082.

Living in the Light: A Guide to Personal and Planetary Transformation, by Shakti Gawain, Bantam Books, 1993; ISBN 0553561049.

Men Are from Mars, Women Are from Venus, by John Gray, HarperCollins, 1992; ISBN 006016848X.

Chapter 17: Raising Kids the Simple Living Way

Books

Born to Win, by Muriel James and Dorothy Jongeward, Perseus Press, 1996; ISBN 0201590441.

The Complete Idiot's Guide to Crafts with Kids, by Georgene Lockwood, Alpha Books, 1998; ISBN 0028624068.

Mary Hunt's Debt-Proof Your Kids, by Mary Hunt, Broadman & Holman Publishers, 1998; ISBN 0805415181.

Games for Girl Scouts, Girl Scouts of the USA, 1969; ISBN 0884413470.

Hopscotch, Hangman, Hot Potato, & Ha Ha Ha: A Rulebook of Children's Games, by Jack Maquire, Simon & Schuster, 1992; ISBN 0671763326.

Hand Clap! "Miss Mary Mack" and 42 Other Hand-Clapping Games for Kids, by Sara Bernstein, Adams Media Corporation, 1994; ISBN 1558504265.

Homecoming: Reclaiming and Championing Your Inner Child, by John Bradshaw, Bantam Doubleday Dell, 1992; ISBN 0553353896.

P.E.T.: Parent Effectiveness Training, by Thomas Gordon, New American Library Trade, 1975; ISBN 0452264618.

Simplify Your Life with Kids: 100 Ways to Make Family Life Easier and More Fun, by Elaine St. James, Andrews McMeel Publishing, 2000; ISBN 0740706640.

Web Sites

Mother-ease: www.motherease.com; 1-800-416-1475

Bummis: www.bummis.com; 1-888-828-6647

EcoBaby: www.ecobaby.com; 1-800-ECOBABY

Chapter 18: When You Know How to Play, Who Needs Recreation?

Books

Amusing Ourselves to Death: Public Discourse in the Age of Show Business, by Neil Postman, Viking Press, 1986; ISBN 0140094385.

The Complete Idiot's Guide to Gardening, by Jane O'Connor and Emma Sweeney, Alpha Books, 1997; ISBN 0028610962.

No Logo: Taking Aim at the Brand Bullies, by Naomi Klein, Picador USA, 2000; ISBN 0312203438.

Shows About Nothing: Nihilism in Popular Culture from "The Exorcist" to "Seinfeld", by Thomas S. Hibbs, Spence Publishing, 1999; ISBN 1890626171.

Magazines

Sky and Telescope Magazine
Sky Publishing Corporation
P.O. Box 9111
Belmont, MA 02478-9111
1-800-253-0245
www.skypub.com

Web Sites

Great Books Foundation: greatbooks.org/

Chapter 19: Circle of Community: You Can't Do It Alone

Books

Building Communities from the Inside Out: A Path Toward Finding and Mobilizing a Community Assets, by John P. Kretzmann and John L. McKnight, ACTA Publications, 1997; ISBN 087946108X.

Changing Places: Rebuilding Community in the Age of Sprawl, by Richard Moe and Carter Wilkie, Henry Holt & Company, Inc, 1999; ISBN 0805061843.

Cyberville: Clicks, Culture, and the Creation of an Online Town, by Stacy Horn, Warner Books, 1998; ISBN 044651909X.

Once There Were Greenfields: How Urban Sprawl Is Undermining Americas's Environment, Economy, and Social Fabric, by F. Kaid Benfield, Donald D. T. Chen and Matthew D. Raimi, Natural Resource Defense, 1999; ISBN 1893340171.

Time Dollars: How to Build Community Through Social Capital, by Edgar S. Cahn, 2000, ISBN 1885429231.

Magazines

World Watch Magazine
Worldwatch Institute
1776 Massachusetts Ave., N.W.
Washington, D.C. 20036-1904
202-452-1999
www.worldwatch.org/mag

Organizations

American Community Garden Association
100 N. 20th Street, 5th Floor
Philadelphia, PA 109103-1495
215-988-8785
E-mail: sallymcc@libertynet.org

Womanshare
680 West End Avenue
New York, NY 10025
212-662-9746
E-mail: Wshare@aol.com.

E. F. Schumacher Society
140 Jug End Road
Great Barrington, MA 01230
413-528-1737
www.schumachersociety.org

Web Sites

The Sustainable Communities Network: www.sustanable.org

Northwest Earth Institute: www.nwei.com

Seeds of Simplicity, the Simplicity Circles Project: www.seedsofsimplicity.org/cecile.htm
To see if there are any simplicity circle study groups in your area: www.simplicitycircles.com.

Chapter 20: The Politics of Paring Down

Books

Graceful Simplicity: Toward a Philosophy and Politics of Simple Living, by Jerome Segal, Henry Holt & Company, Inc, 1999; ISBN 0805056793.

Hometown Money: How to Enrich Your Community with Local Currency, by Paul Glover, order from: Ithaca Money, Box 6578, Ithaca, NY. 14851, (607) 272-4330.

How to Save Your Neighborhood, City, or Town: The Sierra Club Guide to Community Organizing, by Maritza Pick, Sierra Club Books, 1993; ISBN 0871565226.

Local Currencies in Community Development or too much mngwotngwotiki is bad for you, by Tony Savdie and Tim Cohen-Mitchell, Center for International Education; 1997; ISBN 1889536016.

The Overworked American: The Unexpected Decline of Leisure, by Juliet B. Schor, Basic Books, 1993; ISBN 046505434X.

Rethinking Our Centralized Monetary System: The Case for a System of Local Currencies, by Lewis Solomon, Praeger Publishers Text, 1996; ISBN 0275953769.

Small Is Beautiful: Economics As If People Mattered, by E.F. Schumacher, Hartley & Marks, 1999; ISBN 0881791695.

Organizations

E. F. Schumacher Society
140 Jug End Road
Great Barrington, MA 01230
413-528-1737

E-mail: efssociety@aol.com
www.schumachersociety.org

Ithaca Hours
The local currency exchange for Ithaca, New York
P.O. Box 6731
Ithaca, NY 14851
607-272-3738
E-mail: ithacahours@lightlink.com
www.ithacahours.org.

GANE and the Economics Working Group
3407 34th Places N.W.
Washington, DC 20016
202-244-0561
www.greenecon.org/gane.

Shorter Work-Time Group
c/o Barbara Brandt
69 Dover Street #1
Somerville, MA 02144
617-628-5558
www.swt.org/

Society for the Reduction of Human Labor
c/o Benjamin Hunnicutt
1610 East College Street
Iowa City, IA 52245
E-mail: hunnicut@blue.weeg.uiowa.edu

Web Sites

Paul Glover's (Ithaca Hours founder) site: www.lightlink.com/hours/ithacahours/.

The TimeWork Web: www.vcn.bc.ca/timework/

Chapter 21: New Directions in Education

Books

10 Traits of Highly Successful Schools: How You Can Know If Your School Is a Good One, by Elaine K. McEwan, Harold Shaw Publishing, 1999; ISBN 087788840X.

Angry Parents, Failing Schools: What's Wrong with the Public Schools & What You Can Do About It, by Elaine K. McEwan, Harold Shaw Publishing, 1998; ISBN 0877880190.

Charter Schools in Action: Renewing Public Education, by Chester E. Finn Jr., Gregg Vanourek, and Bruno V. Manno, Princeton University Press, 2000; ISBN 0691004803.

Dumbing Down Our Kids: Why American Children Feel Good About Themselves but Can't Read, Write, or Add, by Charles J. Sykes, St. Martin's Press, 1996; ISBN 0312148232.

Dumbing Us Down: The Hidden Curriculum of Compulsory Schooling, by Taylor Gatto, New Society Publishing, 1991; ISBN 086571231X.

Homeschooling Handbook: From Preschool to High School: A Parent's Guide, by Mary Griffith, Prima Publishing, 1999; ISBN 0761517278.

How Children Fail, by John Holt, Perseus Press, 1995; ISBN 0201484021.

How Children Learn, by John Holt, Perseus Press, 1995; ISBN 0201484048.

The Montessori Method, by Maria Montessori, Schocken Books, 1989; ISBN 0805209220.

Peak Learning: How to Create Your Own Lifelong Education Program for Personal Enlightenment and Professional Success, by Ronald Gross, J. P. Tarcher, 1999; ISBN 087477957X.

Peterson's Guide to Distance Learning Programs, 2000 Peterson's Guides, 1999; ISBN 0768902576.

Rudolf Steiner Education: The Waldorf Schools, by Francis Edmonds, Rudolf Steiner Press, 1987; ISBN 0854403442.

Study Circles: Coming Together for Personal Growth and Social Change, by Leonard Oliver, Seven Locks Pr, 1987; ISBN 093202047X.

The Unschooling Handbook: How to Use the Whole World as Your Child's Classroom, by Mary Griffith, Prima Publishing, 1998; ISBN 0761512764.

Organizations

Elderhostel
75 Federal Street
Boston, MA 02110-1941
877-426-8056
www.elderhostel.org

Study Circles Resource Center
P.O. Box 203
697 Pomfret St.
Pomfret, CT 06258
860-928-2616
E-mail: scrc@neca.com

Web Sites

About.com Home-schooling: about.com/education/homeschooling/

Chapter 22: Future Planet: Living With the Natural Order

Books

Awakening Earth: Exploring the Evolution of Human Culture and Consciousness, by Duane Elgin, Millennium Project, 1993; ISBN 0688116213.

Home! A Bioregional Reader, by Van Andruss, Christopher Plant, Judith Plant, Eleanor Wright, New Society Publishing, 1990; ISBN 1550920073.

Let the Mountains Talk, Let the Rivers Run: A Call to Those Who Would Save the Earth, by David Brower, New Society Publishing, 2000; ISBN 0865714118.

Chapter 23: What's Rich? Redefining Wealth for the Simple Life

Books

A Call for Connection: Solutions for Creating a Whole New Culture, by Gail Bernice Holland, New World Library, 1998; ISBN 157731039X.

Index

U

V

Y-Z